Trailblazers

Trailblazers

Test pilots in action

Compiled

by

Christopher Hounsfield

Pen & Sword
AVIATION

First published in
Great Britain in 2008
By Pen and Sword Aviation
An imprint of
Pen and Sword Books Ltd
47 Church Street
Barnsley
South Yorkshire
S70 2AS

ISBN 978 1 84415 748 8

A CIP record for this book is available from the British Library

Typeset in Palatino Linotype by Lamorna Publishing Services
Printed and bound by Biddles Ltd

Pen and Sword Books Ltd incorporates the imprints of Pen and Sword
Aviation, Pen and Sword Maritime, Pen and Sword Military, Wharncliffe
Local History, Pen and Sword Select, Pen and Sword Military Classics and
Leo Cooper.

For a complete list of Pen and Sword titles please contact
Pen and Sword Books Limited
47 Church Street, Barnsley, South Yorkshire, S70 2AS, England
E-mail: enquiries@pen-and-sword.co.uk
Website: www.pen-and-sword.co.uk

Flying may not be all plain sailing, but the fun of it is worth the price

Amelia Earhart, legendary test pilot
(1897 – 1937)

Buckinghamshire County Council	
2671686	
Askews	Dec-2009
629.13453	£19.99
TRA	AYL

Contents

Acknowledgements

Once the idea had been sown in my head, the thought of putting the book into practice appeared to be straightforward. However it was not to be so easy. It would have been nearly impossible without the lynchpin that was Shawna Mullen; the web and publications administrator and office manager for the Society of Experimental Test Pilots (SETP) based in California. She received my first enquiring email regarding contact with test pilots, and willingly forwarded a number of requests from me to the membership. Without Shawna's assistance, this book would not have happened and the snowball effect that did occur, would have remained very small.

As it was, there were pilots who were prepared to come forward and volunteer their stories and tales, as well as initiate a 'chain' message, and I must thank Tony Blackman, in particular, Vlad Yakimov and Kapil Bharghava for putting me in touch with other pilots who would otherwise have been out of touch.

I would especially like to acknowledge a number of pilots who did write, but whose stories I was I was unable to include. I very much hope this is merely the first anthology. To me Trailblazers is a living project that will be ongoing. A number of writers were unable to put together a story in the time available, and some have been in contact since the manuscript was submitted.

My wife Louisa was incredibly patient, while I took over the computer and the entire dining room table, with piles of manuscripts and pictures, for months, and then smiled when I had the audacity to ask her to read through the finished bundle of paper.

It is the test pilots who have made this possible and I hope I have done justice to their stories. We really do owe them all a great deal.

Glossary

AGL – Above Ground Level.

Aileron – The hinged control surfaces attached to the trailing edge of the wing of a fixed-wing aircraft.

Angle-of-attack – Angle between the chord line of the aerofoil or wing and the relative air stream.

ASI – Air Speed Indicator.

ATC – Air Traffic Control.

Autorotation – The phenomenon which results in the rotation of, and lift generation by, a rotorcraft's primary rotor through purely aerodynamic forces.

Ceiling – The maximum height to which an aircraft can climb.

Chase aircraft – An aircraft flown in proximity to another aircraft normally to observe its performance during training or testing.

Damping – A means to reduce the effect of oscillation and vibration, particularly with regard to aircraft engines.

Dihedral – The upward angle from horizontal in a fixed-wing aircraft from root to tip.

Drag – The total resistance of an aircraft along its line of flight.

EFTS – Empire Flight Test School.

Elevators – Control surfaces, usually at the rear of an aircraft, which control the aircraft's orientation by changing the pitch of the aircraft

Elevons – Aircraft control surfaces that combine the functions of the elevator (used for pitch control) and the aileron (used for roll control).

Feathered propeller – A propeller whose blades have been rotated so that the leading and trailing edges are nearly parallel with the aircraft.

Flameout – An emergency condition caused by a major loss of engine power.

Flight Envelope – the capabilities of an aircraft in terms of speed and altitude.

Flutter – A self-starting vibration that occurs when the wings bend under aerodynamic load.

HUD – Head Up Display. A transparent display that presents data without obstructing the user's view.

IAS – Indicated Air Speed (the airspeed as shown by the indicator).

ILS – Instrument Landing System.

INS – Inertial Navigation System.

KCAS – Knots Calibrated Air Speed.
KIAS – Knots Indicated Air Speed.
Kinetic energy – The energy of motion.
Mach – The speed of sound (at ground level approx 670mph/1,072km/h).
MSL – Mean Sea Level.
NACA – National Advisory Committee for Aeronautics (pre-cursor to NASA).
Nacelle – The structure surrounding an aircraft engine.
OAT – Outside Air Temperature.
Ornithopter – Flapping wing aircraft.
PIO – Pilot Induced Oscillation. A phenomena when a pilot overcorrects his
steering creating a swinging motion.
Pitch – The angle by which the nose of an aircraft is inclined up or down from
the horizontal.
Rotate – The speed at which an aircraft can leave the ground on take-off.
SAS – Stability Augmentation System.
SETP – Society of Experimental Test Pilots
Slats – The aerodynamic surfaces on the leading edge of the wing, when
deployed, allow the wing to operate at a higher angle-of-attack.
Stall – A condition in which an aircraft experiences an interruption of airflow
resulting in
loss of lift and a tendency to fall.
STOVL – Short Take-Off and Vertical Landing.
Telemetry – The automatic transmission and measurement of data from remote
sources by wire or radio or other means.
Test bed/cell – A platform for experimentation for large development projects.
Thermocouple – A widely used type of temperature sensor.
Thrust vectoring – The ability to direct the thrust from an aircraft's main
engines in a direction other than parallel to the vehicle's longitudinal axis.
Trim – A way in which to balance and stabilize an aircraft once in flight, in
order to relieve flight control pressure,
UHF – Ultra High Frequency (radio).
Vector – To change direction of the aircraft or to guide an aircraft in flight by
issuing appropriate headings.
VTOL – Vertical Take-Off and Landing.
'X' – Experimental aircraft/mission.
Yaw – The turn of an aircraft. When the rudder is turned to one side, the
aeroplane moves left or right.
'Z' – Zulu. A pre-prepared, agreed time or Coordinated Universal Time (UTC).

Introduction

An anthology that tries to embody modern test piloting is near impossible. There are many hundreds (probably thousands) of books, which successfully describe the flying history of just about every aircraft that has taken to the skies. There are also a similar number of autobiographies from test pilots and pioneers that dot the world's bookshelves. A collection of this kind does not try to rival any of these studies, but aims to divert and entertain by exploring the test pilot margins of experience.

When I first took over as editor of *Aerospace Testing International* several years ago, the magazine dealt purely with current newsworthy test projects and technology. However, as a closet historian, it seemed enormously important to me to include past, as well as present, exploits of test flying, and the massive technological developments driving man's further attempts to conquer gravity.

A regular feature based on this idea was therefore introduced into the magazine, and George J. Marrett was the first test pilot I managed to contact. George was a Vietnam veteran, and a test pilot on the F-4 Phantom. He wrote an article and sent some pictures; from that moment on I was mesmerized.

His article was followed by John Farley's experience with the Fairey Delta 2, Dennis Newton wrote about the race to get the LearFan airborne and the legendary Alex Henshaw, Spitfire test pilot, discussed a complete equipment failure. However, as the magazine is published quarterly, 12 months had only produced four of these fascinating stories, and I wanted more.

I did more research, but was surprised I could not find a single anthology, or even generic publication based on the experiences of test pilots. A collection of anecdotes and stories from test pilots seems like an obvious 'must-read', and so my mission began. I have sought stories that illuminate the mentality of people who epitomize the great age of flying to the edge of space and below.

I did not want this to be a collection of well documented tales from the 'great and the good': Chuck Yeager (sound barrier), Hans-Werner Lerche,

(German Second World War pilot), Gerry Sayer, test pilot of Britain's first jet aircraft, Neil Armstrong and so on. I wanted it to be a first-hand and exclusive tribute to the whole fraternity of test piloting that genuinely supercedes creed, national boundary and politics.

All the stories in this book encapsulate the general spirit of test flying, sometimes humorously, sometimes proudly, sometimes tragically. What proved interesting was the editorial briefing I gave to the pilot writers, and their reaction to it. The aim of the book was not to bring together a collection of broad descriptions of flights and the test programme of particular aircraft, but to collate a selection of snapshots. This snapshot may be just a part of a major programme; possibly one memorable flight; even just a few seconds of enormous excitement but a memory that embodied everything about their test flying experiences.

However when I explained my aim, most pilots were somewhat perplexed (in the nicest way). They felt a compulsion to write about the science, the technology, the test programme. It was natural; it was their job to evaluate an aircraft and report the technical facts, not what went wrong, how they coped, the stress they underwent, the physical and mental pressure or the near-death experience

My first experience of meeting a test pilot was when I was a young Army officer in 15/19 King's Royal Hussars. After a bad accident on exercise I was posted to Royal Air Force Headley Court located south of London as it was the rehabilitation centre for all serving men in the UK's armed services but was run by the RAF.

The officers lived in a beautiful and very old country house with the most amazing facilities. As might be expected, the majority of inmates were from the Army, but there were a couple of pilots, one from the Fleet Air Arm who was a subtly flamboyant Harrier pilot (ejection injury), and one RAF Tornado pilot (burns injury). Compared with my somewhat pretentious and peacock display, I was surprised at their cool, logical, mathematical and calm approach to what they did as a job and to their injuries. The pilots had a unique attitude that comes across in this book. The Army also tended to drink much more in the bar.

There are not many test pilots in the world; test pilots are a rare breed and have a rare quality to go to the extreme. There are only limited places, and they have to be at the pinnacle of their game. The type of aircraft, civil/military, rotary/fixed, small outfit/huge corporation may differ but they share a common trait: What, for us would be one of the most exhilarating rides in one's life (even as a passenger), to a test pilot is just a day in the office, but there is still a desire to take it to the 'max'.

Most of us take flying in complete safety for granted. Someone else has taken all the risks needed to ensure our fast and safe travel. Even in modern times with all the computer technology and wizardry that goes into the design of a modern airliner or fighter jet, someone still has to step up, climb into the cockpit and take to the air for the first time, in a completely untested machine.

I was a member of the press when I witnessed the first ever take-off and successful flight of the monolithic Airbus A380 in 2005. It was an amazing event, tens of thousands of people lining the periphery of Toulouse Airport, and massive minute-by-minute worldwide press coverage. Very shortly afterwards I spoke to the chief test pilot, and senior vice-president with Airbus, Captain Claude Lelaie. My question: 'How was it sitting at the end of the runway, in the largest civil aircraft in the world, which has never flown before and being watched by the world?' His answer: 'I was not really nervous, we were trained for this. It took a little longer to prepare for the first flight, because of the extra procedures. Otherwise it was fully standard. We decided we wanted to be right on time. The official time announced for first take-off was 10:30, but actually it was 10:29. So, we missed it by one minute, which isn't too bad,' he explained nonchalantly, as if he had just driven the 10:30 out of the railway station according to the timetable.

This is a unique, but limited collection of anecdotes written first-hand or adapted specifically for this book. There is only one pre-Second World War entry: John Macready. He was an incredible pilot and pioneer who died in 1991. His story was put together especially by his devoted pilot daughter, Sally quoting his original log books, notes and diaries, and it demands inclusion.

Otherwise, the book covers the years from 1942 up until the present day. From the naval Buccaneer to the B-45; the unique V-22 Osprey to the sublime Vulcan bomber, and the U2 spy plane to the Saab Gripen fighter jet. Some stories describe true milestones in aviation, such as Jean Pinet's traumatic experiences with Concorde; some tell a tragic but uplifting tale like Dave Gollings with the Canadair Challenger; many are very funny. Carl Lyday's adventure, with an inverted F-111, had many a dinner guest eagerly listening to me. But all the narratives are delivered with varying degrees of humility, bravery, pride and modesty.

About half of this selection is from pilots from the USA. This was not intentional but is probably, in part, due to the destination of my original enquiry (the Society of Experimental Test Pilots (SETP) in California) and partly maybe because its pilots were more enthusiastic to discuss their experiences, particularly in their own language. Otherwise stories came from France, Canada, UK, Germany, Switzerland, India, Russia, Sweden and Brazil. It is a shame that, despite some effort, no pilots came forward from other prolific aircraft manufacturing countries. Perhaps,…next time. However, all pilots, American or otherwise, very plainly feel a great sense of brotherhood that crosses national boundaries, pride and political belief: it is about furthering flight.

It is hoped this book will appeal to all those who wish to dip into an amazing and exciting fraternity and share just a tiny bit of what it must be like to soar through the air in a ground-breaking aircraft: Aviation enthusiasts, ageing and young pilots, engineers, adventurers, people who like a good story, aeronautical theorists, historians, young pilots in the making and the next generation – 'Trailblazers' of the future.

Much thought went into the order of anecdotes. It was arranged to mix old and new, US and other, plus the different types of machines. But it was a very deliberate decision to finish with John A. Harper who, to me, epitomized the test pilot creed. His story is the shortest, and free of any ambiguity. He wrote a short piece describing frankly how he and his crew went in the air to test a B-45 in 1952. The wings fell off, three men baled out, but only two survived. That was it; another day in the office. I contacted him to request if he might be able to expand the account in order fit in with the length of the other stories and asked if, maybe, he could throw in a few more adjectives. His reply was: 'Chris, this was how it happened and how I remember it. If you don't want it, don't use it.' I have!

This book is also a tribute to Alex Henshaw, the legendary Spitfire test pilot who sadly died shortly after completing the adaptation of his story. It is the smallest of a vast amount of insights into the great man, but in *The Times* obituary it said:

> Of the 30,000 Spitfire test flights carried out at Castle Bromwich in that time, Henshaw flew a prodigious 10 per cent. Once, after flying a Spitfire inverted at 50 feet over Birmingham city centre, he was nearly arrested. He was also the only person to barrel-roll a Lancaster bomber.

In 2005, aged 92, he flew a Spitfire again, but for the last time. He died in 2007.

This volume has been an absolute pleasure to compile, and an honour to coordinate. Any enjoyment that readers gather from these pages is entirely down to the endeavours of the band of brothers who wrote them. Many pilots took off; not all of them came back.

Christopher Hounsfield
2008

Chapter 1

From 1969-70 George Cooper served as the assistant director of safety aviation at NASA headquarters.

George E. Cooper
The Douglas XSB2D-1
A Surprise Visit

The highly decorated World War II Pilot George E. Cooper recalls an unexpected meeting with an old farming friend.

After serving as a fighter pilot in World War II, I returned to civilian life in the spring of 1945. My wife Louise and I were living with her parents on their prune and apricot ranch in Saratoga, then a small agricultural town in the Santa Clara Valley, south of San Francisco, later to become famous as 'Silicon Valley'. Because we were hoping to build a house on the farm that Louise's parents had offered us, I began looking for various employment possibilities in the area. I interviewed for some engineering jobs, but none really appealed that much to me. In my heart of hearts, I wanted to continue flying.

I think it was through military contacts that I learned about Ames Aeronautical Laboratory at the Moffett Field Naval Air Station. The National Advisory Committee for Aeronautics (NACA, which was the precursor of NASA) had founded Ames at the beginning of the war as a second research facility, that was both close to West Coast aircraft manufacturers and complemented its original laboratory at Langley Field, Virginia. I heard that Ames was now expanding its aeronautical projects and using test pilots in its flight research. Since it was only about 12 miles north-east of Saratoga, near the town of Sunnyvale at the southern end of the San Francisco Bay, I decided to find out if they might be interested in a former Air Force fighter pilot who had an engineering degree, even though it was not in aeronautics. I drove over to Moffett Field and went to the administration office. But when I inquired about the possibility of a flying job, I was flatly turned down by the woman at the front desk. 'We have no openings for pilots,' she said.

I still hoped that I could find a job in aviation, and I began attending interviews with commercial airlines. To become a commercial pilot, it was necessary for me to change my Air Force status to that of a civilian pilot with an FAA license. This involved taking a required medical examination with an FAA-designated physician. I found a local doctor who was FAA-certified and made an appointment with him for a pilot's physical.

After he completed the exam, we were chatting, and I happened to mention my interest in Ames. He volunteered that he had done the medical certification for one of its test pilots, a fellow named James Nissen who lived nearby in Los Altos. Dissatisfied by the response that I had received from the front office, I decided to contact him to learn what was really going on at Ames and what its future needs for pilots might be. Finding that he was listed in the local phone book, I called him the next day. I introduced myself and explained my interest in Ames. He agreed to meet with me that afternoon. I drove directly there and knocked on the door. He invited me in, and I told him what the woman in the administration office had said, that the program wasn't looking for more pilots.

'She doesn't know what she's talking about,' he said immediately. 'We really need pilots. In fact, we have to borrow pilots from the Navy right now.' After further conversation about my flying experience, he invited me to come out and meet his boss, Bill McAvoy, head of flight operations.

I went to Ames a day later for an interview with Bill. I was very pleased when he agreed with Jim that his program could use more flyers and that my experience qualified me as a suitable addition to his division. He sent a request through NACA's administrative channels to hire me as an engineering test pilot, and within a few days I was quite relieved to hear that I would be offered the job.

After all the necessary forms were completed, I finally reported for work on August 4, 1945. At the time, there were two branches at Ames devoted to flight: Flight Operations and Flight Engineering. Their war-time objectives were now changing to post-war objectives. The first was to respond to the military services' requests to solve some of their planes' handling problems and to document the stability and control of their aircraft. The second objective was to find ways of safely attaining higher speeds and extension of the aircrafts' flight envelopes. Through this latter research we were to define new criteria and specifications for the design of future military aircraft.

I very much enjoyed those early months at Ames because of the wide variety of aircraft available. Many of the planes were twin or multi-engine aircraft, which were of special interest to me because during the war I had been piloting single engine fighter planes almost exclusively. In my first weeks I started out flying co-pilot with Jim Nissen on multi-pilot aircraft while also beginning to fly the many single-pilot aircraft that were also to be tested. Soon I was flying nearly all of the planes being tested at Ames, sometimes making three or four flights a day, and I also was serving as the project pilot on several research studies.

Despite the heavy daily flight schedule, I liked the fact that I was flying many different types of aircraft and was accumulating valuable experience. I was usually assigned to pilot the various aircraft in which handling and stability problems had been identified. The planes I tested during those first months included the Bell P-39N Airacobra, P-51D Mustang, F6F Hellcat, B-25, P-47D Thunderbolt, A-26B Invader, R4D (the naval version of the DC3), the C-82 (a cargo aircraft), the C-46 (for icing research), and the Lockheed 12. I also flew the US Navy's F7F-3 Tigercat, which was an interesting aircraft in that it had plenty of power but had been designed with a marginal amount of directional control during takeoff. This meant that, should it lose one of its engines during a high-power takeoff, it would yaw dangerously and had to be controlled very rapidly with the rudder. During this time we were also starting to research jet aircraft, which began with our testing the P-80.

During those first months at Ames, however, I spent much of my time testing the El Segundo XSB2D-1 (later designated as the BDT-1). Built by Douglas Aircraft at the end of the war as a follow-on to the Douglas SBD (sometimes called the Dauntless Divebomber), it was powered by the Wright 3360 engine. This particular engine would go on to dubious fame by giving commercial airlines considerable trouble. For example, TWA selected it for its fleet of Lockheed Constellations, which then suffered more than an average number of in-flight engine shutdowns.

The XSB2D-1 had numerous problems, which included too much drag and too little power. Ames had been trying to solve these problems by testing it in what we called the '40 x 80' wind tunnel. Completed in 1944, this wind tunnel covered eight acres and, based on its 40-foot high by 80-foot wide test section, was the largest wind tunnel in the world. Because of its size, it was possible to mount the complete instrumented airplane on support struts in the test section and operate it with the engine running. With the war almost over, there was no chance that the XSB2D-1 would ever go into service as a dive bomber. As a result, Ames was able to retain the plane to use for other research and development studies of aircraft design.

After its problems were presumably solved, it was released from the wind tunnel for in-flight tests. I became involved in several of these projects using it as a test bed. One of them was to evaluate different propellers' designs during maximum power ground runs and in-flight performances. The engineer who formulated this study was Welko Gasich, who occupied the rear cockpit during our test flights of the plane. (Welco would later go on to become senior vice-president at Northrop Aircraft Company.)

On January 10, 1946, we took the XSB2D-1 up for what was probably our sixth or seventh test flight. We were climbing out at about 6,000 feet above the town of Los Gatos, about 15 miles south-west of Moffett Field. We were en route to our test area over the Santa Cruz Mountains when we heard 'pop, pop, pop,' much like the backfire of a car. It's the sound that any test pilot hates to hear; it almost always means a serious problem. Although we didn't know what had happened, I immediately turned the plane to head east and back to Moffett Field.

Soon I was getting only intermittent power. Fortunately, my original 6,000 feet altitude allowed me to maintain a safe airspeed while we were slowly losing altitude. Still, I thought we would be able to make it back to Moffett, and Welko radioed the tower to alert them to a possible emergency landing. He continued answering their questions, but I wasn't able to speak on the radio because I was too busy maneuvering the plane. I dropped the nose again to try to maintain flying speed and keep the plane on its route to the landing field.

Suddenly, when we were over the town of Sunnyvale, about 1½ miles from the runway, the cockpit became ominously silent. I knew immediately that the engine had failed completely. With no alternative but to continue lowering the nose to try to maintain flying speed, I had to make a quick decision. Despite some close calls while in the Air Force, I had never been forced to bale out, but I knew I would be prepared if necessary. Nevertheless, I had always thought that my first choice should be to try to land the airplane if it was still controllable and any suitable terrain was available. That, indeed, was my choice now, especially since we had lost so much altitude that we were already too low for a safe bale out. We were over an area of scattered homes interspersed with small orchards. I quickly decided to avoid the homes directly ahead to lessen the possibility of any injuries to people on the ground. I made a limited turn to the right and aimed for an orchard that had fewer houses surrounding it.

Putting us into a dive, I was still able to control the plane. I aimed the nose between the orchard rows, which were about 25 feet apart, so that the body of the plane would fit exactly between them in order so as to avoid a more serious crash. I left the landing gear retracted as we began our descent toward the orchard and planned to wait until the very last moment before lowering the flaps. This would enable the airplane to lose enough speed to reduce the impact at touch down. We descended into the orchard with the wings shearing trees on both sides from the tops at the beginning of the row where we first entered and down to the trunks, when the plane hit the ground with a minor jolt and slid on its belly along the row. The trees looked as if they were so many matchsticks snapping as we came through and finally stopped at the base of the last trees. All in all, we mowed down 84 prune trees in our landing.

As I was climbing out of the cockpit onto the wing, a pick-up truck raced up to the plane in a cloud of dust. Out jumped John Alonzo, a farmer in Sunnyvale whom I knew because he also owned orchards near my in-laws in Saratoga. He gazed in bewilderment at the plane's torn wings and his sheared-off prune trees. Recognizing me standing on the wing next to the cockpit, he stared as if he had just seen a ghost.

'My God, my God, George,' he called. 'What happened?'

The newly trimmed rows of plum trees courtesy of George Cooper, January 1946.

George Cooper's heavily pregnant wife only discovered about the accident from the press coverage.

'Well, John,' I replied, 'You keep asking me to drop in on you sometime, so here I am.'

By then Welko had gotten down from his cockpit and assured me that he was also uninjured. We accepted John's offer to drive us back to his house at the side of the orchard so that we could use his telephone. He was still so

The project was eventually cancelled after the aircraft proved too heavy and unreliable and the Navy decided it needed a single-seat aircraft.

excited that he forgot to turn around, and we went full throttle in reverse for a quarter-mile between the rows of prune trees. Once we were inside his home, he reached for a bottle of bourbon in a kitchen cupboard and, with shaking hands, said, 'I think we need a drink.' We declined, and I phoned Jim Nissen at Ames to report that we were okay and to ask him to send someone to retrieve the plane and pick us up as soon as possible. A crowd was already gathering in the orchard, and we didn't think it safe to have so many curious people milling around.

A half-hour later a crew arrived with a truck and trailer. They loaded the plane on the trailer, and we climbed into the truck. When we arrived back at Moffett, we examined the plane and found that there had been a fire in the engine's induction system. Neither then nor later could we determine its cause, but the plane was so badly damaged that it was never flown again.

The Douglas XSB2D-1 was an experimental scout bomber derived from the Dauntless

I had little time for further debriefing that day, however, because I had to rush to meet Louise at the hospital for her last check-up before the anticipated delivery date of our first child. (Our son Bill was born the following month, on February 2, 1946.) Despite my crash landing that afternoon, I managed to make it to the hospital only a few minutes late. I decided not to mention to either Louise or her doctor why I had been slightly delayed.

My little secret was exposed the following day when the local newspaper ran a story about our emergency landing and featured a photograph of our plane sitting in the middle of the shorn prune trees.

TESTIMONIAL

Born in 1916, George Cooper grew up in Southern California and in 1940 received a degree in mining engineering from the University of California at Berkeley. During the Second World War, he served as a fighter pilot in the 412th Fighter Squadron of the USAAF. After flying top cover over Normandy Beaches on D-Day, he completed 81 ground attack missions in a P47 Thunderbolt over German territory, and in air combat, he shot down four German planes. He was awarded 17 air medals as well as the Distinguished Flying Cross with Palm. After joining Ames Aeronautical Laboratory as a test pilot in 1945, he took aeronautical engineering graduate courses at Stanford. Promoted to chief aeronautical research pilot in 1951, he was named chief of flight operations in 1958. In 1969-70, he served as the assistant director of safety aviation at NASA headquarters in Washington, DC. Although he retired from Ames in 1973, he remained a consultant to its director for the following year and continued as a military and commercial airlines consultant for more than 20 years.

In 1973, he began to pursue his long interest in viticulture and winemaking. In 1994 the winery was licensed and bonded and began commercially marketing its wines under the 'Cooper-Garrod' label. The winery has won numerous awards and high ratings from wine reviewers.

Although saddened by the death of his beloved wife Louise in the spring of 2007, he continues to be involved in winemaking, attends his various aeronautical associations meetings and spends time with his four children, Bill, Jim, Barbara and David, and his 11 grandchildren.

Chapter 2

John Farley was associated with the Harrier development programme for 19 years.

John Farley – FD2
Learn the Hard Way

John Farley is famous as the chief test pilot on the Harrier programme. However, here he recalls a slight hiccup with the record-breaking FD2.

I don't know if many people can recall what they were doing on the 4 November 1964, but my memory of that day is very clear. My boss, Squadron Leader Jack Henderson, stuck his head round my office door, said, 'Lunch', and disappeared. As it was 12:30, I dropped what I was doing and followed him out of Aero Flight pilots' block at RAE Bedford.

Parked in a slot right by the entrance was a plain dark green Bedford van which served as our runabout. By the time I arrived Jack was already in the driving seat and his deputy, Lieutenant Commander Paul Millett, was joining

him in the front so I made for the back double doors. The back of the van was completely empty and I squatted down on the wheel arch for the short drive to the mess, just outside the airfield boundary. As a Flight Lieutenant posted in at the beginning of the year, I was the most junior of the four service test pilots whose collective job was to fly a variety of aircraft for the civilian scientists at Bedford. The fourth, Flight Lieutenant Clive Rustin, was away that day.

There were no windows in the back so I watched the road ahead through the wire mesh divider between me and the cab, the better to keep my perch on the wheel arch, as Jack was not hanging about. Halfway to the mess I realized that he and Paul were talking about me. Essentially Jack was asking Paul's advice on whether I was ready to be launched in the 'Fred', as WG777 the Fairey Delta FD2 was affectionately known. Paul clearly had his reservations. Thanks to its reheated Avon engine, the FD2 accelerated faster than most aircraft of that era and Paul was afraid I would get left behind and so exceed the limiting speed for getting the wheels locked up and raising the droop nose. He made a big point to Jack that the last time this happened the thing had been up on jacks for weeks while the hanger crew tried to readjust the various gear and nose linkages, micro-switches and sequence valves involved.

On the return journey after lunch, Jack and Paul continued their debate about whether I was fit to be let loose in the Fred. With hindsight their whole conversation was a big stage managed exercise, but it did not seem like that to me at the time.

I had not been back in my office many minutes before Jack came in asking 'Would you like to fly the Fred this afternoon, John?' I thought, 'Oh shit,' but heard myself say 'Of course, Jack'. 'Come to my office and I will brief you' he replied.

Later, as you can imagine, when I opened the throttle to roll, there was no way I was going to let this thing run away with me, and nothing was going to stop me getting the nose high enough to nail the speed below the dreaded 250 knots. After unstuck, at about 170 knots, I quickly selected the gear and nose up and got on with a pretty determined pull which settled the IAS at 220 knots. From this position of advantage I watched all the bits do their thing and was rewarded with a full blown sequence of lights and doll's eyes showing that retraction was happening and finally that the aircraft was clean. (doll's eyes were round magnetic indicators, a bit less than an inch in diameter, that showed either black, when all was tucked away, or white, if bits were still travelling. They were much in fashion in those days)

Once clean, the best climb speed for the Fred was 450 knots IAS changing to .85 Mach at about 13,000 feet, give or take a bit, depending on the temperature of the day. Therefore I lowered the nose and started to let the speed build up.

With all the experimental aircraft on Aero Flight it was normal to use 'continuous voice', this being a system that allowed you to transmit on one frequency to ATC and receive on another. This meant it was like a phone call so either of you could interrupt the other and the pilot could speak his mind without having to wait or even press a transmit button. There was a room on the ground in the pilots' block where a safety pilot could join in on the conversation, plus watch real time telemetry data from the aircraft. On top of this you had your own dedicated air traffic controller who just looked after you. Sounds great, and indeed was, but it did mean that the ground pilot as well as ATC could hear every breath you took, so those on the ground were never in much doubt about how well you were getting on, or not, as the case may be.

That afternoon I had none other than Jock Connell, the Bedford SATCO looking after me. Clearly with Jack Henderson as my safety pilot (and it sounded as if Paul was by his side), the first team were handling this flight.

Then it happened...

As the speed reached 450 knots the aircraft went into a violent pitching oscillation. I had never experienced a PIO (Pilot Induced Oscillation) before, nor had Jack mentioned the possibility of one in his brief. Luckily, from the depths of my apprenticeship, I remembered a conversation with an RAE test pilot where he had told me that when guys got into a PIO (thanks to these new fangled powered flying controls), the only way to recover was to let go of the stick. I did just that and the oscillation stopped dead. Just then Jock Connell came up with, '97, amber one five miles ahead turn right 180 on to east'. I quickly put in a bunch of right aileron, aiming for a 60 degree bank before pulling round to avoid the amber way. Immediately the Fred started another oscillation. This time it was the mother of all lateral oscillations. A roll PIO. I let go of the stick as if it was on fire and at once the aircraft became steady as a rock. Of course my heading had hardly changed so now Jock was shouting for me to turn immediately.

I am sure you get the picture. Every time I tried to control the flight path in pitch or roll I just set off a huge PIO. I did get it round roughly on to east and I did keep it climbing but in the process I had this wild oscillatory ride which knocked all the stuffing out of me. I was too busy to speak, just panting and grunting, while I tried to decide what to do. At one point I dimly heard Jack enquire whether I had got it trimmed yet. I also thought I could hear Paul laughing in the background. Goodness knows what the joke was, it all seemed a pretty poor show to me.

A minute or two later, roughly on east and going through 3,500 feet I let go of the stick and closed the throttle to give myself a much needed physical breather while I decided what to do. Clearly I could not control this monster to better than 20 degrees of heading and several thousand feet. To land it was

out of the question but I needed a rest before I jumped out. At idle power my speed was slowing and now approaching 200 knots so I gingerly got hold of the stick with the aim of getting the aircraft down to a more reasonable height. Thirty seconds later I realized the Fred was now a doddle to fly so I continued to descend at this speed. At 10,000 feet all was still well. Jock even had me on a steer for base. I added some power and levelled off at 200 knots. No problem.

To cut a long story short, I drifted down into the circuit and landed perfectly normally, but as I taxied my brain was churning. Clearly I was not cut out for this sort of work and, as I taxied slowly to my parking spot on the Aero Flight apron, I was rehearsing my resignation speech to Jack. This was just as well because Jack and Paul were standing with the ground crew and clearly waiting for me. I shut it down, the ground crew put the ladder up to the cockpit and I got down, noticing that Jack and Paul were still enjoying some sort of joke.

As I approached them I started with, 'I'm sorry Jack' but he put his hand up to silence me and told the ground crew to put the hydraulic ground rig on the aircraft and turn it on. With this and the Houchin electrical rig running, Jack turned to me and, shouting over the noise of the two rigs, said 'Get back in, stand on the seat and face the back'. Wondering what on earth all this was about I mutely did as

On 10 March 1956 the FD2 broke the World Air Speed Record raising it to 1,132 mph.

instructed. 'Now push the stick forward with your foot.' I turned round on the seat to do this and Jack shouted 'No – do it facing the back and watch the controls'. Again I did as he said and felt the stick go fully forward under my boot. For a second or so I was amazed to see no movement of the controls, then suddenly all the trailing edge surfaces went down.

Back in Jack's office he put me in the picture. When the Fred was designed in the 1950s, fully powered flying controls were in their infancy and people were learning about them all the time. In the Fred's case it had none of the more modern filtration systems and so, after a fair bit of flying, silt built up in the operating fluid resulting in significant lags between the pilot's input to the servo valve and the subsequent movement of the actuator. Lags in any

The Fairey Delta 2 ended up being an early and effective prototype for Concorde.

control system are very bad news. If you wonder why, you have only to imagine driving a car fast with a small built-in delay between you moving the steering wheel and the front wheels turning. If you were to make a normal correction, nothing would happen so you would then put in a bit more input. Suddenly the thing would bite and you would realize you now had more than you needed. Then, as you tried to correct the other way, it would happen all over again, leading to a nice weaving progress up the motorway.

Knowing that the Fred was due a major hydraulic system flush and clean, Jack and Paul decided to use the opportunity to give me some valuable on-the-job training regarding the effects of lags. Today such things are taught rather more formally at test pilot schools, using variable stability aeroplanes where an instructor in the back seat can dial in a whole range of flying control problems although I suspect such modern experiences are perhaps a little less memorable when compared with the one Jack set up for me.

Back to that lunchtime journey in the van… As I suggested earlier, the conversation I 'overheard' was clearly deliberately staged for my benefit. They wanted me to be concentrating so hard on checking the gear and nose retraction sequence that I would simply fail to notice how nicely the Fred handled below 250 knots. Later, at high speed, when more control precision was needed, I would trip over the lag effects and learn my invaluable lesson. Which doubtless explains why the first team were up for this trip and everyone was laughing while it was going on, except me.

The FD2 was developed in order to investigate flight and control at transonic and supersonic speeds.

Incidentally WG777 was the airfame that Peter Twiss used to raise the world's airspeed record by no less than 310 mph to 1,132 mph in 1956. By 1966 it had been fitted with an ogee wing as part of the Concorde research programme and reborn as the Bristol T221. In this guise it came with a nice modern hydraulic system taking all the fun out of life.

TESTIMONIAL

John Farley OBE did his engineering training as a student apprentice at the Royal Aircraft Establishment, Farnborough UK, between 1950 and 1955. He then joined the RAF for pilot training on Piston Provosts and Vampires. After a first tour on Hunters in Germany, he became a flying instructor on Jet Provosts at the RAF College Cranwell before joining the Empire Test Pilots' School course in 1963 where he was awarded the Patuxent Shield and a distinguished pass. Following ETPS he was posted as a test pilot to the Royal Aircraft Establishment Aerodynamics Research Flight at Bedford where he flew all the UK research aircraft then flying, including the Fairey Delta FD2. This tour involved more than 40 different types and, in 1964, as RAE project pilot on the P1127 prototype, he started what was to become 19 years of Harrier programme test flying at Dunsfold. He was appointed Deputy Chief Test Pilot at Dunsfold in 1971 and Chief Test Pilot in 1978. He checked out the original USMC evaluators of the Harrier in 1968 and, following the US purchase of the aeroplane, he worked on the Harrier II development programme at St Louis, Whiteman AFB and Edwards AFTC where, in 1982, he managed more than two hours gliding in a Harrier during engine-related trials over the lake bed. He has flown 80 plus different types and in 1990 became the first western test pilot invited by the Russians to fly the MiG-29. He retired from freelance test piloting in 1996 but continues to consult on flight test programmes.

Chapter 3

After pioneering the Skyhook retriever system, Pete Purvis became an F-14 test pilot in 1971.

Pete Purvis – F-14A Tomcat
The Day I Shot Myself Down

It is a dubious accolade to have been shot down by one's own missile, but, as Pete Purvis proved, some things are just going to happen.

My friends have often introduced me with the unforgiving phrase: 'Hey, I'd like you to meet the guy who shot himself down. This honor belongs to myself and another Grumman test pilot, Tommy Attridge, who managed to fly his F-11F-1 fighter into a hail of 20mm rounds he had just fired during supersonic gunnery tests. Several years later, as a test pilot for Grumman Aerospace, flying out of Point Mugu, California, I found a more modern way to do this using a Sparrow missile and the No. 6 F-14A Tomcat, which, at the time, was the Navy's fighter of the future.

More than three decades later, that day, June 20, 1973 remains extremely sharp in my memory, with good reason.

It wasn't a dark stormy night. The midday sun was bright in the clear southern sky. The Californian Channel Islands off Point Mugu stood out in blue and gray, in stark relief against the glistening ocean below as Bill 'Tank' Sherman and I flew west towards the test area in the Pacific Missile Test Range. Tank and I had known each other since we were in the same class in the Navy's F-4 replacement air group training. He already had a combat tour under his belt as a Navy Radar Intercept Officer (IRO) and was good at his business: Analytical, competent and cool, the kind of pilot you wanted to have along when things got hectic. I learned the real value of a good IRO over North Vietnam while flying combat missions in the F-4B Phantom from the USS *Coral Sea.*

One of the myriad development tests of a tactical airplane is weapons separation, whether those weapons are bombs or missiles. That day, we were testing a critical point in the Sparrow missile launch envelope. We weren't testing the missile's ability to kill airplanes, only its ability to clear our airplane safely when fired. The crucial test point took place at Mach 0.95, at 5,000 feet altitude and at zero g, and it consisted of firing Raytheon AIM-7 Sparrow missiles from the farthest aft station (Number 4) in the 'tunnel'; that is under the F-14 between the two engines where most missiles are mounted in semi-submerged launches in the tunnel, with two of its eight cruciform wings (four forward, four aft) inserted into the slots in each launcher. These triangular fins are 16 inches wide and, when the missile is attached to the launcher, stick into the bottom of the fuselage.

The test point for that day was in the heart of the low-altitude transonic range where the high-dynamic pressure flow fields close to the fuselage are mysterious. The zero g launch parameter meant the missile would not get any help from gravity as it was pushed away from the airplane by the two semicircular feet embedded in the launcher mechanism. Each of these feet was attached to a cylinder containing a small explosive charge that was set off by pulling the trigger on the stick.

This particular launch was not thought to be risky from a pure separation standpoint, because preceding Sparrow launches from the F-14 wing pylon, forward and mid-fuselage positions in identical flight conditions had demonstrated favorable release dynamics and good clearance between the missile and the aircraft throughout the entire launch sequence. In fact, the missile company Raytheon, on the basis of its own aerodynamic analysis, was concerned that the missile would severely pitch nose down, as it had on two of the three prior launches at this condition, and

The variable wing geometry gives the Tomcat a span of 68ft at 20 degrees of sweep and 38ft at 68 degrees.

possibly be so far below the aircraft as it passed the F-14's nose radar that it could, in the real world for which it was designed, lose the rear antenna radar signal and compromise the target acquisition portion of the missile trajectory.

Raytheon engineers had predicted a two-foot clearance. Independent Grumman wind tunnel tests confirmed the Raytheon analysis. However, this was not to be the case for this launch.

Hal Farley, the other Grumman test pilot sharing the missile separation program, and I had flown an extensive build-up series to get to this critical data point. Flight-test programs are very orderly evolutions. Engineers and test pilots study historical and forecast data carefully as test points progress from the mundane to the hazardous. This one was no different. Neither Hal nor I had flown missile separation tests before this series. And they didn't cover it at the Navy Test Pilot School, either. One of our Grumman colleagues, Don Evans, a former Edwards USAF test pilot and one of the most experienced sticks in the outfit, had warned us during flight test 'bonus' discussions, that for other than test flights, high air-speed tests and structural demos, weapons separations were the most perilous, primarily because of their unpredictable nature. Hal and I listened to Don, but his thoughts didn't sink in until we did a bit of on-the-job training. We soon learned that, once they departed the mother airplane, 'stores' sometimes had minds of their own; they sailed away and were known to barrel roll over the top or, perhaps, disintegrate ahead of the airplane. Once you've seen that happen, you become wary of staying too close when chasing the test airplane. We often had eager Navy pilots flying photo chase, and we had to warn them, in no uncertain terms, that this wasn't a Blue Angels' try-out.

During the preflight briefing, the engineers once again displayed graphs that showed the predicted missile-to-fuselage clearance, as a function of the time after trigger pull. As expected, clearance was seen to be tight. But we had the utmost confidence in Grumman's separation engineer, Tom Reilly, and his data. All previous launch data used during build-ups had come out on the money. We were good to go.

The test missile was a dummy AIM-7E-2; an obsolescent model of the Sparrow with the same form, fire and function as the AIM 7-F, the missile scheduled for the Fleet. The 7E2's casing, however, was slightly thinner than the 7F's.

The rest of the briefing was routine. After the regular ground checks, we took off and flew directly to our test location about 80 miles offshore between Santa Rosa and San Nicolas Islands, directly west of Los Angeles.

The test crew has two primary jobs: First, to hit a specific data point (aircraft attitude, altitudem airspeed, g loading) in the most efficient manner, and then relate unusual phenomena and analysis to the folks back on the ground. On this day, the second part was covered by several million dollars' worth of test instrumentation. This was very fortunate, because things were about to get exciting.

We hit our point in the sky (567 KIAS, 5,000 feet, 0g) and I pulled the trigger: 'Ka-whumpf'! A much louder 'ka-whumpf' than we had ever experienced before. The missile appeared in my peripheral vision as it passed from beneath the left nacelle. It was tumbling end over end, spewing fire. That's weird!

My first thought was, 'I'll bet stray foreign debris pieces enter the left engine'. My instant analysis seemed to be confirmed a few seconds later when the master caution light flashed in front of me. My eyes jumped to the caution panel, which had begun to light up like a pinball machine!

'HORIZONTAL TAIL' and 'RUDDER AUTHORITY', numerous lesser lights, and 'BLEED DUCT' (that's the one that usually came on before fire warning lights). I disregarded all but the 'bleed duct' light and tried to punch it out by turning off the bleed air source. That didn't work! Now the chase plane told me I was venting fuel, and had 'a pretty good fire going'.

'How good is that?' I asked in my cool-guy, smart-ass best, 'there's the left fire warning light!' I shut down the left engine which didn't work either. As I reached for the left fuel shut-off handle the nose pitched up violently, so sharply in fact that the force of more than 10g curled me into a fetal position. I couldn't reach either the face curtain or the alternate handle between my legs. It didn't take long for me to figure out that I was no longer in control of the situation. 'Eject, Tank, eject,' were my thoughts and, as the high g force (data said it peaked at 1.3 seconds) bled off to a point at which one of us could reach the face curtain, either Tank or I initiated the ejection sequence and in just one second we went from raucous noise and confusion to almost complete peace and quiet.

The ejection was smooth, and after my body completed about four somersaults the chute opened. The opening shock was gentler than I had expected. In fact, I hardly noticed it. All the action from missile launch to our ejection took only 39 seconds; it seemed much longer. We had ejected at an estimated 350 knots, having bled off 150 to 200 knots in the pitch up, and at 7,000 feet, 2,000 feet higher than we started. Post-accident analysis of the instrumentation showed the violent nose-up maneuver was caused by a full nose-up stabilator command, the result of a probable burn-through of the control rod that actuated nose-down commands. Had the stabilator command gone full nose-down, this would not be written.

As I stopped swinging in the chute, I saw Tank about 75 yards away and 100 feet below me. We waved at each other to indicate we were in good shape. We both waved at Fritz, who circled until he was low on fuel. We had hoped to wave at a helicopter, but to travel 80 miles in a helo flying at 120 knots takes a long time, even though it launched a few minutes after we ejected. Our airplane descended in a slow, shallow left spiral, burning fiercely in a long plume reaching from the trailing edge of the wing to well beyond the tail. On impact, it broke up and scattered pieces across a 100 foot radius. The largest chunk was the left portion of the tail section that floated in a pool of pink hydraulic fluid.

The parachute ride was calm, serene and long. The only noise was the chase plane roaring by several times. As I hung in the chute, my thoughts turned to the next phase: water survival. The sea below was calm. My first thought was 'did the crash sound reveille to the sharks, who must be lurking hungrily below awaiting their next meal?' Oddly, that was the last time I thought of sharks for the rest of the day because my mind soon became otherwise engaged. Sharks weren't something I could control, but water entry was, so I began to go through my water survival tactics. I pulled the right handle of the seat pan to release my life raft, which was supposed to remain attached to the pan on the end of a long yellow lanyard, or so I'd been told. I peered carefully below, but saw no raft or shadow on the water. Pulled the left one. Still no sign.

Bear in mind that the last time I had hung in a parachute harness was in preflight some 16 years before, and then not for very long. I wasn't about to perform a creative search for my life raft using chute steering or other acrobatics best left to the 82nd Airborne. Nor did I care to enter the water in other than the prescribed manner, so I gingerly walked my fingers up the risers and found the parachute's quick-release fittings, so I could actuate them when I hit the water to avoid becoming tangled in parachute and shrouds; yet another way to die.

After what seemed like a very long time hanging below the chute, the water suddenly rushed up at me, an event that, according to survival school anecdotes, signaled impending water entry. I plummeted about 10 feet under, then bobbed to the top while trying to actuate my life vest all the way. In my state of diminished IQ, I had forgotten that very basic step on the way down. I flailed about the surface, kicking, treading water with one hand and searching for the life-vest toggle with the other, then treading water with both. My addled brain realized that this maneuver wasn't going to be a long-term survival technique. It is better to stick your head under water, submerge if you must, open your eyes and find the damned toggles, or you're going to die. Doing so, I found the right one, pulled it, and once again ascended to the surface, this time from about eight feet down. Next, find the left toggle. Now that I was at least floating, I figured I didn't need to perform my immersion act again, so I somewhat calmly found the left toggle and inflated the rest of the life vest that contained most of the neck collar and thus, lots more comfort.

Now, where was the raft? Because I hadn't seen either the raft or its shadow on the way down, I assumed it hadn't inflated but it must be on the water nearby. I couldn't turn around very well because of my stiff neck. I soon saw the raft about five yards away out of the corner of my eye. I remembered rafts being yellow, but this one was black and at first glance seemed partially inflated. Both illusions were caused by the protective cover draped over the raft's side. I pulled on the lanyard and pulled the vessel to me.

Now the fun began. The time had come to board the raft. I remembered the 'method' from earlier days in water survival training: 'Face the low end of the raft, grab the sides, pull it toward you, do a snap roll, and you'll be in a nice, comfortable position on your back.' Right. But this approach didn't consider that the person boarding the raft still had his seat pan-strapped to his butt. The outcome of this trick was an inverted raft parked on top of my head. I flipped the raft and rested.

Soon I hoisted myself into the raft on my stomach, rested, then tried to complete a sneaky slow-roll. After about 45 degrees of roll, I became hung up on something. My oxygen hose was still connected to the seat pan. I fumbled around and eventually freed the hose. I disconnected the pan, and very carefully pushed it to the foot of the raft, I certainly didn't need to puncture it now. About now, my tired and befuddled mind decided to take stock of the situation and sort out priorities. I am in my raft and floating nicely; it's pretty calm, and I have better things to do now than flail about trying to get flat on my back in this raft.

Where's Tank? I figured he was behind me because he yelled from that direction a few minutes ago. I had replied by waving my arms, I was too weak to do much else after flailing about, and I was nauseous from swallowing seawater.

I turned on my Guard channel beeper, mainly to see if it would work. Half the world knew where we were, probably including the Soviets who regularly shadowed Pacific Missile Range operations with trawlers offshore. Planes had been flying around us when we ejected: two F-4s, Bloodhound 21, an S-2 used by PMR for range clearance. We also carried a PRC-90 survival radio, which is much better suited for talking to other humans, so I stowed the Guard beeper and pulled out the PRC, connected the earphone plug to the plug on my hardhat (this was probably the most coherent thing I'd done since jettisoning the airplane) turned to Guard transmit/receive and held a short confab with Tank. We were both fine. We were the only people talking on Guard, so I attempted to raise someone on Plead Control, PMR's main range-control frequency. Success. Bloodhound 21 flew low overhead, and we began conversing. Where was the cavalry? It was about 10 minutes away, in two helicopters.

Relieved, I tried to get comfortable. I first sighted the helo as he passed the foot of my raft several hundred yards away, and headed for the wreckage. Almost in unison, both Bloodhound 21 and I let him know neither Tank nor

I were at the wreckage. 'I'm at your nine o'clock' (I was really at his three; another good argument for giving direction first, then clock code.) I vectored him to me over the radio.

He quickly locked on. 'You don't need a smoke.' I was happy to hear that. If lighting a flare followed the trend of my misadventures of the past hour, I probably would have doused myself in orange smoke or opened the wrong end and burned myself.

'Do you have any difficulty?' asked the helo pilot.

'I'm hung up on something in the raft,' I said.

'I'll drop a swimmer,' he said.

After about 30 seconds, he splashed down about five yards away, disconnected me from whatever had me hung up, then guided me toward the horse collar being lowered by the second crewman. Using sign language, he told me to get out of the raft. Hesitant to leave the security of my new found home, I somewhat reluctantly obeyed. Strange thoughts race through the mind at times.

I got into the horse collar the right way on the first attempt (getting in the wrong way is probably the most common mistake in rescues). As I came abreast of the helo's door, the crewman grabbed me and pulled me in. I let him do everything his way. At this point, I wasn't about to insert my own inputs, the wisdom of which I had begun to suspect not long after entering the water nearly an hour before.

I saw the other helo getting close to Tank, who had a flare in his hand that was billowing immense clouds of orange smoke. I walked forward in the aircraft and watched as the crewman hoisted the swimmer aboard. Both helped me out of my flight gear. Then I strapped myself onto the canvas bench along the left bulkhead, looked out the open door at the welcome sight of the ocean now below me and smoked one of several cigarettes offered by the crewman as we flew to the beach some 40 minutes away.

Naturally, a larger welcoming committee had gathered on the ramp to meet us: Captain Clyde Tuomela, the Navy's Mugu F-14 program manager; Commander 'Smoke' Wilson, his deputy; Mike Bennett, Grumman's local flight test manager; Hal Farley, and a host of others. Tom Brancati, Grumman's manger at Point Mugu, happened, at the time, to be en route to Washington to brief the Navy on program progress. You don't lose a hand-built development airplane costing untold millions every day, so Tom, after being notified of the loss of the F-14 flight as he passed through Dulles airport, had to gather his data and thoughts quickly to explain this one. We had lost two aircraft previously: The first on the second ever F-14 flight when the hydraulic system failed, and the second, the carrier suitability demonstration airplane, which crashed into the water during an air show practice, killing the F-14 project pilot, Bill Miller, who had ejected earlier from the first, along with Bob Smyth, the director of Grumman's flight test.

One tenet of the fighter pilot's creed is: 'I would rather die than look bad.' You have got to look cool as you dismount, just as though nothing had happened; kind of John Wayne-like. Yeah, right! As I stepped down from the helicopter and my feet hit the ground, I began to shiver uncontrollably, and I had great difficulty talking. The thermal shock from flailing around in the 60 degree ocean for almost an hour had hit. This embarrassing state didn't wear off until later in sick bay, after I had belted down four large, raw brandies.

That evening, Tank and I had our Grumman bowling league scheduled. We went. Luckily, neither of us dropped a ball on our foot.

Pete Purvis completed 101 combat missions in the F-4 Phantom in Vietnam.

TESTIMONIAL

Pete Purvis was born on December 1, 1934 in Cleveland, Ohio where his first exposure to aviation came while sitting atop the family 1937 Ford watching the Cleveland Air Races. After high school, he spent the next four years at the US Naval Academy where he encountered his first Grumman aircraft.

Purvis flew his first Grumman aircraft, an S2F-1 Tracker, while assigned to VS-32 at NAS Quonset Point, Rhode Island. He soon decided that there was more to flying than chugging along at 100 feet and was eventually selected to attend the US Navy Test Pilot School where he was assigned to the Service Test Division.

One of his most interesting projects was the Skyhook Covert Aerial Retriever System invented by Robert Fulton, who was a direct descendant of the steamboat inventor. He achieved several firsts for Skyhook, such as the first live pick-up at night and the first simultaneous snatch of two people. After three years at NATC, in 1968, Purvis resigned his commission to join Westinghouse in Baltimore as an engineering test pilot. Grumman called in

1971 and offered him the opportunity to become an F-14 experimental test pilot. By early 1975, flight test activity at Point Mugu had waned, so he joined Grumman International as director of Washington operations and, in 1981, he became affiliated with Tracor Aerospace. He changed course in 1988 but, due to the recession of the early 1990s and fading government projects, he changed back to aerospace where he has worked as a consultant since 1993.

Chapter 4

Jean Pinet became the President and Secretary General of the Air and Space Academy Europe.

Jean Pinet – Concorde Moment of Madness

It lasted just a short time, but a few crazy moments nearly put paid to the entire Concorde test programme.

We had been flying Concorde at Mach 2 for more than three months, on both sides of the Channel. The British 002 was to have been the first to reach Mach 2 but it was pipped to the post by 001. Number 002 had been held up by an unfortunate technical delay and Brian Trubshaw, BAC flight test director, had sportingly agreed to let André Turcat achieve the legendary Mach 2 first, with the up-and-running 001.

The trials moved forward at a rapid pace and we discovered a layer of the atmosphere that we had only previously touched on with our military aircraft. With Concorde we stayed there for hours on end, despite the limitations of the prototypes' heavy fuel consumption. The Olympus engines had not yet reached their nominal performance and we were obliged to keep the reheat (or afterburner) lit most of the time in upper supersonic flight, in order to maintain Mach 2.

In reheat extra fuel is injected between the last stage of the Low Pressure (LP) turbine and the first exhaust pipe (primary nozzle) giving extra thrust from the whole engine and its nozzle.

The four reheats, one per engine, were operated by means of four 'on-off' switches placed behind the throttle on the centreline pylon between the two pilots. Air was fed to the engines via four air intakes, one per engine, mounted side by side in pairs in two engine-nacelles, one under each wing. The advantage in terms of reduced drag was obvious. The wind tunnel trials, though, showed that in supersonic flight a sudden problem on one of the engines had every chance of contaminating its partner through the interference of the shock waves from one intake to the other, despite the small protective fence situated between the two.

We knew then that failure of one engine at Mach 2 would lead to failure of its adjacent engine, leading to a strong yawing movement, itself causing a strong sideslip which might well affect the two surviving engines and transform the aircraft into the fastest glider in the world. However, an automatic rudder deflection system was installed, in order to prevent strong dynamic sideslip.

Engine air intakes are very sophisticated. Airflow at Mach 2 generates a whole system of shock waves which slow the stream of air down from 600m/sec in front of the aircraft to 200m/sec in front of the engine, while keeping up an excellent thermodynamic performance. Engines, which in supersonic cruise are constantly at maximum power, are highly sensitive to any interference and they can react violently with a low pressure compressor stall, in other words by suddenly refusing to accept the air fed to it. The brutal arrest of a 200kg/sec airflow arriving at 600m/sec can create certain problems. Normally the refused airflow is deflected downward through a dump door located in front of the engine and automatically opened by the air intake computer when needed.

In order to bring the shock wave system under control and enable the feat, unequalled to this day, of a 0.96 thermodynamic efficiency for the compression in the air intake, two articulated surfaces called air intake ramps, operated by hydraulic actuators, were installed in the ceiling of each of the rectangular channels capturing the air in front of the engines. Each of these ramps was the size of a large dining table and both, mechanically synchronized, were lowered or raised by means of controls managed by their corresponding air intake computer, at this time a complicated analogue computer, which matched the shape to the Mach number, the engine rating and other parameters such as sideslip.

At the time, this was the least known aspect of the aircraft; it was defined

The rear ramp appeared stuck in the front engine inlet, in which could just be made out the first compressor blades.

almost entirely by calculations, since no simulator and no full-scale wind tunnel existed yet for trials. Its analogue settings were very sophisticated but not easy to adjust, so we were moving forward cautiously with our Mach 2 trials.

On 26 January 1971, we were performing a more or less routine flight to measure the aircraft's function and performance at Mach 2, with a new rating designed to improve performance on Engine 4 (a slight increase in rotation of the low pressure mobile was designed to increase the air flow and consequently the thrust).

The test crews were by now taking turns to carry out the tests and the pilots were swapping between left or right seats in the cockpit.

On the day in question, Gilbert Defer was on the left, I was on the right, Michel Rétif was in the flight engineer's seat, Claude Durand in the main flight observer's seat and Jean Conche at the engine observer's station. With them was Francis Gillon, representative of the official French CEV.

The four-man crew in November 1970 with Pinet at the Captain's controls.

Hubert Guyonnet was on the fourth seat in the cockpit and carried out the radio tests.

After take-off from Toulouse, we accelerated into supersonic speed over the Atlantic abeam Arcachon and our flight path led us to north-west Ireland. Two reheats, 1 and 3 were on because the very high stratospheric temperature did not allow for Mach 2 flight without them.

Everything was going well. In the previous flight the crew had encountered strong turbulence, which is quite rare in the stratosphere, and had duly informed us. So far, no problem had occurred on the aircraft.

We were returning to Toulouse, heading south, just off Ireland. Our programme included subsonic flight tests so we prepared to decelerate. Gilbert was flying the aircraft. Michel and the engineers signalled that all was normal and ready for deceleration and descent.

We were at 15,300m altitude, at Mach 2, with a CAS of 530 knots (indicated airspeed corrected for air density and compressibility), in other words at maximum dynamic pressure in normal use.

On Concorde the right seat was the one from which the fewest systems manoeuvres could be carried out. A pilot's role there was more to actively help the others by monitoring programmes and checklists and by handling all secondary commands such as landing gear, droop nose, radio navigation, communications, and some essential engine commands excluding the throttle, for example the reheat switches.

Concorde was the first civil airliner to have an analogue fly-by-wire control system.

Procedures stipulated that before using the throttles to reduce the engine speed, one had to switch off the reheats. Gilbert asked me to do so, after which he could gradually throttle back the engines in order to avoid a bumpy transition. We had been advised during our early training on Olympus power plants to avoid touching the throttles in the event of engine stall.

As a safety measure I decided to cut off the afterburners one at a time, checking that all was well as each went off. First reheat 1, registering the slight jolt signalling the corresponding decrease in thrust. Then 3…

We were instantaneously plunged into a frenzied and crazy universe. The deafening noise of a canon firing off 300 shots per minute right by our side was coupled with a dreadful and terrible shuddering. Our submarine-like world (the metallic, totally opaque visor of the prototype was in the high position) was shaken at a frequency of five oscillations per second and with an amplitude four to five times greater or lesser than that of gravity (later the recorders showed oscillations of an amplitude well exceeding the maximum recorded range of plus and minus 3g). To the extent that we were seeing double, our eyeballs incapable of following the enforced oscillations.

At supersonic speed the aircraft stretched by nearly a foot. A large gap opened up on the flight deck between the engineer's console and the bulkhead.

Gilbert had the reflex of a test pilot: to get as quickly as possible out of the zone of maximum kinetic energy in which we had found ourselves and decelerate immediately. He set all four throttles right back without hesitating.

During this time I tried, or rather we all tried, to answer the questions, 'What is going on? What can be causing this terrifying phenomenon?' and especially, 'How can we stop it?'

Suspecting a massive engine problem I tried to decipher the indications of the engine instruments on the dashboard through the fog of disturbed vision and in the midst of the hail of electric warning lights and captions falling from the overhead panel. No interphone contact was possible between us.

I could vaguely make out that engines 3 and 4 rotation speeds seemed to be slower than the other two, especially number 4.

Something had to be done. Gilbert was flying the aircraft and had his hands full. I had a foolish impulse, probably dictated by the imperious mind-set need 'to do something' to stop the nightmare, despite the fact that I had, at my direct disposal, few commands seemingly linked to the phenomenon. Remembering my distant training, I tried to increase the level of rotation to engine 4. Of course this had no result and I quickly and definitively cut it back. With a terrible feeling of impotence and ineffectiveness I searched desperately for something to do from my isolated corner on the right.

Then it all stopped, as abruptly as it had begun. How much time had the incident lasted? Thirty seconds? A minute? When the flight recorders were analysed we found out it had lasted...only 12 seconds! And yet I have the distinct impression of having had a whole stream of thoughts, come up with heaps of ideas, suppositions and above all to have searched and searched and searched for solutions. It was as if my brain had suddenly gone into overdrive. But it was, above all, the failure, the realization that I had not been able to do anything or even to understand anything, which will remain with me forever.

It is little consolation that the rest of the crew did not understand anything either and, apart from Gilbert, were just as powerless.

The aircraft was slowing down and engine 3 which had seemed to be off switched itself back on automatically. Number 4, though, was well and truly dead.

Michel did a quick scan of his instruments. He also noted that 4 was off, but according to his air intakes position indicators, all four air intakes were working properly, which reassured us. With our flight experience in this altitude remaining limited, the most likely hypothesis to result from our post mortem, was that we had been faced with massively high stratospheric turbulence. But nobody really believed it. Presently at high subsonic 0.90 Mach, everything seemed to be working properly, so we decided to relight engine 4 since it was still a long way back to Toulouse.

Michel carried out the necessary manoeuvres. The engine started up again, idled at an average rotation speed and cut off after 20 seconds, leaving us mystified and this time worried, despite the normality of all indications.

Gilbert wisely decided not to try a new ignition and Claude left his post to cast an eye at an instrument that had been mounted on the prototype in order to inspect the landing gear and engines if necessary: a hyposcope, a kind of periscope going out through the floor rather than the ceiling. After a few seconds the interphone delivered the message: 'Shit, guys (stuttering...) we've lost air intake 4...!'

He went on to describe the gaping hole in the air entry in question, which seemed to be missing its ramps, and had traces of structural damage on the nacelle.

Gilbert's reaction was swift, the dynamic air pressure and, therefore, the speed had to be reduced. But we could not judge the exact extent of the damage. Were the wing and flight controls affected? And what about engine 3?

We decided to return to the minimum CAS of 250 knots and a lower altitude and to reroute towards the Fairford airstrip in the UK where our British colleagues and the 002 were awaiting us. I informed everyone of the problem and our decision, adding that if nothing untoward occurred we would try to reach Toulouse, since we still had enough fuel to make it.

Approaching Fairford, nothing out of the ordinary had occurred so we decided to continue, all possible airstrips having been alerted by radar stations from the flight test centre controllers who were following us on their screens.

At low speed, now that we knew what had happened and had nothing else to do but wait to arrive, time passed slowly and we exchanged few words, each of us lost in his thoughts and hypotheses. Engine 3 was, of course, carefully monitored. Personally, I was thinking of the anecdote about the unfortunate man in his toilet, whose house falls down around him when he pulled the flush! I had the impression we had gone through a similar experience.

Gilbert landed very gingerly because we did not fully trust engine 3. But everything went without a hitch. On the tarmac a large welcoming committee was awaiting us and, as soon as the engines were cut, there was a rush towards the right hand engine nacelle.

Gilbert and I got out first and were welcomed at the bottom of the ladder by André Turcat and Jean Franchi, who had broken away from the crowd contemplating the right nacelle.

They shared the same calm, dazed attitude, and the same expression; a mix of incredulity and frustration. It was André who spoke first: 'To think we weren't on this flight, how unlucky can you get…(they meant it).' Yes, it was supposed to be a routine test flight.

The sight of the right nacelle was impressive. As we approached, the spectators parted to let us past, all wearing the same incredulous, respectful expression, as if we had been saved by a miracle.

The ramps of intake number 4, the two 'dining tables', had disappeared, leaving a gaping hole above, in which the control kinematics were intact, and revealing some stubs of the ramp attachment rods.

In fact, only the front ramp had completely disappeared, clearly ejected and blown forward, (a staggering thought considering the speed we had been flying), slipped under the nacelle, damaging it, and along the protective fairing of one of the right-hand elevons' servo-controls, without touching it; a miracle. The rear ramp, or rather what remained of it, seemed stuck in the front engine inlet, in which could just be made out the first compressor blades, or rather what was left of them, which was not much.

The volume of metal that the engine had swallowed without exploding was impressive: no vital part of the aircraft had been touched, no hydraulic circuit, no fuel tank. I still remember to this day stories of the American supersonic B58 Hustler bomber, for

Air intake 4 lost its ramps and the nacelle was severely damaged.

which engine failure at Mach 2 led to the probable loss of the aircraft. Our civilian Concorde had only been shaken! The trust I already felt in the machine was fully borne out by this incident, which I did not at all regret having experienced, especially when I saw the envy written all over the faces of our friends, Turcat and Franchi.

But we had to know what had happened and why, and also why the ramp suspensions had given way. We soon understood why.

It was me who had unknowingly started the phenomenon off by stopping the engine 3 reheat. The normal, but brutal, arrest of fuel from the reheat had obviously prevented combustion and thus counter pressure behind the LP turbine. Due to the engine modification that had been carried out before the flight, the halt was not accompanied by the normal, predicted concomitant movement of the area decrease in the primary nozzle that was to compensate the fall in pressure. The LP turbine had gone into overdrive, carrying with it the LP compressor which, not appreciating this treatment, had protested by stalling. The stall had itself caused a brutal displacement of the air intake shock waves which subsequently stalled also (with an upstream unsteady, shock waves move away from the air intake throat). It influenced the adjacent air intake 4 which stalled, leading to the stall of its own engine. These stalls generated a massive overpressure above the ramps and, despite the dump door, those of air intake 4 decided to detach from their weak attachments..

A lack of understanding of the phenomena at work (it was the first air intake stall experienced) had led to approximations at design stage in the calculations of the ramp supports which had ended up undersized.

There was another error. Instead of position sensors being placed on the ramps themselves, they had been fitted on the hydraulic engine control shafts. This was why Michel Rétif was under the impression they were in their correct position, because the hydraulic engines, untouched by the damage, continued to function properly, unaware that their ramps no longer existed, thus giving us a false sense of normality.

The measurements taken during this incident led to the air intake structure being completely overhauled and three months later we resumed testing.

Subsequently we deliberately provoked air intake stalls on numerous occasions so as to regulate it, this time by means of more capable digital calculators. Although without danger, but still impressive, it bore no relation in terms of intensity to that stall without ramps...

From my point-of-view, I had the indelible feeling of impotence and failure during the incident and this caused me to reflect on the likely reaction of a regular airline pilot. This aircraft was destined to be placed in the hands of normal airline pilots, and not to remain the domain of test pilots.

At the time I accepted the offer of founding and becoming head of a training centre for future Airbus customers. The project was called

Aeroformation, and had the firm aim of including Concorde training, and this Concorde training was to include reactions to air intake and engine stalls.

A certain French President probably harbours an uneasy memory. One day much later we were flying with our first production aircraft, Concorde 1, on the way back from Saudi Arabia. That time I was on the left and Gilbert on the right, Michel again in the third seat! But that is another story.

Concorde 001 was the first to fly in 1969 with an all French crew.

TESTIMONIAL

Jean Pinet was born in Toulouse on 13 September 1929. From 1952-1956 he served in the French Air Force as a fighter pilot, including a stint training with the USAF.

From 1956-1965 he was transferred to the Centre d'Essais en Vol, in charge of air-to-air and air-to-ground missiles flight tests. He spent the last three years of this period appointed to Erprobungsstelle 61 der Bundeswehr, Manching in Germany, in charge of the German missiles flight tests (Oberregierungsbaurat) on F104-G and G91. From 1965 until 1994 he worked with Sud-Aviation / Aerospatiale in charge of Concorde handling qualities and flight controls, flight and simulator tests, development and certification, also flight and maintenance training at Aerospatiale and Aeroformation with the Caravelle and Concorde. With Airbus Industrie he set up and managed the GIE Aeroformation, the Airbus training centre. He was the founder of Aeroformation, managing director and flight instructor

As well as numerous other activities in the aerospace industry he is a former President and Secretary General of the Air and Space Academy (Europe). He remains a consultant in aeronautics for Thomson Training and Simulation and Groupe Aeroconseil. He is an Officer of Légion d'Honneur and Officer of Ordre National du Mérite.

Chapter 5

G. Warren Hall has flown more than 65 different types of aircraft including the X-14B, XV-15, AD-1 Swing Wing and the Rotor Systems Research Aircraft.

G. Warren Hall –
Rotor Systems Research Aircraft
From Rotors to Wings...the First Flight

The truly historic first flight of the Rotor Systems Research Aircraft, a NASA project which was a helicopter flying without rotors.

It was early morning on Tuesday, May 8, 1984...one of those really ideal mornings at Edwards Air Force Base that comes only with patience. There was little or no wind; the morning air was chilly; the ground crew was complaining about how the temperature had dropped as the sun began its climb over the hills of the rocket site to the east of the Edwards dry lake bed. This was not our first attempt to fly the fixed wing Rotor Systems Research Aircraft (RSRA). The previous Friday we had begun the same early morning routine only to find that winds, which had been forecast to be 10 knots or less, were gusting from 30 to 37 knots, a full 70 degrees off the runway. A disappointed crew and lots of supporters of the program knew the answer to the question: 'Will we fly today?' without it even being asked.

The RSRA was a unique research aircraft designed specifically to flight test advanced helicopter rotors. It had flown as a helicopter, a compound helicopter, (combination fixed and rotary wing aircraft) and now, for the first time, as an airplane. The RSRA was unique in that it was possible to explosively jettison an errant rotor in flight, thus converting from a compound helicopter to a fixed-wing aircraft. The airplane configuration was originally considered only as an emergency mode in the event it was necessary to jettison an unstable rotor in flight. Recently, it was deemed necessary to flight test the RSRA in the airplane configuration to demonstrate the versatility of the fixed-wing craft to fly without a rotor. It was also a great opportunity to obtain 'rotor' data. This data would be used to determine the capability of the basic airplane to overpower a new sophisticated X-wing rotor, expected to be flight tested on the RSRA in 1986.

The RSRA was powered by two 8,250 lb General Electric TF-34 turbo fan engines and two General Electric T-58 1500 shaft horsepower engines. The wing was unique in that its incidence angle relative to the fuselage could be changed in flight.

This is the story of the first flight of the fixed wing RSRA at the NASA Dryden Flight Test Facility at Edwards

The program began to investigate ways to increase the speed of rotor aircraft, as well as their performance, reliability and safety.

Air Force Base, California. I was the first person ever to fly the same aircraft as a helicopter, compound helicopter, and fixed wing airplane.

The morning was perfect. The ground crew had arisen at one o'clock that morning. The RSRA was on the line and humming with activity when the flight crew arose at three o'clock. Portable lights pierced the darkness as the shiny white airplane was carefully prepared for this important first flight. The noise from electric carts shattered the quietness of the desert calm. The airplane and its sophisticated electronic system that would dutifully report the craft's structural health were meticulously checked and re-checked. Red,

The concept uniquely gave the RSRA the vertical flight stability of a helicopter and the horizontal cruise capability of a conventional aircraft.

yellow and green lights signaled to Lonnie Phillips, the instrumentation technician, that all systems were ready to go.

By 05:00 the telemetry room, the structural facility (call sign 'NASA TM'), and the control room (call sign 'NASA 1') had all completed the numerous preflight checks required to ensure that their complex instrumentation was ready. At 05:15 sharp, the overhead speakers crackled with a radio call from the RSRA (call sign 'NASA 740') to NASA TM. It was the instrumentation engineer, Zoltan Szoboszlay, reporting that the vital telemetry link between the aircraft and the ground test facility was ready for checkout.

Other activities were taking place. Over at the US Army flight test facility, the Army flight crew for the 'Firebird' were busy preparing for its all important, but hopefully not required, mission. The Firebird was a UH-1H 'Huey' helicopter specially modified with a fire suppressing apparatus and manned by a highly trained crew who were to stand by in the event of a mishap. The Firebird was to orbit south of the runway during our takeoff and landing, and trail the RSRA out to the flight test area.

The crew for 'NASA 701', the chase aircraft, a Beechcraft Super Kingair, had already completed its preflight checks and was ready to start engines. It was also checking the flight test area for turbulence and winds before the RSRA flight.

It was 05:20; the ready room telephone rang and Rube Erickson, the test director, told us that the airplane would be ready for the pilots by the time we got there. The pilot's preflight was more of a ritual than anything else, for the crew chief, Gary Jackman, and our highly competent inspector, Frank Presbury, had checked and double checked the

The purpose of the 1984 tests was to demonstrate the fixed-wing capability of the helicopter/airplane hybrid and explore its flight envelope.

RSRA in every detail. Pat Morris, was an Army test pilot assigned to NASA. He was the co-pilot and occupied the left seat and I the right. We met at the tail wheel. Since I had already kicked the main wheel tires, it probably wasn't necessary to kick the tail wheel again, but then why not?

As we mounted the entry stair, the many 'Good lucks' from the ground crew were appreciated apprehensively. A quick check of the instrumentation circuit breaker panel, showed several breakers pulled to protect delicate flight instrumentation during the preflight checks. All were reset. Heat from the electronic equipment made the cockpit seem cozy and warm. It felt comforting after the chilly desert air outside.

The ejection seats were certainly uncomfortable and I sure would like to have known who designed the lap belt attachment. This was the most difficult seat to strap into I'd ever seen. Pat reminded me not to forget my leg restraints. At last, we were all strapped in, ear plugs in, beanie cap on, and last, but not least, helmet and gloves fitted. Pat was already talking on the interphone as I plugged in my radio cord. 'Good morning, Gary, how do you read?' I complained again about the decrease in temperature.

'NASA TM, this is NASA 740, how do you read?'

The aircraft was equipped with 14 load cells to measure main-rotor thrust, torque, drag, wing lift and auxiliary engine thrust.

'Loud and clear.'

'All stations check in.'

'Firebird, are you up?'

From the safety plane, a curt military: 'Yes sir! We're ready to go.'

'NASA 1?'

'Good morning 740, it looks like a nice day for a first flight.' That was Don Mallick, a seasoned senior NASA test pilot. He was to monitor our flight and coordinate any ground activities we needed; a good man to have on your test team.

'NASA 701, do you copy?'

'NASA 701 here, we're taxiing out at this time...'

Good, I guessed the Air Force folks were already in the tower. The NASA photo and ground crew also checked in.

Pat, with his normal military efficiency shouted, 'Are you ready for the checklist?'

'Sure, go ahead.'

We started the checklist about ten minutes ahead of schedule. The pre-start checklist was soon complete, and I started number one engine. The lights dimmed in response to the high power drain of the electric starter as the number one T-58 engine engaged. 15 per cent...Pat flipped the boost pump switch on. 20 per cent...throttle around the horn...one, two, three, four, five...come on. Swoosh! There was a large and noticeable increase in noise over our heads as the engine lights off. The engine gauges came alive quickly. We watched the engine temperature intently. On Friday it had gone much higher than I liked. Oil pressure okay, starter dropout. It was a good start! Pat remarked, 'All hydraulic pressures are up.'

As I advanced the throttle forward to 104 per cent rpm, both generators came on the line.

'Gary, we're ready for external air and you can clear the left TF-34.'

This was one of two large jet engines on either side of the fuselage that allowed us to fly as a fixed wing airplane.

'You've got air and it's clear.'

Pat completed the fuel check and I pressed the starter button. 10 per cent, throttle out of the detent. The engine lights off.

'Pat, make a note that the fuel flow indicator didn't register on start. You watch the starter and I'll keep track of the temperature.'

'Disconnect external air.'

We were now on our own. It seemed like it took forever, but each hydraulic control system had to be checked, as well as the electronic portions of the flight control system. In my 19 years of active flight testing, this was by far the most complex airplane I had ever flown.

'NASA 740, NASA 701, over.' It was Cliff McKeithan, an Army Lieutenant

Colonel, in the chase airplane.

'Go ahead, 701.'

'The test area is free of turbulence from the surface to 10,000 feet. Conditions are perfect; we'll remain airborne and pick you up on takeoff.'

At long last, the checklist was complete. We would start the fourth engine when we got through with the three and a half mile taxi. It saved fuel and reduced the wear on the brakes.

Pat was already calling Edwards ground control for taxi clearance:

'Eddie ground, this is NASA 740 at the NASA ramp, taxi for take-off. Pull the chocks, Gary.'

A cheery 'Good Luck, guys,' and Gary signaled Ron Gardner to pull the chocks. Both hustled off to NASA 11, a van that was to follow us out to the runway in case we had a problem.

'Well, Pat, we've waited for this a long time.'

'It's a great day for it,' was his reply.

We passed the tower:

'NASA 740, this is Eddie ground, what is your aircraft designation?'

Pat replied, 'We're the R-S-R-A...Romeo, Sierra, Romeo, Alpha, over.'

'What's that?'

'The Rotor Systems Research Aircraft.'

'Where's your rotor? Are you going to be a helicopter tomorrow?'

It must have been the same controller who was on duty when we flew the airplane into Edwards in the compound configuration.

'No, we're going to be a fixed wing airplane for a while.'

We started the second TF-34 engine and give the instruments one last check.

'TM, we're ready for the takeoff unless you see some reason there for us not to.'

'Everything looks good here, you're cleared to go.'

The SAS (Stability Augmentation System) was on, tail wheel to go.

' Well, Pat, this is it.'

'Good Luck, Warren,' was his reply.

Power came on, brakes off...fan speed 50 per cent, 40 knots, 80 knots, 100 knots. Boy, this thing really accelerated...80 per cent on both engines, feels good...115, 120, 125 knots...stick back slowly...hmmm, it didn't lift off as quickly as I expected it would, but we were airborne. 130, 140, 145 knots, this thing really climbed.

'Are you ready for the gear up?'

'Roger, raise the gear.'

150, 155, easy now, we wanted to climb out at 150 knots...stick back some more...I didn't think it would climb this steeply. I bet 701 can't keep up. Air speed decreasing to 150.

'Are you ready for the flaps?'

'Uh, sure, flaps up. You know, Pat, this thing is really shaking. It feels like something's wrong in the back of the airplane.'

'TM, we're getting quite a bit of high frequency shaking in the back of the airplane. Do you see that?'

'Yeah 740, we see it on the horizontal stabilizer, we're checking it out.'

'TM, 740, we are also getting a noticeable longitudinal chugging in the airplane. I don't feel it laterally, only in the longitudinal axis.'

Wow! We're through 7,000 feet already. Better start easing off on the power if I'm going to stop at 10,000 feet. Hmmm, the chugging has stopped but there is a noticeable vibration in the back of the airplane, which was worrying.

'TM, 740, What do you see on the horizontal stabilizer?'

'It's showing a lot of activity but it's within limits. You're cleared to proceed.'

'740 Roger.'

'TM, I'd like to feel this thing out for a few minutes and then we'll continue the flight card.'

The aircraft was actually pretty stable in pitch, but occasionally I noticed a marked tendency for the airplane to slide out from underneath me laterally.

'Pat, I'm still concerned about the shaking in the back of the airplane.'

'Me too, Warren.'

'NASA 701, this is 740, do you feel any turbulence?'

'Nawh, it is nice and smooth here.'

I was afraid of that.

'Do you see anything moving on the back of the airplane?'

'No, we don't.'

'TM, 740, We'd like to incrementally turn off the SAS, to see if it might be causing the shaking.'

Control agreed and all for SAS were shut off one-by-one.

'Still no change…TM, the SAS is coming back on, we don't feel any change.'

'We're suggesting a wing incidence change to see if that might affect the shaking,' (hydraulic pistons allow the RSRA to vary the angle between the wing and fuselage when commanded by the pilots).

'Roger, you're cleared to increase the wing incidence to seven and a half degrees.'

'Roger TM, record "on" wing coming to seven and a half degrees, it's record number 22...We don't see any difference here and besides we're getting thirteen and a half degrees angle of attack and the stall light blinks on occasionally. TM, we're putting the wing back to five degrees, it is record 23, over.'

'TM Roger.'

'TM, we'd like to extend the flaps to see if that helps, over.'

'Roger, go ahead 740.'

'It is record 24 and the flaps are coming to 15 degrees.'

Wow, suddenly it felt much better. It was as smooth as glass now. The anxious moments seemed over. This was the way it should feel.

'TM, lowering the flaps has stopped the shaking.'

'TM Roger, we see that here, the tail has really calmed down. It looks good here.'

'And it sure feels better up here. We're going to raise the flaps in increments to see if we feel any change...Flaps coming to ten degrees. Still feels good. Flaps coming to five degrees...still good. Okay, we're going to leave the flaps at five degrees and get on with the flight card. Fuel is 3,200 lbs.'

We held at 150 knots and backed down on the tail rotor rpm, careful as we got to 95 per cent. It looked like 94 per cent was the best we were going to do as it dropped off rapidly below 94 per cent.

'What's next Pat?'

'We're to extend the gear and flaps and feel out the landing configuration and establish two sets of side-slip conditions to load up the landing gear door.' (The left landing gear door had been redesigned following an in-flight failure on a compound helicopter flight a few months back.)

I was now beginning to like this airplane more. It was nice and stable, almost too stable. It especially felt good in the landing configuration.

'I'm going to practice a flare and wave off.'

OK, slowing to 125, 120, power on,...good. Good pitch response, nose coming up, good acceleration.

'Tell TM we're ready to take the gear doors out to their maximum speed now. What increments do they want?'

'Ten knot increments.'

'TM, 740 how long a record to you want?'

'Two minutes each, 740.'

'Roger. Punch the clock for me, would you Pat?'

'There's three degrees, four, five, right on five. Hold it right there. Good.'

'About 15 more seconds to go. Good record.'

'TM we'd like to be heading home with about 1,800 lbs of fuel and we show 2230 at this time.'

We were now on our way back, and I knew the chase plane needed to shoot some film. NASA 701 eased up and to our right.

'How about dropping down just a little 740.'

'Okay, but come on 701, keep her coming down or we'll be too high to land.'

'We've got your pictures, 740, you have the lead.'

'Let's put the gear down to get a little more drag so we can get down. Call the tower, Pat, tell them we want a straight in to a low approach.'

The landing checklist was complete.

'Give me full flaps now or we'll never get down.'

'Full flaps.'

I was extremely impressed with how stable the airplane was. I was looking for 140 knots and made a note that it was difficult to match up the power on the TF-34s. That must be what was causing the lateral shuffle I felt. Power coming on to help stop the rate of descent.

'Looking good.'

That was Pat providing encouragement and expressing his anxiety at the same time. Careful. There was more sink rate than I would have liked. The Edwards runway is always a little deceiving because it is twice as wide as most runways. But it sure was nice to have 15,000 feet of concrete to land on.

The speed looked good and we kept her coming down. We were over the approach end, powered back, another sudden lateral shuffle. 130 knots, 125, and we leveled off.

'120.'

'OK Pat, we're taking it around.'

Throttles coming up...60 per cent, 70 per cent, 80 per cent. That should be good enough.

'Set flaps to 15 degrees.'

We turned downwind. It looked like we were the only airplane in the pattern. We were now on the downwind at 3,800 feet.

'Well Pat, it really feels quite good. We'll land this time. I think I'll extend the turn to base leg to give myself a little more time to get stabilized on the final approach.'

'NASA 740, you're cleared to land, the wind is calm.'

With full flaps we were over the runway and approaching touchdown...easy...where was the runway? We should have touched down by now. Speed 120, still floating, I eased off on the power, lateral shuffle – touchdown! Out of the blue came a sudden oscillation right at touchdown, but to no avail. I couldn't really tell if we were on the ground. Speed 105 knots and stick back. I never felt the tail wheel touch. We must have been closer to a three point landing attitude than I thought. I had expected the full flaps to make it feel more nose down.

We used the entire runway as there was no reason to abuse the brakes. I shut down, the right TF-34 helped slow us down. Pat chimed in with relieved excitement, 'Good job, good job!'

'TM, 740 is exiting at the end, the record is off.'

Don Mallick enthusiastically shared our excitement,

'Congratulations, NASA 740, an excellent first flight!'

'Thanks Don.'

The excitement of those moments was always hard to capture, but we had taxied half way back to the ramp before either one of us realized we had forgotten to call the tower for clearance back to the NASA line.

Sheepishly, 'Eddie ground, NASA 740 for taxi to the NASA ramp.'

'Eddie ground roger, we've got you covered, you're cleared to the NASA ramp. Good flight!'

TESTIMONIAL

G. Warren Hall learned to fly while working as a 'line boy' at Northfield Airport in Richmond, Virginia. He earned his private pilot's license at 18 years old. After graduation from the University of Virginia in 1960, with a degree in Aeronautical Engineering, he became a naval aviator logging more than 300 carrier landing in the F-3B Demon and F-4B Phantom II aircraft.

He began his flight test career in 1965 as an engineering test pilot with Cornell Aeronautical Laboratory of Cornell University where he logged more than 100 hours in the Bell X-22A V/STOL aircraft. He has a Masters Degree in Aerospace Engineering and an MBA from the State University of New York at Buffalo. He joined NASA Ames Research Center as a Research Test Pilot in 1977. He has flown more than 65 different types of aircraft including the X-14B, XV-15, AD-1 Swing Wing and the unique Rotor Systems Research Aircraft. He is a Fellow in the Society of Experimental Test Pilots.

He completed 28 years of military service before retiring as the Commander of the California Air National Guard's 129th Rescue and Recovery Group at Moffett Field, California with the rank of Colonel.

In 1993, the San Francisco Chapter of the American Institute of Aeronautics and Astronautics designed Mr Hall a 'Living Legend of Aerospace'. In November 2004, he was inducted in the Virginia Aviation Hall of Fame.

Chapter 6

Kapil Bhargava flew Spitfires and Vampires before attending the Empire Test Pilots School in UK to graduate as one of India's pioneer test pilots.

Kapil Bhargava – Messerschmitt HA-300 Against all Odds

Indian Kapil Bhargava flew the maiden flight of the HA-300 for the Egyptians, with German support. The last aircraft from the legendary Willy Messerschmitt, it was also the smallest supersonic fighter ever made.

Professor Willy Messerschmitt was arguably the world's finest aircraft constructor. During the Second World War he manufactured more than 35,000 Me-109s: more than any other fighter in history.

After the war, all German designers and scientists were prohibited by the Allies to undertake any research for defence purposes. Professor Messerschmitt was even limited in his movements within Germany. He set up a new firm, Hispano Aviacion, in Spain and started designing an ultra-light fighter aircraft in 1951. Only a delta-shaped plywood glider without a tail was built. Its first flight, being towed by a CASA C- 2.111 (the Spanish

Heinkel He-111), was abandoned due to instability before becoming fully airborne.

Eventually it was the Egyptians who took over the HA-300 project. A German design team moved to Helwan, south of Cairo. The shift of the project from Spain to Egypt resulted in the letters HA (originally Hispano Aviacion) referring to Helwan Aircraft, at least as far as the Egyptians were concerned. The HA-300 was an extremely ambitious development project. It was an ultra-light, single seat, delta-shaped fighter aircraft with a separate tail plane. It was Messerschmitt's last design and the only truly supersonic one. He was already famous for the Me-109 and Me-262, but the HA-300 was the smallest jet fighter aircraft ever designed and flown. Even the Gnat was bigger. Its delta wing was swept at 57.5 degrees and its thickness/chord ratio was just 3 per cent. This was perhaps the thinnest duralumin wing ever flown for a fighter aircraft. Messerschmitt was well ahead of his time in the concept of his first supersonic design; unfortunately, he did not have an adequate industrial base from which to launch it. If he could have done this work in a developed country, the HA-300 may well have been a success.

Clearly, the HA-300 would have had amazing performance due to its lightness and very high thrust to weight ratio. These would have allowed it to go up almost vertically and reach 12,000 metres in only two and a half minutes from brakes off. But, the thinness of its wing also meant that flutter was very likely. Its very small wingspan of just 5.84 metres meant that damping in roll at high altitude would have been very low, which could result in inertia coupling at high rates of roll. The rudder was also quite high above the centre line. The HA-300 was never tested for inertia coupling, but it did show slight adverse bank on use of rudder.

The Indian participation in Egypt's aircraft industry was the direct result of a close understanding between Pandit Nehru and President Gamal Abdul Nasser. Suffice it to say that I was deputed by the Indian Air Force to work as a test pilot in the Egyptian Aircraft Factory 36 at Helwan. The Egyptians had no qualified test pilots, and the project needed one. The German experts at Helwan had wanted a European test pilot, but none were available. When I arrived at Helwan in June 1963, I was escorted to meet Fritz Schaeffer who was the former test pilot of Heinkel and had flown the world's first jet fighter in 1941. As the man in charge of the flight test group, he bluntly told me I was not wanted and should not dream of flying the HA-300. I could keep myself amused with the HA-200 (Saeta) twin engine basic trainer aircraft, Messerschmitt's last but one design, being produced under licence at Helwan. Air Marshal M. Sidky Mahmoud, Commander Egyptian Air Force (CAS), expressed his inability to force the Germans to use my services.

I pointed out that if the Egyptians had no use for me, I would prefer to return to India, as test pilots were not exactly in surplus there. The Air Marshal then suggested that, although I would normally be engaged in the production testing of the HA-200, I should simultaneously 'keep an eye on the HA-300'.

The situation changed somewhat dramatically a few days later, however, when it was decided that the HA-300 would be taxied in front of President Gamal Abdul Nasser during the Egyptian Republic Day celebrations in July 1963. Since no other test pilot was available, the German staff conceded that I might be permitted to taxi their prototype fighter. In their opinion, I was unlikely to do much harm merely taxiing the aircraft!

The performance of this 'simple exercise' proved rather more complex than had been anticipated, owing to a number of factors. The damping of the nose oleo leg was unsatisfactory and resulted in the aircraft pitching violently on encountering the slightest roughness on the runway surface. The self-centring action of the nose wheel was so powerful that the wheel tended to skid and jump sideways rather than turn. Tremendous effort was put into reaching a reasonably acceptable compromise between nose wheel shimmying and turning stiffness, and it was only then possible to demonstrate gentle taxiing of the aircraft in front of the President.

This occasion was the only time I met President Nasser in person. He was accompanied by Anwar El Sadat, who later succeeded him. I explained to President Nasser the layout and the most interesting features of the HA-300 and was asked my personal opinion of the Helwan fighter. In my reply, I endeavoured to imply that, left to the foreign staff alone, the HA-300 would make an interesting research project for their own objectives, but would never be developed into an effective weapon system. He just smiled. I concluded that he had his reasons for persisting with the project, and under the control of foreigners. He must have believed that a successful flight test would be sufficient to strengthen his hand in international negotiations.

In October 1963, when the Germans failed to hire any European test pilot, I was asked by the Egyptian Air Chief to conduct its maiden flight. I told him that the aircraft was a death trap and I was not willing to fly it. A number of messages between Professor Messerschmitt and myself were relayed by the Air Chief.

On being told of my fears, Messerschmitt said that he had not wanted, 'A bloody Indian pilot,' as he was sure to be cowardly. My response was that I was not just chicken, I was shit-scared. I explained cordially I would be very dead if I attempted to fly the aircraft before its deficiencies were removed.

To settle the dispute we invited Wing Commander Suranjan Das from HAL (Hindustan Aircraft (later Aeronautics) Limited) to give his opinion on the aircraft's hazardous design features. He took my list of dangerous features and completely confirmed my views. He sent six copies of my report, with a covering letter, informing all concerned authorities that no Indian test pilot should be permitted to fly the aircraft until its shortcomings were eliminated. In this way I became the only pilot available for the HA-300 V-1's first flight.

My most memorable encounter with Professor Messerschmitt soon followed. One day, I was told that the Professor wanted me in his conference room. On entering it, I saw that it was laid out like a kangaroo court. At the head of some long tables was Messerschmitt with an interpreter beside him. Senior Germans were seated on one side, with their Egyptian counterparts opposite them. The bottom end had one seat for me, the accused. Messerschmitt asked me through his interpreter why I was so insistent on the modifications, which I had claimed were essential to ensure safety. By then I was quite angry and replied that I was not really interested in the modifications but they were my conditions to fly the aircraft; otherwise another test pilot could be hired and I would happily go back home to India.

There were many German red faces on hearing this answer. The word ultimatum buzzed around between them. People did not issue an ultimatum to Professor Messerschmitt. However, he calmed his team down and told me that, while he might agree to make the changes, he wanted to know why I was so adamant to have them done. Still seething with rage, I said that a technical lecture was necessary and I would proceed to give it if he really wanted. He quietly agreed to listen.

I reminded Messerschmitt that the contract for the aircraft specified the design to conform to the British Air Publication-970 (AP) requirements, which laid down the design criteria for military aircraft. The nineteen points listed by me were all in serious breach of the AP.

A few of faults were so obvious that it was a wonder that the design team did not anticipate them in any way. For example, the integral fuel tanks had leaked and flexible rubber tanks were inserted to counter the problem. Some of these had also leaked. Yet, the only indication for fuel contents was a totalizer gauge showing the fuel entering the engine. The pilot would only realize that all his fuel had leaked after his engine cut. The fuel system had apparently been designed with a preoccupation for unlimited inverted flying. Firstly, there was no requirement for such a facility and secondly, the Orpheus engine's oil system would, in any case, have limited the maximum duration of inverted flight to about 10 seconds. Also, the direct supply tank to the engine was the smallest in the system and any failure of air transfer pressure would produce a flameout within two minutes. The tail plane trim was operated by a single-pole switch on the stick carrying the entire current of the large motor, without any protection against a trim runaway. Rudder flutter was forecast at Mach 0.56, yet its damper was powered by a single hydraulic system. Other design deficiencies, too many to list here, were also massively dangerous and unacceptable to me as a qualified test pilot.

Messerschmitt did not take long to realize that I was right in my concern for the aircraft's safety. It takes a truly great man to admit that he is wrong. The Professor got up from his chair and shook my hand. He said that he had not realized how far his team had fallen back in design expertise. He assured me that all required actions would be taken and he would instruct his staff to follow my directions. It took just six months after this meeting for me to declare the aircraft ready for flight.

The first flight on 7 March 1964 was as much routine as the maiden flight of any revolutionary fighter aircraft can ever be. There was absolutely no trouble of any kind in its short duration of just over 12 minutes. The excitement came after the flight.

When we were sipping champagne, Messerschmitt shook my hand and held it for a while. He was trembling. I asked him what the matter was and why he was so tense. He replied, 'When I think of what could have happened.' I told him that we had done all our worrying on the ground with every contingency planned for. The safety of the aircraft was the issue with which we had been struggling for six months. He said that while that was all very well, so many of his earlier prototypes had crashed on the first or an early flight. I lightly replied that he should have listened more to his test pilots and not threatened to send them off to the Russian Front if they disagreed with him. He smiled.

Our safety precautions allowed the two prototype aircraft (V-1 and V-2) to complete 135 flights without a single accident. For me, the aircraft was very pleasant to fly. Its control forces had been adjusted to meet my requests and the aircraft's response in rates of roll and stick force per g was exactly as I liked. I was able to take the V-2 (Second Prototype) to Mach 1.13. During flutter testing Major Sobhy El Tawil, trained by me as a test pilot, encountered flutter when a thruster on the left wing was fired. He followed the briefing exactly and did not allow aerodynamic loads to increase. Instead, he throttled back and gently eased out of the dive. He returned safely with a cracked inner hinge of the left flap/aileron. The German staff was very impressed with his airmanship. This was, literally, the only safety hazard experienced on the aircraft during its entire history. The HA-300's maximum speed and ceiling were limited as all flying was done with the Orpheus 703 engine.

The engine choice for the HA-300 was a critical problem. In the end the British Orpheus engine was chosen.

The foreign technical staff, working on the HA-300 airframe and the E-300 engine, wholeheartedly embraced proposals for a collaboration with India in the venture. The principal motive of the Egyptians was presumably to get

India to share the cost of developing the E-300 engine, which was offered as an option for India's own HF-24 Marut. For Brandner and his team, Indian collaboration provided the opportunity to flight test the engine in a really suitable airframe. Four prototype E-300 engines had each completed 2,000 hours static running in test cells before the ninth prototype engine had begun flight trials beneath the wing of an An-12. This installation was proving

After three prototypes and the development of the E300 engine, the HA-300 project was abandoned in 1969.

somewhat less than satisfactory owing to the limited flight envelope possible.

India had built an HF-24 with reheated Orpheus engines and for this development HAL had enlarged the rear end of the aircraft. Consequently, it was a relatively simple job to adapt an HF-24 airframe, powered by a pair of normal Orpheus engines, but easily modified to replace one or both with E-300s. This aircraft, referred to as the IBX, was flight tested in India with normal Orpheus engines and again in Egypt after delivery and reassembly at Helwan. Shortly thereafter, an E-300 was installed in the starboard engine bay. A team from HAL supported the flight testing of this aircraft, despite the technical and logistical difficulties resulting from the distance between Bangalore and Helwan, well over 100 flights being performed and the E-300 being declared ready for installation in the single-engine aircraft, the HA-300.

Apart from just over a dozen flights performed by me, all flight testing of the IBX was undertaken by Wing Commander I.M. Chopra who later became chief test pilot at Bangalore and finally retired as chairman of HAL. The contribution to the development of the E-300 engine made by him and Group Captain (later Air Marshal) C.S. Naik, a Cranfield graduate, was invaluable, especially since few of the local technical staff possessed much knowledge or experience of flight testing and analytical techniques.

Professor Messerschmitt asked Professor K.W. Tank, who had just finished his assignment with HAL, to stay in Helwan to help complete the development of the HA-300. Indian policy makers, including the CAS, were quite confused about collaboration with Egypt. According to them both countries would use the HF-24 fitted with the E-300 engine. The Indian authorities had not realized that the Egyptians were not interested in the HF-24. When this became clear, official Indian enthusiasm for the E-300 also disappeared. This was the death knell of the HA-300 project. Foreign experts working at Helwan began to drift away. The Egyptians also ran out of patience and money, and closed the project in May 1969. My attempts to fly the V-3 with the E-300 engine, designed specifically for the HA-300, did not succeed due to problems with the engine.

Messerschmitt and I parted as good friends and with high regard for each other. He, along with Professor Tank, paid me a great compliment by asking me to join the Panavia flight test management group. This was obviously not possible for me, as I was still a serving Indian Air Force officer. The first flight of the HA-300 was the highlight of my sixteen-year long test-flying career.

In 1991, Daimler-Benz Aerospace AG (DASA) bought up the H-300 V-1 and airlifted it to Germany. Apprentices of MBB at Manching. under proper supervision, worked for five and a half years to restore it for exhibition at the Deutsches Museum. My article on the HA-300, published in 1980 in a UK aviation magazine, enabled DASA and the Messerschmitt Stiftung (Foundation) to trace me in Bangalore. The Foundation then invited me to attend a ceremony on 26 March 1997 for DASA to hand over the aircraft to the Deutsches Museum.

Mr Aloysius Rauen was Senior Vice President of the Military Aircraft Division of DASA. He traced the history of Professor Messerschmitt's work in Spain from 1951 till the definition of the HA-300 to its final form. He concluded that due to various constraints, the HA-300 could not be produced as a fighter but its concept led to the emergence of the MiG-21 in USSR.

Now the HA-300 is in Munich's Deutsches Museum at Schleissheim just

north of Munich. Hopefully, visitors will look at the HA-300 and be deeply impressed that there was real genius behind its concept. By coincidence, or by design, the aircraft just behind the HA-300 was the HF-24 Marut, as the last project of Professor Kurt Tank, taken from HAL Bangalore to the Deutsches Museum.

In 1991 Daimler-Benz Aerospace bought and restored an HA-300 which is now on display at the Deutsches Museum outside Munich.

Even though my long stint in Egypt jeopardized my career opportunities in the IAF, I never regretted being deputed for this job. I shall forever cherish the memory of having handled the last design of an exceptional aeronautical designer and manufacturer and having earned due recognition from him.

TESTIMONIAL

Kapil Bhargava was born on 21 August 1928 and commissioned into the Indian Air Force in October 1950 after studying for a BSc in physics, chemistry and maths. He qualified as a pilot attack instructor in Leconfield, UK in 1953 and as a test pilot from the Empire Test Pilot School in the UK in 1956.

Bhargava retired from the IAF in 1976. During the previous quarter of a century, he was a fighter pilot; test pilot at Short Brothers and Hunting Percival Ltd and chief test pilot at HAL until 1960. The following year he was a test pilot at AV Roe & Co on the Avro 748. After his six year period as chief test pilot at Helwan. he became Commanding Officer at A&ATU (Aircraft & Armament Testing Unit), then first Commandant ASTE (Aircraft & Systems Testing Establishment).

From 1984 Bhargava was made executive director (flight operations & safety) for Hindustan Aeronautics Ltd before being made a technical consultant (India) to GEC-Marconi Avionics Ltd, UK.

He has flown 79 aircraft types. Group Captain Bhargava has had a keen interest in safety and reliability of aircraft and systems. His task as group executive in Hindustan Aeronautics Ltd (HAL) was to promote flight safety. His major safety achievement was the solution, in 1984, of drag damper problems in Alouette III helicopters. None of these have been lost due to this problem since then. Currently, he is a freelance writer on professional subjects and home computing. He was elected Honorary Fellow of the Aeronautical Society of India in December 2003.

Chapter 7

As part of the JSF program, Art Tomassetti was the lead pilot for the X-35 Test Team. He was the only US government pilot to fly all three variants of the aircraft.

Art Tomassetti – X-35B
'X' Marks the Mission

A test pilot recalls and repeats the dreams of another legendary pilot more than half a decade before him in a ground-breaking jet fighter.

Just 14.5 hours; it doesn't seem like a lot of flight time. In fact most pilots who have flown multiple aircraft might not even care to mention a type in which their flight time was that low. But when the aircraft designator starts with an 'X', then 14.5 hours can be significant. In fact 29 minutes of those 14 hours were particularly noteworthy.

It was July 19, 2001; Edwards Air Force Base, California. Around mid-afternoon I wandered into the flight test spaces looking for Paul Bloxham, one of our STOVL test conductors. I was hoping that he would have the test cards ready for the next day's mission. These cards outlined the test events that would be conducted during the sortie. He said he was still finishing them up but could show me the copy. As I looked over the cards I noted that there were three flights planned for the next morning; the first would continue to expand the flight envelope for the aircraft and gather more data for flying qualities. It all seemed very straightforward.

The second flight was to start with a short takeoff. After getting the gear up and transitioning from Short Take Off and Vertical Landing (STOVL) to conventional mode, the plan was to climb to 25,000 feet and perform a supersonic dash out to Mach 1.05. With this done I would complete some additional handling maneuvers and then return for a vertical landing. It took a minute to sink in but as I looked up from the pages at Paul, he had a smile on his face, 'This is the mission X profile,' I said. He nodded his head.

Mission X was a planned flight event for the X-35B that was intended to showcase the fact that the airplane could perform all the required STOVL maneuvers and had the airspeed performance of conventional non-STOVL airplanes. This was to be achieved by completing a short takeoff in STOVL mode, a level supersonic run in conventional mode, and then a vertical landing again in STOVL mode. It probably doesn't sound like a big deal and other aircraft had accomplished these events before. The big deal was that no other aircraft had ever done these events together in one flight. The Harrier comes the closest with being able to do all the events, but required a very steep dive to break the sound barrier and go supersonic.

The third flight would be a quick demo of a vertical takeoff from the landing pad at Edwards Air Force Base. I hadn't heard much talk of the mission X flight recently and didn't think it was going to take place that week, let alone with me as the pilot scheduled to fly it. Once the surprise started to wear off, the reality began to sink in. Tomorrow was going to be a busy day.

The flight briefs would probably begin between 05:00 and 06:00. It was already 15:30 and there was still work to do before heading out for the day. There was a crew day rule in effect, which meant that everyone was expected to have 10 to 12 hours off between events. This meant that the leadership would start getting people on their way home between 17:00 and 18:00. I started thinking to myself that it sure would be nice to get in the simulator to practice the flight events before having to perform them in the aircraft tomorrow.

Most people would assume that if there is fear involved in test flying, it is related to the danger of the endeavor. The truth is that, for most test pilots, the fear involved is the fear of screwing up. The simulator was located at the Lockheed Martin Skunkworks facility in Palmdale about 30 minutes drive from Edwards. I called down to the facility and spoke to the lead engineer there and asked if they would be willing to keep the simulator open for me to come down later in the evening. He said they could. I added that I also needed him to keep it to himself because I would probably be pushing my crew day a bit. Without a hesitation he said that wouldn't be a problem.

I finished up my work at Edwards and headed down to the simulator building. Everything was ready and I was able to practice the sequence a couple of times until I felt comfortable with my performance. Trying to get everything on the test cards done for the mission X flight was going to be tight on fuel, so I wanted to make sure I had it down fairly well. The simulator team was great, as they had been throughout the months and weeks leading up to flying the airplane, and accommodated my request to reset, repeat, and modify the practice runs as I went through. Once I was comfortable with the maneuvers and sequence, I thanked the crew and headed home. Needless to say, sleeping didn't come easy that night. I kept going over the sequence in my head as well as all the normal procedures, what-ifs and lessons learned, from my prior flights in the aircraft.

July 20, 2001. When the alarm went off I got ready quickly and headed up to Edwards. As I arrived at the hangar I saw the airplane was outside. That was a good sign; it meant that they were completing the fueling and the checks before flight. If you came down the hill toward the hangar before your brief, and didn't see the airplane outside, that was not a good sign and probably meant the airplane had a problem.

The first check, when I walked in the hangar, was the weather, specifically the winds. Everything looked like it would be within limits for the morning's events. I asked the test conductor how we were looking and he said everything looked good. We started the brief on time and it was all very straightforward. We discussed that it was going to be difficult to get all the maneuvers complete with the fuel available for the mission X flight, and considered what we would cut out in order to make sure we got the big three events done. We also talked about the vertical takeoff from the pad, since this would be another first for the airplane. Finally, we discussed timing for the morning, as we were trying to complete everything before 10:00. We were trying to meet the deadline because there was going to be a memorial service for a pilot and aerial photographer who had been killed in an F-16 crash earlier that week. The photographer had worked with our program and had become a friend of mine. One thing every pilot learns is that you have to be able to compartmentalize your feelings, such that they don't distract from the job of flying. Today would be a day I would get to practice that skill.

Once the brief broke up, everyone went off to the places where they needed to be. The engineers walked towards the data trailer, which was parked inside a corner of the hangar. From here they would monitor all the telemetry from the airplane and direct the flight. I walked off to another trailer, which was parked close by, to get into my flight gear. The lead government engineer, Andy Maack, walked with me. Andy had become a close friend over the past few years, working on the program. I guess he probably knew me well enough at that point to recognize that I seemed a bit quieter than normal for this morning's event. For as long as I live, I will never forget the brief conversation that took place next. Andrew looked over to me and said,

'You know, they taught monkeys how to fly rocket ships, this isn't really that hard.' A smile began to appear on my face and he said, 'Just go out there and have fun, you'll do fine.' I thanked him, shook his hand and said, 'See you in a bit,' and I walked into the flight equipment trailer and he walked over to the data trailer. I suited up in my flight gear and walked out to the airplane.

Pre-flight of an aircraft can be something of a ritual. While there are some obvious things you can check, there are many things you cannot check. You can't open every panel and check every hydraulic connection or electrical circuit.

I did my walk around the airplane and gave it my customary pat on the nose. Call me superstitious, but I had been doing that since my first combat flight ten years earlier in Desert Storm. Since I had come back safe from every flight since then, I wasn't about to mess with a good thing. I climbed up the ladder to the airplane and started getting strapped in. Once settled, I started going through the checklists. Very quickly I was in contact with the control room and they took over the process of calling out the items on the checklist to complete. Quickly we progressed through getting the avionics equipment up and running, engine start, and pre-takeoff checks; everything was running smoothly.

My primary safety and photo chase aircraft for the day was an F-16 and it reported over the radio that it would be ready on time. Before taxiing to the runway, the aircraft had to complete and pass something called an Integrated Built-In-Test or IBIT. This test checked all the numerous functions of the airplane, including primary flight control functions. From the pilot's seat, it required pressing one button and then sitting back for a few minutes as the automatic checks were done. This was an interesting process because the computers took control of the airplane and moved the flight control surfaces like the rudders and flaps as well as moving the stick and throttle inside the craft. This test would also convert the airplane to STOVL mode.

To convert from a conventional airplane to a STOVL airplane, several things occurred. Eight propulsion doors had to open. The clutch to drive the lift fan from the engine power had to engage, and the computers had to switch over to new flight and engine control schemes. Sitting in the cockpit there was a definite sensation of a transformation taking place. At this point we ran into a problem because we lost the telemetry connection to the control room. This took several minutes to correct before we could try the IBIT again.

Once complete, the display would show all the faults that were discovered. Some of these were okay to go fly with and others were not. My luck seemed to be back on track and none of the codes that showed up would prevent us from flying. As I taxied out toward the runway the 'Plane Captain' gave me a smart salute and I was on my way. Approaching the runway I saw the F-16 chase aircraft waiting and gave it thumbs up as I went by. The control room said everything looked good and we were cleared for takeoff.

Lockheed was joined by partners Northrop Grumman and British Aerospace in developing an aircraft resembling the larger F-22.

The first flight went well; a short takeoff followed by some handling qualities evaluation at 5,000 feet and a slow landing at 80 knots. I conducted a hot refuel which means they refilled the fuel tank with the engine running. Once refueled, I taxied back to the runway for Mission X. This takeoff would be an automatic short takeoff. It meant the aircraft would automatically move the thrust vector to a preset angle for takeoff once the appropriate speed was reached. I anxiously set everything up for the maneuver and, once cleared by the control room and the tower, I pushed the throttle up to full power and released the brakes. The aircraft accelerated quickly, giving a good push back into the seat. At 100 knots I pressed the button for the automatic short takeoff, the thrust vector changed from 28 degrees to 40 degrees and the aircraft jumped off the ground. The nose continued to rise approaching the point where I started to get a little uncomfortable, so I got on the controls and prevented it from going any further. I raised the gear and began the steep climb to 25,000 feet.

I could see the chase airplanes struggling to keep up. Upon reaching altitude I leveled off and moved the throttle to maximum. Within a second or two the afterburner kicked in and the aircraft began to accelerate. To be honest, going supersonic in a modern jet fighter today is not very impressive, in fact, unless you are watching the airspeed indication, you might not even realize it had actually happened. Today was a little different; over the dry lakebed of Edwards Air Force Base, 54 years earlier, a 24-year-old Chuck Yeager first broke the sound barrier in level flight. Here I was, in about the same piece of sky, about to repeat that event.

There wasn't much time to dwell on this since the speed was increasing rapidly. The Mach indication crossed through 1.0 and at 1.05 I brought the throttle back and began to decelerate. I started a descent down to the next test altitude and began to set up for the next move. I was a little behind on fuel and started to realize that I probably wasn't going to be able to complete the full set of items planned, before I had to start back to the field. I relayed this to the control room and they agreed. We would complete two more items and then start back. The maneuvers went off without a hitch and I started back towards the airfield.

As we approached the runway I slowed the aircraft down to lower the landing gear and converted from 'conventional' to STOVL mode. I moved the thrust control lever back about an inch, to begin the conversion process.

An additional engine was coupled to the primary engine to provide the lift for vertical flight.

Almost immediately the noises changed and I could feel the aircraft go through its transformation. This process took about 15 seconds and, all the while, the pilot was just along for the ride. Most of my attention was focused on watching the engine instruments and status displays and hoping not to see any warning or caution lights illuminate. The conversion completed with no problems and I began to slow the aircraft down from 180 knots to zero, adjusting the timing and control movements to arrive in a hover at 150 feet over the landing pad.

There is something unusual but very exciting about taking a jet aircraft into a hover. Despite my many years of flying the AV-8B Harrier and the countless hovers I had completed in that aircraft, the feeling never went away. I made small control adjustments to center the aircraft over the pad, using barrels that were placed out at 150 and 300 yards from the pad. Since you could not see directly below the aircraft at that altitude, visual markers had to be set out at a distance to give the pilot some position reference.

Once centered up I was given the 'cleared to land' signal by one of the other pilots, who was acting as an outside observer and talking to me on a portable radio. I reduced the power and the aircraft began a slow descent. At about 40 feet I could see the outline of the landing pad and made last adjustments to the aircraft's position as I continued down. The aircraft touched down, with a little bounce that was normal, and I brought the throttle back to idle.

The pilot who was outside observing, Squadron Leader Justin Paines of the Royal Air Force, gave me a thumbs up, and the

The X-35 STOVL was equipped with a shaft-driven lift-fan system plus roll control jets along the wings.

flight, for all practical purposes, was over. Just like that, an aviation milestone had been achieved. No bands playing, no parades, no big crowds of cheering people; just a test pilot sitting in a new airplane taking a deep breath and being thankful he hadn't screwed anything up. I still needed another trip to the refuel area to take on a little more fuel before attempting the vertical takeoff.

I did make it in time to attend the memorial service that morning. Some might think that something like that would ruin the thrill of accomplishing what we did that morning. In truth, the stark reality of the hazards involved with the business of testing airplanes, contrasted with the excitement of actually being a part of that process, was overwhelming.

TESTIMONIAL

Colonel Art Tomassetti of the US Marine Corps was born in Port Chester, New York on March, 13 1964. He was commissioned from the NROTC program at Northwestern University in June of 1986. Upon receiving his wings, he began flight training in the AV-8B Harrier in 1988. He served with two Fleet Harrier Squadrons, VMA-542 and VMA-513. He made two, 6 month deployments to the Western Pacific and spent 9 months in the Persian Gulf for Operations Desert Shield and Desert Storm. During Operation Desert Storm, he flew 39 combat missions in the AV-8B Harrier throughout the Kuwait theatre of operations.

In 1997, he attended the United States Naval Test Pilot School in Patuxent River. He was assigned to the Strike Aircraft Test Squadron, where he conducted flight tests in both the F/A-18 and AV-8B aircraft. Tomassetti served as a member of the Joint Strike Fighter (JSF) Test Force and became the lead government pilot for the X-35 Test Team. He was the only US government pilot to fly all three variants of the X-35 aircraft and flew the first ever Short Take-Off, level supersonic dash and vertical landing, accomplished on a single flight. From 2002 to 2004 he served as the USMC JSF program integrator at the Lockheed Martin Facility in Fort Worth, Texas.

He reported back to Pax River in 2004 as the chief test pilot for VX-23 and took over as Commanding Officer of the squadron in December 2005. In 2007 Colonel Tomassetti began his current tour as Commanding Officer Marine Aviation Detachment Patuxent River. He has attained over 3,000 flying hours in more than 30 different types of aircraft.

Tomassetti is married to Marchelle and has two children Taryn and DJ.

Chapter 8

Vlad Yakimov was chief test pilot at the Russian Design Bureau.

Vlad Yakimov – Yak-41
Out of the Flying Pan

Vlad Yakimov was the Russian test pilot for the Vertical Short Take-Off and Landing (VSTOL) Yak-41, and on one test flight nearly didn't make it.

It was August 1991 and the management of the A. S. Yakovlev Design Bureau (DB) had made the decision to finally display the Yak-41 or 'Article 48' (as it was called at the time), and immediately everyone began the preparations. It was my idea to present the aircraft so that we would gain further financing from the Defence Ministry (DM), and the DB 'Yak' chief designer, Alexander Dondukov, supported me.

First of all, we went to Severomorsk on the Kola Peninsula, where the head-quarters of the Red-Banner Fleet of the former USSR, now Russia, was stationed. All the admirals and generals of the Northern Fleet were very pleased with the visit, especially when they found out that the aim was to carry out flight trials of the Yak-41, the new supersonic aircraft with Vertical/Short Take-Off and Landings (VSTOL), on the aircraft carrier *Admiral Gorshkov*. By this time, it was already six or seven years since the Yak-38, which was used on boats of that class, had been put into service and everyone was awaiting the appearance of a new aircraft.

Two Yak-41 models were in use at the time, No. 75 and No. 77, and they were both included in this programme. They had different flight control systems: No. 75 ('41-2') was equipped with an Electric Remote Control System (ERCS); No. 77 ('41-3') was fitted out with a Steadiness and Manoeuvrability System (SMS).

These systems were operated automatically, but only as part of the VSTOL, and as part of suspended and transition procedures, acceleration after take-off and braking before landing, depending on the position of the R-79 baseline engine nozzle, working together with two RD-33 lifting engines in these flight procedures.

Yak-41 had the same set-up as Yak-38: one Lifting, Advancing Engine (LEA) and two Lifting Engines (LE), which were situated in the pilot's cockpit and had separate air inlets, which opened and shut automatically depending on the position of the Control Stick of the Lifting Engines (CSLE). They were located on the left-hand panel of the pilot's cockpit and had two fixed positions: 'start' (fully forwards) and 'stop' (fully back).

However, there are fundamental differences between the two planes; Yak-38 had three turbojet engines, whereas Yak-41 had three turbofan engines, which used the procedure of controlled afterburning. Yak-41 was also 30 per cent larger, and had a different design configuration.

We started practical preparations for flights from the deck of the Northern Fleet with A. Sinitsin (at that time he was head pilot) on board No. 75, and myself on board No. 77. Over the next week we practised and tested the vertical and short take-offs and vertical landings on dry land.

There were two problems. Firstly, the concrete strip. This is not a problem for metallic ship decks, but concrete strip surfaces cannot sustain the increased heat (e.g. gas welding) exhaust gases from three engines working in the afterburning process. Our engineers found some kind of white chemical substance (I don't remember what it was called), spread it on parts of the strip and this problem was solved.

The second problem was the brakes. To complete short take-offs, you need three running engines, all of which are driving the plane systems, and the flaps and slats have to be released for take-off. The pilot keeps the plane's brakes on, engages the automatic ejector on the Control Stick (CS), pushes the button 'short take-off' on the control console (both nozzles on the lifting engines move to the position of 15 degrees backward), then move CS to 'full afterburning', check that everything is engaged, release the brakes and start take-off. At a speed of Vi (50km/h) the nozzle automatically moves to the 67 degrees position and the plane turns away, gathers the undercarriage in and accelerates until you reach normal flight.

When the brakes were fully clamped after engaging the full afterburning procedure, the plane started to 'skid' and the anti-skid system started to kick in. There was the possibility that the rubber of the principle undercarriage wheels could get torn.

After discovering the problem, I suggested making special shoes for the principle wheels. Now, when the plane stopped on the starting line these shoes were placed beneath each wheel and they 'gripped' the wheels. Then the pilot carried out all the operations for a short take-off and the plane kept its position until the brakes were released and then it moved across the shoes and embarked on its flight. The problem was solved.

Both aircraft were on dry land at the Severomorsk aerodrome, and our next task was to prepare for the first ever landing on the deck of the aircraft carrier *Admiral Gorshkov*.

The plan was to carry out a test flight in the vicinity of the ship in a helicopter to inspect the flight area, define characteristic points for approach and landing on the deck and simulate some approaches to the deck, for example, with the same profile of the Yak-41. All worked very well. Now, in our opinion everything was ready and the day after we would fly to the ship.

Today was the day. To my surprise, the night before I had slept like a baby and felt totally refreshed and energized.

We arrived at the aerodrome. Our engineers had prepared both planes. I should mention that the weather in this region is very changeable, but on this day everything went in our favour, there was light cloud and brilliant visibility. We put on NLSS (Naval Life-Saving Suits), which were bright orange diving suits made completely of rubber, with special hermetic boots, and went to the planes.

A. Sinitsin in No. 75 was first, and after he had landed on the deck of the ship in about 15 minutes, I was going to take-off. I wished him luck and went to wait my turn with my '77'. He took off.

Half an hour went by with no information. An hour, nothing, an hour and a half, complete silence, no information about what I was supposed to do. I should mention that all this time I was wearing the NLSS without any form of ventilation within the suit. This suit was not designed to make it easy to walk. The most comfortable position to be in when wearing it was the sitting position. As a result of this, most of the time I was sitting in the plane as if flying, then I would get up, do my 'morning exercises', stretch my muscles a bit and then sit down again. I repeated this every 20-25 minutes. Nobody knew what was happening.

Finally, after two hours, a helicopter arrived from the ship bringing our technical equipment, and the pilot of the helicopter said that I would soon get authorization for take-off. After almost three hours of waiting, I finally got the authorization.

I took off in the plane in the direction of Vayenga Bay and immediately saw the ship. There was enough fuel so I decided to do a couple of demonstration approaches nearby. When I was broadside to the superstructure of the ship, I engaged the afterburner and completed a military turn to the left towards

Severomorsk and rose to a height of 350 metres above the bay, at a distance of 3km from the ship. The second passage took place with two ascending rolls at a climb angle of 75 degrees. Then, having made a turn to the right, I carried out the approach, completing it successfully with a vertical landing on the deck. After I had stopped the engines, when I was getting down the steps, the sailors lifted me off them and started throwing me up and catching me in their arms with shouts of joy.

The Admiral Gorshkov *aircraft carrier moored off the Kola Peninsula on the roof of Europe.*

Then they put me down on the deck and we drank mouthfuls of cognac, right there on the deck next to the aircraft. I took off my helmet and asked where the first plane was. I was told that it was in the ship's hanger because the tail unit and the nozzles of the baseline engine were damaged during landing. Now I understood why I had had to wait for so long.

When I took off my NLSS all my clothes were completely soaked as if I had just got out of a swimming pool.

One week later, the weather was better than it had been on any of the days before and we decided to fly. We carried out brief pre-flight preparations. My task was to complete a short take-off from the deck, fly in a circle, make the approach and then carry out a vertical landing on deck.

I put on the NLSS and went to my plane. It was on the deck in the technical position for starting, warming up the engines and testing the systems. I took the report about the readiness of the plane, carried out an external inspection and sat in the cockpit. I inspected the equipment, fastened the seat belt system, checked the locking straps of the ejector seat, closed the cockpit window and checked it.

I then started the engines, leaving them idling, checked the hydraulics, navigation and autopilot, and released the flaps and slats into the position for take-off. The plane moved into the take-off position on the deck with the shoes in place. I asked the flight officials for authorization for take-off and received their confirmation.

CSLE starts (fully forward as far as it will go), a quick glance in the mirror – the air inlet fold is open, there is a green light on the dashboard. Indicators LE1 and LE2, 15 seconds, control jets are engaged, I engaged the

The Yak-41 drops onto the deck of the carrier.

automatic ejection, pressed the 'short take-off' button. CS was now set to 'full afterburning' and I released the brakes. We smoothly and majestically moved across the shoes; five seconds and the nozzle automatically shifted into the short take-off position, I brought the lever towards myself and everything pulled away from the deck of the ship and we began to climb.

I finished accelerating at a height of 120 metres and a distance of 1.5km from the ship. At an altitude of 500 metres, I completed a left-hand turn so that I could carry out a circular approach. I followed this with a second turn so that the approach system was facing the ship. I suddenly became aware of medium strength turbulence and drifting from the left to the right of 15 degrees, I thought that during landing the drift would be from the right to the left. I should mention that approaches for landing on the ship could only be completed visually as there was no autopilot to carry out the flight of the plane.

I released the undercarriage, flaps and slats, fully tightened the ejector seat mechanism and completed a second turn to carry out a straight approach. The operator informed me of the distance from the deck, but I knew that this information might not be accurate. Therefore, I descended in the general direction of the stern of the ship, I launched the LE – CSLE forward as far as it would go, glanced at the LE indicator, direction and speed reduction, the control jet engaged. Distance: 1.7 km, speed: 200km/h, height: 70 metres, descent: -2m/sec, I engaged afterburner, the nozzle was now completely vertical and I moved afterburning nearer to full capacity. I now had to hover at 10 metres above the deck, or 23 metres from the water.

I could see the spray created by the jets from my engines and became aware of the vibration along the vertical axis of the plane. I pressed harder on the right pedal to maintain the direction of travel. Three hundred metres from the edge of the stern, the nose of the plane was 18 degrees to the right of the axes of the deck. I gently pressed the nozzle switch to bring the plane into lengthways movement and approached the deck, crossing the edge of the stern with the nozzles vertical position. The nose of the plane was 35 degrees to the right of the axes, with the right pedal fully pressed and the lever moved to the same side; to my left was the superstructure of the ship. In front I could see Severomorsk with its houses on the hills. There was no question of accelerating on this side to land at the aerodrome, which was straight ahead, as I was not convinced that I would be able to complete the manoeuvre (acceleration) without putting the town and its houses at risk. There was only one option, land vertically on the deck.

I pulled slightly on the CS to decrease traction, and therefore produce a descent. Almost at once I felt that the plane was going down as if the engine traction was failing. I instinctively put the CS to full afterburning, and saw that my fall had been checked and gently touched down on the deck.

But without warning, things took a turn for the worse. There was an explosion and huge flames leapt all around the cockpit. Instantly, I put the CS to 'stop' (which controls all three engines at once). My next thought was: Now they will start to put out the fire on the plane, I'll unfasten my seatbelt, throw off the emergency cockpit window and get out through the left-hand side. With my left hand I opened the lock on my left shoulder strap. With the finger of my left hand I pressed the radio station button on the CS and said: 'Start the fire fighting system and I'll get out of the cockpit!' There was no reaction and no answer. I took the strap in my left hand again, placed it in the lock socket, closed the latch and checked that it was closed. Then I spoke into the radio again: 'Is anyone going to put out the fire?!' Again there was total silence. There was only one thing to do to avoid being burned alive. With my right hand I seized the ejector button and pressed it, while saying into the radio connection: 'To hell with you, I'm getting out!' (this was 26 seconds from the moment of the explosion).

The seat came out very smoothly, meaning that my eyes stayed open and I saw the whole process – the cockpit window glass breaking and my 'flight' in the seat. The next feeling was hanging in mid-air (45 metres above the deck); I instinctively looked at the canopy of my parachute – everything was okay! I looked down, oh God; I was heading straight for the fire again!

Luckily though at the last moment, a gust of turbulence from the tuning call of the ship blew the parachute beyond the fire to the right-hand side of the ship. Here there was another danger, the second deck, which had the ship's weaponry positioned along it. What a great place to break my arms, legs, ribs or whatever else to pieces. But again I was lucky, I drifted two metres beyond the rails and plopped into the water.

Yakimov's aircraft moments after erupting into a fireball.

I looked around and unfastened the left strap of the parachute; there was an inflatable boat nearby, which I pulled towards me using the rope. My suit had also filled with air and I was in no danger of drowning. A rescue helicopter approached and hovered nearby, its propeller caused terrible downdraft on the surface of the water and I gave a sign with my hands that it should not come any closer, as I had seen that a motorboat had been launched from the ship and it was heading towards me. When it approached, the sailors pulled me onto the motorboat with the parachute. When I was on board the boat, I saw that the plane was still shrouded in fire and black smoke. When we arrived back at the ship, I was immediately taken to the ship's hospital and they took off my NLSS, thanks to which only my socks were slightly wet, and I was put in a bed. The doctor, an old lieutenant, ordered everyone out of the room and asked me how I was feeling. I answered that I was fine. He started to measure my blood pressure and my pulse. He did this once, then again, and then a third time and I asked him what he was doing. He answered: 'I can't understand, your blood pressure is 120/75mm and your pulse is 74.' I said that these were my normal values and instead of measuring them, it would be better if he gave me something to drink. He did this, and gave me 50g of neat medicinal alcohol!

This was what happened on the day that I was reborn. I have the armrest from my ejector seat to remind me of the events of that day; my mechanics gave it to me as a present.

The Yak-41 was a specialist VSTOL aircraft for the Russian Navy.

TESTIMONIAL

Vlad Yakimov started to fly in 1974 at the age of 19, as a military cadet at Stavropol High Military School for pilots and navigators, of Air Defence of the USSR. Here he flew the L-29, UTI MiG-15 and MiG-17.

After he finished in 1977, Yakimov went to the Moscow District Air Defence as an engineer fighter-pilot, flying: Su 7UB, Su-9, MiG-23UB, MiG-23P, MiG-23ML. Here he held a variety of positions from pilot to deputy squadron commander and pilot instructor.

From 1984 to 1987, he was with the Military Academy and was then made Deputy Commander in Chief of a fighter regiment in the Far East. By the end of the 1980s, he was a test pilot for the Ministry of the Aviation Industry of the USSR. Until 1991, Yakimov was the test pilot at Yakovlev's Design Bureau, working on the V/STO and V/SL programmes project. This was before he became chief test pilot of the Design Bureau. He has flown 54 types of aircraft with 4,200 hours.

Chapter 9

Shawn Healey is currently serving as the government chief test pilot of the VH-1 Integrated Test Team (Presidential Helicopters Program).

Shawn D. Healy – MV-22 Osprey
Out of Balance

Lieutenant Colonel Shawn D. Healy recalls a momentary, but large loss of balance during natural icing flight tests of the revolutionary, but sometimes controversial, MV-22 Osprey tiltrotor aircraft.

It was a brisk morning at Halifax International Airport, Nova Scotia, Canada on January 22, 2006 as I walked down the pathway, cut through four foot snow drifts, leading to our work spaces adjacent to the Air Canada hangar. The V-22 Integrated Test Team (ITT) detachment was preparing for another day of natural icing survey testing.

So far this had been a very successful icing season; a far cry from our first natural icing survey testing during the winter of 1999 into 2000, using our engineering, manufacturing and development test aircraft, Osprey 8. Over the past few icing seasons, we had been making tremendous gains in our testing with our low rate initial production test aircraft, Osprey 24, affectionately known as Chilly Willy. This natural icing survey detachment was to be the capstone icing season for the V-22 ITT; the culminating point of many years of development and prerequisite testing.

The six-month detachment was to be the final icing season. No more chances to complete the test plan objectives in order to clear the Osprey's operational flight envelope, which was specified as icing conditions up to moderate intensities and down to -20°C ambient temperatures. The Osprey's Ice Protection System (IPS) was designed to be fully automatic in that the system would detect icing conditions and provide full anti-ice/de-ice protection for the aircraft. The only pilot action would be to ensure that the IPS was selected to its automatic mode. This was an enhancing characteristic from an operational perspective, but the technical complexities associated with this automation made it a challenge from the developmental perspective.

The main scope of our testing this season was not only evaluating the performance of a fully functional IPS, but also IPS degraded modes. IPS degraded modes testing involved deliberately inducing various IPS subsystem failures during an icing encounter, to evaluate the validity of the degraded mode algorithms and system performance under the failed condition. Today's flight test event was to be a degraded modes test of the IPS.

I had just set down my mug of coffee on my desk when the fax machine kicked in. It began printing the day's weather forecast along with icing potential products from the military weather forecaster at CFB Shearwater. The forecasters at Shearwater were worth their weight in gold in helping us locate icing conditions. The first page of the fax was for Halifax International and I scanned the METAR that read current conditions as 'WIND 350/23 G29 VISIBILITY 15SM FEW40 OAT -6°C DEW POINT -17°C ALT 30.29,' not very promising. We were on detachment for icing conditions, so good weather was bad and bad weather was good. Things soon started to look much better as I thumbed through the forecast around Cape Breton Island, near Sydney in northern Nova Scotia. The forecast projected severe clear ice within the altitude band of 2,800 to 3,900 feet MSL (Mean Sea Level, or true altitude); light rime ice (ice from fog) within the altitude band of 3,900 to 5,600 feet MSL, and the temperature band -5 to -20°C...good news.

We needed the data at the lower temperature band (around -20°C) and it looked like we would have almost 2,000 feet to work the light rime icing. Natural icing survey testing is not merely flying in any icy condition, but requires specific temperature bands and liquid water content combinations as part of the test build-up procedure and flight test matrix.

The test team assembled for the flight test brief in our makeshift ready room in the Air Canada hangar. Osprey 24 would be piloted by me and Major Stephen 'Chuck' Augustin, USMC. Nick Heiner (NAVAIR) would be the flight test engineer and Jason Patterson (Boeing) would be the test director. Nick and Jason would be manning the IPS instrumentation equipment housed in the Osprey's cabin. They would be responsible for implementing changes, called profiles, into the IPS while in flight. Chuck and I could enable the various IPS selection modes, essentially on/off, but Nick and Jason had principle control and monitoring of the IPS system during the conduct of the tests.

The IPS profiles for the flight were selected based on the predicted temperatures of -11° to -20°C. The IPS rotor profile Number 3 was selected to increase the 'element-on-time' for specific rotor zones along the Osprey's proprotor (the large tilting propellers) blades. Anti-ice profile Number 2 was selected for the degraded modes portion of the test. It would simulate a proprotor blade parting strip failure by setting the temperatures to below freezing.

We would be flying with the default IPS software configuration and then Nick and Jason would load the particular profiles in flight for the icing encounter. The flight test brief concluded with a review of the hazards identified in the test hazard analysis. The particular hazards that concerned us the most were the potential for engine damage due to ice ingestion, in the event of an engine anti-ice subsystem failure, and the potential for aircraft structural damage and proprotor blade damage due to ice impacts. The icing tests were conducted with the Osprey configured in 'airplane' mode at 200

The V-22 completed more than 1,000 flight hours during icing tests in Nova Scotia.

Knots Calibrated Airspeed (KCAS), so ice shed from the front of the tiltrotor had the potential to be struck by the proprotor blades. Case in point: during the 2004-2005 icing season, damage was sustained to a proprotor blade as a result of the blade impacting a large ice chunk from the windshield wiper assembly; 18 inches of composite material was smashed from the trailing edge of the proprotor blade.

Ice build-up and shedding from the windshield wipers had now been virtually eliminated for this round of testing, by a windshield wiper fairing design change to Chilly Willy, but there were other areas of potential ice accretion on the nose of the aircraft that we had to consider. To give the correct perspective, Osprey 24 had gathered several inches of ice during some of our icing encounters during the season, so the size of the ice that was detaching could be extremely significant; it should be mentioned that if a heavy lump of ice actually hit a proprotor blade tip, it would do so at 450 mph.

We completed our aircrew brief and suited up for the flight, donning our complete ensemble that made up the anti-exposure suit. With paperwork signed off and pre-flight inspection complete, we climbed aboard the aircraft and strapped on our parachutes.

Start up was uneventful and with clearance from Halifax Ground Control, we taxied Chilly Willy along Taxiway C for a departure from Runway 05. At 16:39Z, I brought the Osprey into a hover. A check of the Osprey's cockpit displays revealed all systems normal, and with that I began to transition the tiltrotor from helicopter mode to airplane mode. I caught the huge 38 foot diameter tip-path-plane of the Osprey's proprotors in my periphery as the massive proprotor blades wisped past my cockpit side window and just a few feet behind me.

In airplane mode, the proprotor blades swung nearly 10 feet below the aircraft underside and came within a mere 12 inches of the side of the aircraft fuselage. The transition took just 15 seconds; we were now a turbo-prop airplane climbing to 5,000 feet MSL on a northerly heading towards Cape Breton Island.

After a short while we approached an overcast cloud layer in the vicinity of Port Hawkesbury that seemed to increase in thickness towards Cape St Lawrence at the northern-most end of Nova Scotia. The top of the cloud layer appeared to be around 5,000 feet MSL but increased in altitude as it extended northward. We completed our pre-immersion checklist and at 17:05Z, Osprey 24 slipped subtly beneath the tops of the grey clouds to commence a cloud survey.

The purpose of the cloud survey was to determine the altitude that would provide the optimum Liquid Water Content (LWC) and Outside Air Temperature (OAT) combination for our testing. The aircraft system posted an 'ICE DETECTED' advisory less than a minute later, as expected. Chilly Willy had recognized the icing conditions. We continued our descent through the cloud layer while monitoring LWC, OAT, and Median Volume Diameter (MVD, the overall collision efficiency of an iced droplet). We encountered rime ice at light to moderate accretion rates throughout the descent. We discovered the bottom of the cloud layer at 3,500 feet MSL and then initiated a climb. So far, no severe clear icing encountered, and shortly, Osprey 24 exited the top of the cloud layer at 6,000 feet. The cloud survey had taken a matter of nine minutes to complete. Average atmospheric conditions during the immersion were 0.1 grams/meter^3 for LWC, -19°C OAT, and 26 microns MVD. These were the conditions we had been hoping to encounter for our test.

The aircraft is incapable of auto-rotation in the case of engine failure, although one engine can power both propellers.

I flew Chilly Willy above the cloud layer, remaining in clear air, while Nick and Jason determined our optimum test altitude. Chuck, as the project officer responsible for the icing test plan, would be orchestrating the conduct of the test during this next sortie. Jason informed us that he was ready to load 'anti-ice profile Number 2', which was to simulate a failure of the parting strip on each proprotor blade. In order to load the profile into the IPS, the IPS had to be turned off. Chuck selected the IPS to 'OFF' and we waited for the profile to load into the system. I glanced at the OAT presented on my flight display; it read -20°C. Four minutes later the second profile was loaded into the IPS. Chuck selected the mode to automatic, and we were ready to commence. I reviewed the test

The Chilly Willy logo signified the V-22 ice test program in Canada.

hazards and corrective actions in my head one last time. Okay we were ready to go...or so I thought.

At exactly 17:18Z, Osprey 24 re-entered the cloud layer at 7,000 feet MSL as we continued along our northern track. I maintained 200 KCAS during our 300 feet per minute descent and, upon passing 6,000 feet, I glanced at the flight test instrumentation display on the glare shield. It was indicating 0.28 grams/meter^3 for LWC, -24°C OAT, and 22 microns MVD; almost five degrees colder than our cloud survey just several minutes before. The Osprey's IPS was specifically designed to the detailed specification of -20°C OAT. I heard Jason a few seconds later announce that we had now entered a colder air mass and that the OAT had dropped to -24°C. I knew Nick and Jason were keeping a close eye on the ambient conditions in addition to monitoring the Osprey's IPS and external high-speed digital cameras, but now I found myself glancing anxiously, and much more regularly, at the instrumented OAT.

I continued the descent into the darkening grey haze to see if the OAT would start to increase as we approached the target test altitude, and hopefully back to within our OAT specification. I forced my scan back to the primary flight display as Chuck recorded 5 millimeters of ice on the Vernier Accretion Meter (VAM) before clearing it. Jason reported that the IPS was performing as expected and had been keeping us appraised of each IPS proprotor heating cycle. Another IPS proprotor heating cycle occurred at 17:23Z while passing 5,500 feet MSL. I glanced at the flight test instrumentation display again and was pleased to see that OAT had increased to -23°C.

It was at this point I peered outside at Chilly Willy's starboard engine nacelle and to my surprise, noticed that ice had managed to build-up on the engine inlet. Never in all my natural icing survey flights, even the ones where the aircraft had amassed a total of 5 inches of ice during a single immersion, had I observed ice accretion on the engine inlets. Was it because we cold-soaked the engine inlets by turning off the IPS while the profiles were loaded or was it because the engine anti-ice couldn't keep up at -24°C? I didn't know for sure, but there it was. The ice showed up very clearly against the black painted inlet.

The ice that appeared on the aircraft at this OAT and LWC combination formed a smooth glass-like layer that conformed to the contour of the Osprey's surfaces. I reported my findings over the ICS and Chuck confirmed that the port nacelle engine inlet also had ice accretion. I immediately pushed the thrust control lever forward and transitioned Osprey 24 to a climb to vacate the icing layer. Continuing the descent to warmer temperatures was not an option as the icing layer continued down another few thousand feet. Up and out was the quicker way; besides, the digital moving map had us positioned over high terrain. If we continued with the descent, most likely we would find ourselves still in the icing layer by the time we hit our minimum safe altitude. The flight path vector on my primary flight display showed a good climb in concert with the vertical speed indicator.

We were approaching 7,000 feet and almost clear. I quickly checked the engines' display and there were no abnormalities. I started to relax, we were going to be fine, just a little bit longer...and then it happened. The IPS commanded another proprotor heating cycle and the next thing we heard was the thundering roar of the ice impacts against the fuselage from the proprotor blades. We then felt the instantaneous onset of a large and severe 3-Hz vibration. This meant one thing: One of the massive proprotors was out of balance.

If the cockpit was being shaken this intensely, I could only imagine that Nick and Jason had it a great deal worse in the cabin since the anti-vibration system was tuned for the cockpit only. But there was no time to look back and check on them now. I glanced at the starboard nacelle and could see it wagging like a dog's tail on the end of the wing. Jason immediately commanded an IPS 'Proprotor Override'...nothing. Again...still nothing.

The vibration was dramatic and unnerving to say the least. I wondered just how much longer the aircraft could take such a beating before a catastrophic failure occurred. The Osprey is tough, but also complex with many dynamic components. Although the aircraft was being shaken apart we continued, with cool heads, to think through the problem. Our test hazard analysis had not accounted for an asymmetric proprotor ice chunk being shed and causing an out of balance condition. We had to figure this one out and fast. The decision was made to cycle the IPS 'OFF' and then back 'ON' in order to automatically load the default IPS values and clear the profile Number 2 from the system. There was nothing I could do except continue to fly the aircraft and get out of the icing layer. Chuck cycled the IPS OFF and then ON. Seconds later like the end of a tunnel, we leapt out of the cloud layer.

Shortly after cycling the IPS, the remaining ice from the single proprotor blade finally fell away. Almost as quickly as it appeared, the vibration stopped. All systems reported normal and no subsystem failures posted on the aircraft status page as a result of the large vibrations. We aborted the test and steered Chilly Willy toward Halifax. We made an uneventful recovery to Halifax International a short time later.

Post-flight analysis revealed that the left-side proprotor experienced a large vibration 'exceedance'. The actual vibration level recorded, during the asymmetrical proprotor ice fall off point, was as high as 9 inches per second; an order of magnitude well above the Osprey's normal vibration limit. A proper balance in the proprotors ensures that the aircraft remains within its structural design endurance limit loads. It was a wild ride for several minutes, but we were able to work the problem to the correct solution. We gained valuable test data and implemented IPS changes. The Osprey has maintained her balance ever since.

Ice build-up on the leading edge of the empannage (tail) accumulated during severe cold weather tests.

TESTIMONIAL

Lieutenant Colonel Healy is currently serving as the government chief test pilot of the VH-71 Integrated Test Team (Presidential Helicopters Program) at Naval Test Wing Atlantic, Naval Air Warfare Center/Aircraft Division.

He was commissioned a Second Lieutenant in the US Marine Corps upon graduation from Norwich University, the Military College of Vermont. In 1991, he was assigned to HMM-164 where he completed overseas deployments with 15th Marine Expeditionary Unit (Special Operations Capable) in Somalia, and with 11th MEU(SOC) in south-west Asia.

After attending United States Naval Test Pilot School (USNTPS) Healy reported to VT-31 at NAS Corpus Christi, Texas in 1998 for multi-engine propeller transition training. Subsequent to graduation in June 1999, he was reassigned as project test pilot to the V-22 Integrated Test Team. In October 2003, Healy reported to III Marine Expeditionary Force in Okinawa, Japan, where he served on the III MEF Commanding General's staff. Healy transferred to the VH-71 ITT in July 2005. He qualified in the EH-101 and VH-71A aircraft and conducted VH-71 flight tests at AgustaWestland in Yeovil, England. While there, he participated in the British Experimental Rotor Program IV and EH-101 fully articulated tail rotor flight test programs.

Healy has attained more than 4,000 flight hours in more than 40 different aircraft with concurrent designations in helicopters, multi-engine fixed-wing aircraft, and tiltrotors.

Chapter 10

Hugo Piva retired from the Brazilian Air Force in 1987 as a Three Star General with 4,480 flight hours.

Hugo Piva – Beija-Flor (Hummingbird) The Flower Kisser – Pollination of an Industry

A unique helicopter developed with post-war Nazi technology in Brazil kick-started Brazil's now global aerospace industry.

The year 1936 was an eventful one for me. Aged just 8 years old, it was the year I flew my first test flight. Deeply inspired by a movie featuring the Savoia-Marchetti bomber transporting fully equipped Italian paratroopers to battle, I set out to explore the skies. I figured that as a start, a tiny person my size could achieve this with an adult-sized umbrella. In the parlor, I grabbed my father's largest one and set forth to the backyard. Aided by my younger brother and cousins, we placed a tall ladder on top of the external bread oven so I could reach the roof. They handed me the 'parachute' and without flinching, I jumped. Needless to say, it turned inside out, but I had been cautious enough to choose a spot with a tall sand mound leaning against the oven. Not one to give up, we reconvened and I decided that I needed to fasten the tips of the umbrella to the handle in a tight knot. Up I went to the

roof, and out went my parachute. It was huge fun, but I was now out of options, and so gave up on the idea, with the proud feeling that I had been the only one to fly.

Twelve years later, Colonel Casimiro Montenegro of the Brazilian Air Force proposed the idea of creating an advanced technical centre to provide the conditions to develop a solid aeronautical industry in Brazil. So, in 1950, after two years of development, the Ministry of Aeronautics created CTA – Aeronautical Technology Center (later renamed the Aerospace Technology Center), strategically placed between the cities of Rio de Janeiro and São Paulo, in the small town of São Jose dos Campos. CTA had two institutes: ITA – Aeronautical Institute of Technology, the most prestigious engineering school in Brazil, and IPD – Research and Development Institute. There was also the embryo of a third institute to stimulate the creation and development of industries that would use the technologies developed in CTA, and provide employment for engineers graduating from ITA.

At this time Montenegro and Colonel Aldo Weber Vieira da Rosa, director of IPD, wanted to bring projects to CTA that would not only improve local technological expertise but eventually also attract business to Brazil. High on their list of invitees was one of the most respected aeronautical experts at the time, the distinguished Professor Heinrich Focke, designer of the notorious Focke Wulfs, the famous German fighters from the Second World War, and developer of the first successful helicopter. After the war Professor Focke had settled in Holland and had in mind to develop a 'convertiplane' which could take-off and land vertically like a helicopter and cruise horizontally like an airplane. He agreed to stage these projects at CTA as well as a single main rotor, plus double tail rotor helicopter.

Montenegro and Rosa had absolutely no real notion of what such a collaboration could lead to, what resources were required, how much money would be needed, and the amount of time these projects would take. The answers to these were all unknown due to the unique innovative status of the Focke projects. Montenegro and Rosa were worried, as their ultimate goal was different from Focke's: they were more concerned with developing the human element. They wanted to create a market to absorb a new generation of expert engineers graduating from the instituted ITA (Aeronautical Institute of Technology), who would launch Brazil's new era of aeronautics.

Focke arrived in Brazil with his team of sixteen engineers and went to work at a newly constructed hangar at PAR, the aeronautical development branch of IPD. The entire convertiplane was conceived in São Jose; the transmission was a work of art, designed in São Jose, but built under spec by BMW in Germany, then assembled and tested at PAR.

With the convertiplane project under way, Montenegro and Rosa approached the British company Hawker Siddeley with the idea of using its

HS Double Mamba, which featured a turbo shaft of 2,500 to 3,000 shp, to power the convertiplane. The British promised to sell but, after dithering some time, they communicated to us that they would not be able to supply the motor.

Montenegro and Rosa then approached American Wright for their Cyclone aircraft engine, a 2,200hp twin track 18 cylinder motor. Although totally out of spec with Focke's original design, heavier (3,500 lbs) with less power, a very high vibration and noise level, they were otherwise faced with the task of going back to the drawing board. The lack of choice which led them to the Cyclone required a tremendous amount of changes to the convertiplane at a cost which PAR could not easily absorb. The entire project was revamped and a new fuselage built to accommodate the Cyclone, at a cost that bankrupted the project a few years later. Nevertheless, Focke consented to shift his attention to the Beija-Flor helicopter project in 1955. By then I was already enrolled in ITA, eager for my aeronautical engineering degree, after serving five years with the elite fighter plane squadron in Rio de Janeiro.

Small helicopters of the post-war era had one major problem: they were dynamically unstable in pitch and roll. Helicopters were difficult to control in gusts that caused a high frequency oscillation, and the pilot could not let go of the command stick even for a second. Whereas all other helicopters controlled pitch and roll in the main rotor, the Beija-Flor incorporated a lateral control in the main rotor, and pitch and yaw were controlled by the tail rotors, set in a crisscross pattern, at a 90 degree angle; one of my contributions to the project. These improvements enabled the pilot to control the pitch and yaw by changing the blades' angle of attack by moving either the rudders or the stick.

This new arrangement provided excellent longitudinal and directional stability and gave the Beija-Flor a distinct advantage over its competition. However, it was still unstable laterally, requiring further changes to the lever arms of the mechanical stabilizers and the angles of the aerodynamic stabilizing devices.

There is an irony in considering Brazil's position at this time and from a different perspective. While all of these innovations were being incorporated into a cutting edge aircraft for the very first time in São Jose dos Campos, the rest of the country was still largely agrarian in exports and an importer of industrial goods, to the massive advantage of better developed trade partners. Consider, too, that the vast majority of Brazilians could only afford to commute to and from work on a bicycle made in Britain, France or Germany. At the same time Brazil was building and developing a technologically advanced modern helicopter, we did not even have a bicycle factory.

Among the many unique features incorporated into the Beija-Flor was the use of a regular airplane motor, a Continental six cylinder with 250hp,

mounted horizontally. Whereas the typical helicopter of the time had one tail rotor to control direction, Beija-Flor incorporated two intermingled rotors, at a 90 degree angle, to control both pitch and yaw. The fuel tank-normally placed below the vertical engine behind the pilot's back was instead, placed higher than the Beija-Flor's motor, which eliminated the need for a fuel pump, and was therefore lighter, less expensive and a more reliable solution.

The Beija-Flor featured a main rotor with semi-rigid blades that controlled both the up and down movement and the lateral inclination. Unlike all other models, the Beija-Flor's pitch was controlled by the tail rotor, as opposed to the main rotor. The machine also had an auto-rotation safety feature, designed to avoid crash landings in the event of engine failure. A free fall was prevented by allowing the wind to propel the rotor and ensure a soft landing by using the kinetic energy stored in the blades.

To control roll, we worked overtime on an artificial means of stabilization, both mechanical and aerodynamic. The response of the aircraft was very sensitive to any minor adjustment of these devices, and finding the right setting was a painstaking process.

Upon completion of the Beija-Flor design, we had incorporated so many new features that it had practically nothing in common with any other helicopter; it was truly revolutionary.

Most of the improvements proved to be sound solutions, while others failed to perform as well as we had expected. The Beija-Flor design team decided then to work on the stability factors, where we had a clear advantage over the competition. Initial tests concentrated on lateral stability, which became the main objective of the test flights. These tests could be performed at low altitude, therefore the auto rotation system was not implemented, because our resources were limited.

Due to the non-linearity and complexity of Beija-Flor's systems, the controls were completely new to me with every test flight, after the adjustments had been made following the previous test. I flew over 20 test flights in Beija-Flor, the equivalent to flying 20 different helicopters for the first time.

Aside from being Project Beija-Flor's test pilot, my principal design task involved the aerodynamics of the rotors. I was then a Captain in the Brazilian Air Force. Professor Focke's project manager, Herr Begandt oversaw my section, and the senior members of the team were all German. Engineers and technicians working on Beija-Flor were assembled from Germany, Czechoslovakia, Poland, Hungary, Austria, Italy and France, most of whom had previously been in Focke's employ and, of course, the best of the young Brazilian ITA graduates. German and English were the common languages between sections, but in time their Brazilian hosts were able to teach them a basic familiarity with Portuguese. We were impressed with the quickness with which our Eastern bloc partners picked up a new language

The Beija-Flor was the first helicopter to be designed, built and flown in Brazil.

Professor Focke had arrived in Brazil with a small staff that became the core of the project. Once settled in São José dos Campos, they recruited former collaborators they had known in Germany before and during the war, many of whom had fled from the Allies to neighboring countries. All were glad to be working with Focke again, and were looking forward to a new future in a new land. The group was highly competent but very difficult to handle. They had endured the worst hardships imaginable during wartime in Germany and still suffered stress-related losses of home and family. Many of our project members were emotionally and physically scarred, and sometimes demonstrated peculiar and eccentric behavior. As brilliant as each team member was, he was also difficult to deal with on a personal level. Socially pleasant, most of the men were married by now, with families; all except for Herr Bussman, who was a real character.

Bussman was highly proficient in his ability to illustrate complex mechanical devices, a fantastic mechanical designer who could make his hieroglyphic drawings easily understandable. However, his verbal skills were practically non-existent, and it had nothing to do with the language barrier. He could hardly make himself understood in German, his native language, or any other, although he perfectly understood what was said to him. His inability to express himself verbally resulted in a bizarre contract negotiation. After several ineffective attempts to reach an agreement on his employment, we simply handed him a blank piece of paper, which had been

duly signed by management, asking him to fill out the terms of his contract.
He did.

As Project Beija-Flor progressed, a constant flow of homegrown Brazilian
talent came onboard, with the hiring of the best ITA graduates, as well as
technicians from the Air Force and commercial airlines. This was the incuba-
tion period of Brazil's aeronautical industry.

Richard Kurtz, the engineer responsible for maintenance of Beija-Flor, personally checked all systems, especially the engine, before every test flight.
This was a policy that I, as test pilot, insisted on, primarily because the auto
rotation function designed to alleviate the fall after an engine failure was not
connected yet. Kurtz would not let me anywhere near the helicopter until his
pre-flight tests were complete; a non-negotiable ritual. No matter what the
time the test flight was programmed, Kurtz and his mechanics had been
onsite several hours beforehand. Herr Kurtz was a very disciplined and
dedicated person, and I am personally thankful for it!

One might ask, why the team did not finish the auto rotation development
as a high priority? The answer, put simply, is it was a matter of time con-
straint and Spartan resources. No time; no money.

Nothing happened during the first 20 test flights. Although each was a
difficult test, the first 20 were smooth, from a safety point of view. There were
never any failures or heart-stopping events, except, perhaps, for the oscillations; a dance in mid-air with different tempos and tricky steps each flight.
Sometimes the Hummingbird would fly to one side; a strong gust of wind
would make it slide sideways until I could get the rhythm back.

Every test drew a large crowd. The entire crew assembled, down to the
lowliest office clerk. Everyone was so involved in the process that they all felt
like proud owners. But tests were also filled with suspense; nobody knew
what might happen every time the Beija-Flor took to the air. It was an excitement not to be missed.

Constant adjustments kept us from scheduling test flights in advance.
Every department had to sign off on each test, but it was always up to Kurtz
to give the last word. Sometimes this last word would be in the form of a
shout, warning bystanders to clear out of the immediate area, but mostly I
got from Kurtz a thumbs-up and a broad smile.

May 8, 1964, the day of the 21st test flight, Kurtz had run through his
battery of tests and dispatched an assistant to fetch me. I was in my office 200
yards away, preparing for the next flight by reviewing the list of procedures
to be executed. I walked out into a lovely autumn day, a clear blue sky, with
prevailing winds from the south, in line with the runway, laid out especially
for that reason.

For this, the 21st test flight, I was to gauge response at higher horizontal
speed, which I had done before, gradually increasing speed. This was not

new to me or the team. At 14:40, after getting a thumbs-up and now familiar broad smile from Kurtz, I took my customary seat, buckled up, and put on my helmet. The engine was running, and so I took Beija-Flor to a height of about 12 feet above the ground, moved in the four cardinal directions, circled left then right, and found everything in perfect condition. There was some slight oscillation, but nothing unusual, and so I undertook combined movements of turning and sliding in different directions. Next on the agenda were flight commands at differing speeds in combined directions.

Each test proceeded without fault or flaw, followed by a vertical landing. Taking off again I completed another set of combined commands, performed another hovering landing, took off a third time and performed more tests. These maneuvers were conducted at low altitudes, and far enough away from the hangar to assure everyone's safety. I then performed another landing, this time with forward velocity, more like an airplane, taking off immediately, checking its behavior at high speed, but still at a low altitude over the runway.

I had my hands full, and could not communicate with the ground crew (which would have meant hand signals, as the Beija-Flor had no radio). The ground crew understood only what they could see and hear. From my unique perspective I could understand the heart of the machine, what I saw in the instruments, what I felt in command reactions and vibrations, and my pilot's sixth intuitive sense.

The controls checked out, and I continued a straight path over the runway, accelerating. All of a sudden the engine coughed, a sure sign of a technical glitch. Fearing a possible engine failure, I instantly flared back, the engine coughing, but not failing. I decided to return to home base. But the engine stopped as I completed the U-turn and entered the downwash the helicopter had already left behind. When you make a U-turn the wind is rarely exactly in your direction, contributing to moving the turbulence away from your path. But the downward turbulence created by the helicopter was now directly in front of me. This is something that I could not detect from the cockpit, and I felt it only after I ran into it. Normally such turbulence is not a problem, especially if you have enough power to cruise through it, but it was at that exact moment the engine failed.

The kinetic energy in the rotors was not sufficient to hold the aircraft up or prevent the inevitable crash. I tried desperately to hold the Hummingbird with what energy remained in the rotors to soften the landing, but it was not nearly enough and we continued to fall. There was no time for any other maneuver, and we came crashing down before I could take a second breath.

The Beija-Flor was very badly damaged but, amazingly, I walked away without a scratch; our cockpit design insulated the pilot from the kind of injury pilots typically suffered in other helicopters. The only blow I suffered, aside from a pain in the neck from my heavy helmet being knocked, was the loss of our 'child'.

A broken machine is a terrible thing for a test pilot to see. Test pilots need to dissociate the failure of the test with failure of the aircraft. It requires a certain discipline, mental clarity and emotional distance. And yet my first concern was not with me but with the machine: What could have gone wrong?

I mentally traced every step of the test flight trying to think of even the slightest movement that might have caused the mechanical failure which pushed the Hummingbird too far, but I could not find any.

Everyone came charging towards the crash site as I struggled to free myself from the wreckage of Beija-Flor. No-one knew whether I was dead or alive. It was clear that they were more worried for me than the helicopter. They found me unharmed, and it was comforting to feel their deep concern for me. But, I swiftly broke off from the consolations to call a hasty meeting of the engineers to review the accident right away. After this meeting I had the sad task of calling Colonel George Moraes, then director of IPD, and General Montenegro, director of CTA, with the bad news. Both men listened to my report, asked technical questions, and tried to boost my flagging morale as I was devastated by the loss.

A two-seater, the Beija-Flor had its 225hp Continental E225 engine fitted in the nose.

In the months that followed, the Beija-Flor was rebuilt and was again ready to test in March 1965. By this time though, I had departed from the project to attend Cal Tech (in the USA), from where I got my PhD in aeronautics and applied math. I was replaced by Major Ozires Silva as head of PAR and replacing me as Beija-Flor's test pilot was Major Alfenas, an experienced helicopter pilot who took the Hummingbird for granted as just another helicopter. After a few minutes into his first test flight, Alfenas crashed Beija-Flor and destroyed it completely.

This unfortunate accident allowed Ozires to propose that funds be transferred from the Hummingbird to the development of a 16-passenger commuter plane. The core group of engineers raised up in the development of the Convertiplane and Beija-Flor were assigned to the new project, and four years later, when it was transferred to the newly founded Embraer company (Empresa Brasileira de Aeronáutica SA) the whole project was abandoned. By this time I was back at São José dos Campos, starting up Brazil's space program.

TESTIMONIAL

Hugo Piva entered the Brazilian Air Academy in 1945 and became a military pilot after completing academic and flight training (he flew Fairchild PT 19, Vultee BT 15 and North American AT 6). He graduated with the highest honors (academics, sports, marksmanship and flight awards) ever achieved by any student, garnering the only 'Santos Dumont' Medal of Honor ever awarded by the Brazilian Air Force to this day. He then served at Santa Cruz air base in Rio as a fighter pilot, operational in Republican P 47 Thunderbolt and Gloster Meteor VIII.

Piva then went to ITA Aeronautics Institute of Technology, graduating Summa Cum Laude in aeronautical engineering in 1958. He stayed in the Aerospace Technology Center – CTA, in its Research and Development Institute – IPD, specifically, its aircraft department, where he created the Flight Test Group. Here he developed Brazil's aircraft certification process, and personally test flew a very large number and types of aircraft.

He stopped test flying in September 1964 to attend the California Institute of Technology – Cal Tech, to obtain MS and PhD degrees in aeronautics and applied mathematics in 1968. Piva returned to CTA to head the Brazilian space program until 1983, when he was appointed director of the Aerospace Technology Center. He retired from the Brazilian Air Force in 1987 as a three star General with 4,480 flight hours.

He founded Brazil's longest active wine club and after retiring from the Air Force he founded a technical manuals design company, servicing Embraer and automakers.

Chapter 11

Carl Lyday in his pressurised suit, with a rubber seal that separates helmet from flying suit.

Carl V. Lyday – F-111
Keep your Head above Water

During the 1970s the nuclear deterrent was at the forefront of the Cold War. Weapons testing was essential sometimes, with the occasional humorous consequences.

From the early 1970s until the end of the Cold War, the National Command Authorities directed that the F-111E would maintain a five minute nuclear alert status at RAF Upper Heyford, UK. Two B61 nuclear weapons were loaded on the two-seat F-111; nine F-111s were on alert 24/7 inside a triple-fenced alert pad. If world tensions deteriorated, up to 72 F-111s could be loaded with two B61s each. The F-111 was assigned various pre-planned targets throughout the Soviet Eastern Bloc. I was one of those nuclear alert pilots from 1973 until 1975.

With the sophisticated systems in the F-111, we were highly confident of being able to reach the targets and deliver our payload. The F-111 featured a fail-safe terrain following radar which could fly the plane automatically at 200 feet above the ground at night or in the weather, at speeds up to Mach

1.2. The right-seater was both the navigator and weapons systems officer. He was responsible for using the advanced attack radar to navigate to the target, find and identify the target, and then release the bomb. We routinely dropped bombs inside 200 feet, plenty good enough for a nuclear bomb! The right-seater also operated the various highly advanced defensive systems the airplane was equipped with.

After my F-111 assignment, I was selected to attend the USAF Test Pilot School at Edwards Air Force Base, California. I then became an F-111 test pilot, specializing in weapons testing. The B61 nuclear weapon by then had been in the arsenal for many years. Its developer, Sandia Laboratories in Albuquerque continuously upgraded and modified various components of the weapon to improve its reliability and enhance its security features that were installed to prevent unauthorized use. One of the tasks assigned to Mike Billick and me in the late 1970s was to test the new B61 modifications to the extremes of the F-111 envelope to ensure the weapon components and electronics could survive the extreme environments of vibration, aerodynamic heating, parachute opening shock, and ground impact. The electronics in the B61 nuclear weapon were very complex, not only to arm and fire the weapon, but to prevent unauthorized use. For example, before firing, the weapon had to detect that each crew member had set their respective switches correctly and that a special six-digit code had been dialed in by the crew. The six-digit code was securely locked in the command post safe. If the President authorized a launch, this safe would be opened, using the two-man control principle, and the code would be radioed to the crew.

Among other safety features the weapon had to sense that it was dropped at a high airspeed, negating anyone from using it even if they had the code. In addition, the F-111 aircraft had a Unique Signal Generator (USG) that also had to be detected by the bomb before the system would fire. And, there were other classified safeguards. The bottom line was, that one could give a bomb to terrorists and they would never be able to use it. If the weapon was tampered with, a small charge would explode to deform the plutonium pit, rendering it useless. Over the course of two or three years, we dropped the B61, with its modifications, at various conditions, including Mach 1.33 at 100 feet AGL at the Tonopah Test Range in Nevada. We also tried to test a bomb at Mach 2.5 at 60,000 feet which resulted in the following scary event, that in hindsight is rather amusing.

My right-seater for all the B61 test missions flown on the F-111 was Captain Mike Billick. Mike was also a graduate of the USAF Test Pilot School, graduating as a flight test navigator in the class ahead of me at Edwards. Over the many months of this program, we had become as close-knit as an operating room surgical team, knowing exactly what each of us needed to do in the cockpit, often, without words. The planning and preparation for this mission was lengthy and intense. The stated objective was to drop the B61 as high and as fast as the F-111E could go, supposedly Mach 2.5 at 60,000 feet.

The purpose of the test was to see if the electronics in the bomb, including its radar altimeter, could survive the aerodynamic heating, vibration, and extremely low atmospheric pressure at 60,000 feet. The flight conditions would require the two man crew to wear full pressure suits in case of cockpit depressurization or ejection. In order to reach 60,000 feet and Mach 2.5, it would be required to accelerate from cruise conditions, Mach 0.8 at 30,000 feet.

High supersonic aircraft such as the SR-71 and F-111 reach their top Mach by climbing, not diving, which is counterintuitive. The average person would think the top speed of an aircraft is achieved by pointing the nose down and diving towards the earth like an old movie about courageous test pilots. In actual fact, the F-111 and SR-71 reach their top Mach number by accelerating to a specified calibrated airspeed and then climbing while maintaining that airspeed. During the climb, the Mach keeps increasing until the limiting Mach is reached. By the time the F-111 reached 50,000 feet, we'd be at Mach 2.5. At least that's what the charts said we could do!

In order to achieve Mach 2.5 at 50,000 feet, a 350-mile run was required using full afterburner. We were to take off from Edwards AFB, and fly 350 miles north of Sandia's Tonopah Test Range. So much fuel would be used during the acceleration that a tanker was needed in order to refuel just prior to starting the acceleration.

To document the bomb's trajectory, Sandia used huge telescopic cameras. To get stable images, we had to drop the weapon in a small window about 20 minutes after dawn. This was called 'prime time' when the atmosphere was most stable for the photos. Our acceleration run would therefore have to begin while it was still dark which meant a night refuel, in a pressure suit; a very difficult task because the pilot cannot bend his head backwards to look up at the tanker and the boom. Plus, my eye glasses were suspended from the frame of the helmet, further complicating things.

The 350-mile run to the target was to be from north to south. North of the Tonopah Test Range, one is outside restricted airspace and there are several high altitude airways that run east-west that would have to be crossed before we entered the test range. Plus we'd be flying through different Air Traffic Control Centers, requiring near-constant radio communication with air traffic control since we would be in a high-speed climb, not at a constant altitude. At the same time, we had to be in continuous contact with the test range, which was providing radar vectors to get us to line-up perfectly for the weapons drop. It was a very intense period for both me and my right-seater, Mike. The plan was I would work the HF radio with the range while Mike talked to traffic control on the UHF radio.

We dropped off the tanker just before dawn, got our initial clearance from the Air Traffic Control Center (ATC) and began full afterburner acceleration. After less than a minute, the ATC switched us to another frequency. I was talking to the Tonopah Test Range on the HF to get precise headings for the launch of the weapon, but I also could hear my right-seater, Mike Billick, trying to check in with the traffic control guys on the new UHF frequency. No luck.

By this time, we were streaking at about Mach 1.5 and climbing, crossing airways every few minutes. But we had not received further clearance from ATC. I could hear on the intercom that Mike was breathing hard and we were now both concerned about crossing airways without clearance. Fortunately the weather was clear and we could scan for airliners to prevent coming near one. Besides, it was really too late to abort because we'd have to descend back down through the airways which would be even more hazardous than continuing to climb above commercial traffic, so I decided to continue. Mike went back to the original frequency, frantically trying to check in with someone but, by then, we were so far away from the relay antenna that we could only hear garbled responses. Now Mike was trying other published ATC frequencies, but still no contact.

We were rapidly approaching 45,000 feet at Mach 2.0. I knew airliners rarely, if ever, flew above that altitude so once there at least we wouldn't hit one! We were still about 100 miles from the test range, but the aircraft by now was only slightly climbing and the Mach number hung up at Mach 2.29. We kept the heading given by the range controller, but now he was becoming very, very, faint.

Mike, by now, had given up attempts to call ATC, but I could hear him breathing heavily. As we got close to the range boundary, we had milked the airplane to 50,000 feet at Mach 2.29, but it balked there and simply was not going any higher or faster. And, the airplane was feeling very squirrelly, rolling and yawing and pitching, in small uncomfortable, seemingly random movements.

I called Sandia on the HF and told them I couldn't go any higher or faster. They said, 'We'll take what you can get. Altitude is more important than Mach number, so at the appropriate point we'll call for you to 'zoom' (a maneuver where the nose of the aircraft is rapidly pulled up, considerably past what is needed for a normal climb. This causes a very swift increase in altitude and a rapid decrease in airspeed. The 'zoom' must be terminated at some point or the aircraft will run out of airspeed) the aircraft as high as it will go, but at least to 60,000 feet.' At Mach 2.29, distance is covered very rapidly and way before I was ready, I heard: 'Prepare to zoom! 10, 9, 8...' Suddenly, Mike screeched in a high-pitched voice, 'Carl, something is the matter with my suit.' I hurriedly glanced over at him. Inside Mike's pressure suit helmet, I could see through his faceplate that water was up to his chin, only about two inches from covering his mouth.

The controller continued: '... 3, 2, 1, zoom!' Instinctively, I pulled back on the stick and we launched for the moon. Immediately the aircraft stall warning horn blared, there was violent wing rock, and left engine had a severe compressor stall and flamed out. My mind raced. Eject? Mike's going to drown but he will drown floating down so I continued the zoom. 'Mike, you OK?' I shouted as we were in the middle of the maneuver, beyond the point of no return. There was no answer.

Sandia was constantly providing small heading changes, which I heard, but did not process. Those constant calls irritated me as I had my hands more than full. In a tense situation, the least important gets filtered out. I just wanted to keep this 80,000 lb hulk of metal under control. At the zoom attitude, I could not see the ground looking forward and for the first time in my life I was not in control of my machine. As we approached 60,000 feet, I'd had enough of this zoom stuff so I nosed over in a zero-g parabola. 'No, don't!' I heard a gurgle and realized my zero-g maneuver had caused the water to float up and cover Mike's mouth. I quickly pulled back on the stick and the water went back down, but I saw it was still perilously close to covering his mouth. 'Breathe through your nose,' I cried.

'I can't, it's stopped up,' Mike replied, his rapid breathing showing obvious fear and his microphone now garbled. I noted our speed had slowed to Mach 1.8 due to the flame-out and the zoom itself. The aircraft still felt mushy and I felt it would stall again if I increased the back pressure on the stick.

Suddenly, '10 seconds till drop. Arm the weapon,' came the now barely-audible call from the controller on the HF radio. I glanced over to see if Mike was okay. Water was now well over his chin, less than one inch from his mouth. Mike had stretched his neck by tilting his head back as far as he could in the pressure suit to keep his lips above the water. I threw my switch to 'Arm and Release', but with the two-man control principle for nuclear weapons, there was also a switch Mike had to rotate for the weapon to release and function. He had to rotate the switch to one of several possible settings, in this case, 'AIR FF', meaning the weapon would air-burst at a specified height after a free-fall, determined by the bomb's radar altimeter. 'Mike, can you select AIR FF?' I inquired, still way too intent on getting this mission accomplished. Mike replied, 'I think so, but I can't look down so I'll have to feel for the switch.'

Sandia controller: '... 3, 2, 1, Release!'

I pressed the 'pickle' button, felt the 'chunk' as the weapon separated, and called, 'Bomb's away.' I then pulled the throttles to idle and started a glide, which from 60,000 feet seemed to take forever, considering Mike's predicament and the fact we were on one engine, nearly 300 miles from Edwards AFB.

I looked over at Mike. The water was getting higher. 'Jeez, he's gonna die,' I thought. 'And I killed him by not aborting.' Then an old scuba diving maxim came to my head: 'Stop. Breathe. Think. Act.' I realized the solution. Gross, but easy.

The cause of Mike's problem was his suit ventilation system was set too hot. Coupled with the stress and intense workload, Mike had been sweating like a marathon runner. The rubber seal that separates the helmet from the rest of the suit was simply damming up the sweat from his head and face. Although it looked dangerous, and both Mike and I were in a near panic, I suddenly realized the solution. 'Mike, there's nothing more than three or four ounces of moisture. You won't drown in it. Drink it!' Silence.

'Mike, can you hear me?' Even though we sat side-by-side with shoulders occasionally touching, the stiff pressure suit required a really strenuous effort to turn far enough to the right to be able to see him. With no answer from Mike, I had to see if he was conscious, so cranked my body and the helmet around. I'll never forget Mike's look as he slurped the salty mixture with pursed lips. When it was all gone he cranked his suit around to the left to look at me. His sheepish, but very happy grin as he realized he was not going to drown, will never leave me.

After cranking up the left engine, we then had more than 30 very leisurely minutes on the way back to Edwards AFB to laugh, contemplate life, our adventure, and how screwed up the entire mission was. Even the bomb had failed. The radar altimeter evidently pinged on the F-111 and sent the firing signal to detonate when the bomb was only a few hundred feet below us. Had the bomb been real, we would have been vaporized in a nuclear fireball.

Our final mistake on this wild mission ironically provided documentation of it for posterity. After the weapon release, we were so consumed with solving Mike's problem, getting the left engine restarted, and just savoring the fact that we would indeed live, that we failed to turn off the instrumentation tapes. So, they preserved our every word during the flight through the airways without radio contact and the banter that was exchanged during those 30 minutes on the way back to Edwards AFB after the bomb was dropped.

The tapes recorded a now-infamous exchange between Mike and me that brought the wrath of our commander down on us. 'Mike, what are we going to tell the Flying Evaluation Board (FEB) about screaming through four airways at Mach 1.5 without clearance?' (A Flying Evaluation Board is called to see whether a pilot can keep his wings after doing something stupid or foolhardy.) 'I'm not worried,' Mike nonchalantly replied, they don't have FEBs for navigators!' Nothing but raucous laughter was heard on the tapes for the next five minutes. Mike and I had bonded for life.

TESTIMONIAL

Carl Lyday began his military career when he entered the USAF Academy on June 26, 1961. He graduated from the Academy on June 9, 1965 with a degree is basic science. He attended pilot training at Williams AFB, Arizona where he graduated second in his class. After three years as a T-38 instructor pilot at Laughlin, Texas, Carl attended gunnery school, followed by a year at Phan Rang, Vietnam, where he flew 235 combat sorties in the F-100. He received the Distinguished Flying Cross for a classified mission in Laos.

After Vietnam, Carl was assigned to RAF Upper Heyford in the UK, where he flew the F-111E and sat nuclear alert. Carl then attended the USAF Test Pilot School at Edwards AFB. After graduation, he was assigned to Eglin in Florida where he tested various weapons on the F-4 and the F-111, including the mission described in the article. Carl served in various assignments after that, including as a squadron and group commander. He retired on August 1, 1994 after three years as the 46th Test Group Commander at Holloman AFB, New Mexico. Carl accumulated more than 4,400 hours in 55 different aircraft.

At the height of the Cold War, the USA was dedicated to the fighter-bomber and deep strike policy that the F-111 represented.

Chapter 12

Patricia Jones-Bowman and Ornithopter

Patricia Jones-Bowman – Ornithopter
First of the Flappers

A totally unique aircraft, and a machine that falls straight out of the manuscripts of Leonardo da Vinci. But the unflappable Patricia Jones-Bowman has flown the ornithopter, the first functional flapping-wing aircraft.

My dentist and fellow pilot, Joe Fisher, calmly announced, 'They're building an ornithopter at the University Of Toronto,' during a routine check-up in early 1995.

Excitedly, I waved my arms, rolled my eyes and made some weird, 'Oooh. Oooh,' sounds. Conversation was difficult with a mouthful of dental instruments.

'They want to be the first to sustain flight in a purely flapping wing aircraft,' he continued.

'Do they already have a test pilot?' I managed to splutter.

'No,' he replied.

Within two weeks, I had met Professor James Delaurier and his Project Ornithopter (from Greek ornithos 'bird' and pteron 'wing' team at the

University Of Toronto, Institute For Aerospace Sciences (UTIAS) and was accepted as the first test pilot of Ornithopter 'C-GPTR' or just PTR.

Like most people at that time, I thought, to my extreme annoyance, that, 'everything had been done,' in aviation; there was nothing new to discover, there would be no more venturing into the unknown. After all, we had broken the sound barrier and even been to the moon. As I listened to Dr Delaurier, I realized I was wrong, there was, indeed, one more 'unknown' to conquer: flapping wing flight; the last of aviation's firsts!

I was euphoric. This was something that was still within the realm of the individual. Even now, most manned ornithopter research is still being conducted by individuals rather than large organizations. During the following year, construction of the ornithopter continued at fever pitch. It was built in Dr Delaurier's UTIAS wind tunnel laboratory by the UTIAS team and a small army of volunteers, including Joe Foster who built the wing jig, which was needed for the construction of the complex wing spar. Many others also contributed until the lab was filled to overflowing with pieces of ornithopter.

The design was based on the proof-of-concept model that successfully flew in 1991 culminating 25 years of flapping flight research by Dr Delaurier and Jeremy Harris.

Ornithopters must constantly change their wing angle to take advantage of the rush of air.

Since an ornithopter is a purely flapping wing aircraft, the flapping wings provide all of the thrust required and almost all of the lift. There are no propellers, no fixed wings and no other thrust or lift producers of any kind. The wing and the flapping mechanism jointly form the heart of any ornithopter. PTR's wing was of composite construction, aero-elastically tailored to both twist and bend under air loads. It has a 'shearflexing' trailing edge which allows the double-surface wing to twist without wrinkling. The flapping mechanism, designed by Jeremy Harris, consists of a scotch yoke attached to the engine/gearbox and to the wing centre-section. This converts the rotary motion of the engine into the reciprocating vertical motion of the centre-section. Up and down vertical movement of the centre-section causes the wings to rotate around their pivots in a flapping motion. Ailerons are difficult to incorporate into a flapping wing so, there are no ailerons.

PTR uses the rudder to produce yaw which, eventually and indirectly, leads to a roll for turning. A better and more direct solution to lateral control will hopefully be found in the future. A data acquisition system and ballistic parachute were also installed.

By autumn 1996 it was ready for flight testing. We held many brainstorming sessions to discuss the upcoming flight test procedure. Since no manned ornithopter had ever sustained flight, there were no 'ornithopter testing' reports, data, records or books of any kind to consult. We, in fact, were 'writing the book' ourselves. We were about to venture into the unknown and we were all enormously excited.

On October 3, 1996, PTR was transported to Downsview Airport, Ontario and the testing began. Our objective for this, our first test, was just to determine whether PTR would move forward under its own power. We didn't really know. The computer simulations had given predictions for the level cruise condition and the proof-of-concept model which had been hand-launched into level cruising flight never went through an 'accelerate from zero to lift-off' stage so we simply didn't know whether the wing would produce enough thrust to break free and start moving.

If it didn't, a major redesign would be necessary. If it did then we could continue.

To the runway, and the sky!

It was too windy to do the test outside so PTR was pushed to the back of the huge, wartime hangar, turned around and pointed towards the hangar doors which were left open, just in case. I climbed into the cockpit and closed the canopy. With my helmet on and the canopy closed, all was silent, I could no longer hear the chatter of the lab crew and I was now in my own little world.

The lab crew were tapping on the canopy, 'Turn the radio on,' they signaled. They called out the start-up checklist: 'Seatbelt and shoulder harness on?'

I clinched the harness tight and remembered the static tests and being tossed around as the fuselage pitched and heaved.

'Fuel on. Throttle set. Choke set.'

They wheeled up the external battery for starting and plugged it into the connection on the side of the fuselage (too heavy to be carried onboard, which meant that the engine couldn't be restarted in the air).

The green light glowed.

'Clutch?'

'No, it's still unserviceable.'

'Ballistic chute armed?'

'No, not for this test.'

'Ignition switch on, brakes set, controls free and functioning. Clear the wings!'

'Starting now!'

I looked out at the left wing; it started to move slowly, the engine caught and I adjusted the throttle. The wings settled into an idle flapping frequency of 0.5Hz and everyone was beaming. Flapping always had this effect on us.

Now I had to wait while the engine warmed up and the lab crew set up the data acquisition system and video cameras. The instruments were fluctuating wildly, the result of the varying loads imposed during each flapping cycle.

I was being bounced around a little, even at this low flapping frequency. I rode the rhythm, up and forward, down with a 'thunk' and back, up, and then forward again. The signal to, 'Go' jolted me out of my daydreaming.

The calculations predicted, and we devoutly hoped, that PTR would break free and start to move forward at 0.7Hz flapping frequency. Easing the throttle forward, I transmitted a running commentary to the lab crew: '0.55Hz, 0.6Hz, 0.7. Still not moving, certainly being tossed around now, quite difficult to keep the stick centered, instruments fluctuating, 0.75Hz, still nothing, 0.8Hz.'

Suddenly PTR broke free and started to move, picking up speed at a surprising rate! The nose wheel steering was, however, very sensitive. Too twitchy, I thought and had to work hard to keep it straight. The pitching and heaving of the fuselage also posed a problem. As I was being vigorously bounced around, the stick went with me, causing control inputs that I did not intend, and constantly had to correct for.

After merrily flapping our way along the length of the hangar, I throttled back to idle and, amid popping flashbulbs and cheering lab crew, PTR rolled to a triumphant stop with less than 20 feet to the hangar doors.

We were distinctly pleased with ourselves and PTR and immediately made plans to start testing on the runway at the first sign of good weather. With no ailerons and a large average dihedral, taken over the whole flapping cycle, the ornithopter has no crosswind capability and is definitely a 'no-wind' aircraft. All the testing was carried out at dawn when the wind is calm.

At this time we didn't know that it would be another two years before our next milestone would be achieved. We settled down into a routine. Testing would begin as early as possible each summer and continue until winter set in. Our 'hibernation' period each winter was spent repairing the damage to PTR, re-designing and making any required modifications.

We started with low-speed taxi tests and progressed to high-speed tests, acceleration tests, braking tests, roll control tests and every other test that we could think of.

We encountered several problems along the way. Some were expected; others (always the lively ones) were unexpected surprises.

The ornithopter behaves like no other aircraft. During flight, once every second the flapping (and the varying lift) causes the fuselage to pitch from what is normally considered to be an extreme climb attitude to an extreme dive attitude and the wings flap from far above the horizon to far below. This destroys a pilot's normal visual references of aircraft attitude making it difficult to determine whether PTR was on the ground or two feet above it, or whether one wheel was lifting etc. The fuselage pitching and heaving also leads to a turbulent and dramatic ride for the pilot.

The first year's testing ended with the sudden disintegration of the right wing-tip during a run at 25mph. A major modification to the design was carried out during the winter. High speed bouncing brought the second year's testing to an abrupt end causing a flattened nose-wheel, sheared rivets and fuselage damage.

We had reached an impasse.

The year had been spent gradually increasing speed to check the handling characteristics of PTR at 50mph (the predicted take-off speed) and working on a take-off technique that would minimize the pitching and heaving of the fuselage.

We had discovered that a take-off in an ornithopter can't be done in the usual way, by centralizing the stick, accelerating to lift-off speed, then rotating because the pitching and heaving causes bouncing. I, too, constantly was getting bounced around the cockpit, and control became more difficult with increasing speed.

The following year, we started a long series of take-off tests experimenting with different stick positions, speeds and flapping frequencies. Too much 'stick forward' resulted in wheel-barrowing and nose-wheel damage. Too much 'stick back' caused severe bouncing and the test would have to be ended.

To counter this, a computer simulation was written which showed the stick position to be absolutely critical and precise. Stick and elevator positions would now have to be held accurately at various points in the take-off run. An elevator position indicator was needed and one was designed, built and installed on the instrument panel. A lovely instrument, the centre of my universe.

It was designed with a vertical column of colored LED's. Green for various defined positions of 'stick forward/elevator down', red for 'stick back/elevator up' and yellow for 'stick/elevator neutral'. Now I could accurately place the stick in any desired position and radio the lab crew that I was, 'holding 1 Green or 2 red'. Maintaining that position while being tossed around the cockpit is, however, another matter.

Testing resumed at dawn on September 19, 1998. The speed was increased on each run in an effort to attain the 50mph lift-off speed. Very quickly 46mph was reached but at this point we ran into the 'Bounce Barrier'. No matter what we did, at 46mph, PTR would start to bounce wildly and acceleration would cease.

Finally new calculations showed that PTR would have to be held firmly on the ground until 50mph was reached then abruptly lifted off to an altitude that would avoid re-contacting the ground. This is more difficult than it sounds. The lift varies dramatically during the flapping cycle, increasing on the down stroke. When airborne, PTR would follow an oscillating flight path, up, then down, approximately 10 feet, once every second!

On November 8, 1998 we decided to try this technique. I eased in full throttle and held the stick forward until the LED indicator read '2 green'. PTR leapt forward, accelerating straight through the 46mph barrier, finally steadying at 51mph; our fastest speed so far and sufficient for an attempted lift-off.

Thoroughly pleased and smug, we launched into the next test with the objective of conducting a stable and controlled take-off run up to and including an intentional lift-off at the predicted lift-off speed.

At 50mph I brought the stick back firmly and we rose into the air, Our first lift-off!

There was no time to properly savor this feat since it was immediately followed by three ungainly bounces, one of which completely sheared off the nose wheel.

Finally, we rose once more, like a phoenix from the ashes, in a magnificent 'airliner' style take-off, before grinding to a stop on the sheared off nose wheel strut amid ear-splitting screeches and showers of sparks. Our second milestone had been achieved.

The damage to the forward fuselage was significant so, having achieved what we believed to be a first for piloted ornithopters and with me beginning to feel like a 'grizzled veteran', we retreated into our usual winter's hibernation period of 'research and rebuild'.

Testing resumed in August 1999. We hoped that this would be the year we would finally achieve sustained flight. The modifications to PTR had drastically increased the gross weight and the predicted lift-off speed had to be increased to 57mph. We spent August and September practicing lift-offs while waiting for the perfect weather for the flight.

On 15 October 15, the wind was calm and we met at dawn. We didn't know if PTR would reach 57 mph and I wondered what would happen if it did. The pitching and heaving of the fuselage became increasingly severe at speeds above 40 mph and it became increasingly difficult to control.

I climbed into the cockpit; we completed the checklists, and for the first time we armed the ballistic parachute. All was ready. The lab crew gave the signal to go. As I increased throttle I transmitted my usual patter.

'Throttle forward, stick 2 green.'

'Initial pitching quite heavy, 20mph, 30mph, flapping frequency 1.0, increased to 1.1.'

'40 mph, flapping frequency increased to 1.2.'

'50 mph,' I was being bounced around severely; PTR was suddenly extremely difficult to control.

'52 mph, 56 mph, never been this fast before, one more second to lift-off.'

Suddenly we were rolling rapidly and continuously from side to side. What's this? I thought. Something's obviously happened, but no word from the lab crew…throttle back…wait and see…veering off to the right, have to fly it back to the centre line…increase throttle…rudder…it's not responding, we're going over….inverted! We're down…stopped…it was still flapping, even upside down.

I turned the engine off as the lab crew continued to radio: 'Are you okay, are you okay?'

'Yes, I strained, 'though the cockpit is crushed. I can't get out…petrol is leaking…puddle's quite large now.'

'Wait for lab crew…and don't make a spark,' came the fraught reply.

And so, at 56 mph, on the point of lift-off, we had suffered a major structural failure. The right vertical struts buckled in compression and snapped in two. The right wing floated briefly then thrashed and partially disintegrated. The left wing was still flapping and producing lift which caused PTR to roll rapidly inverted. The whole episode, from when the struts failed to when I was hanging upside down from my seatbelt, took a mere five seconds.

We looked at the crash video many times over the next month and determined the cause of the failure. The damage to PTR was severe but we were determined to continue with Project Ornithopter. That winter's hibernation period of research and rebuild was busier than usual but we knew we would again meet at dawn.

The basic airframe of the Canadian ornithopter constructed by a team from the University of Toronto Institute for Aerospace Sciences.

TESTIMONIAL

Patricia Jones-Bowman is British-born and grew up in Hertfordshire, England, but now lives in Canada with her husband and two dogs.

She started flying at the youthful age of 16. Jones-Bowman holds a Commercial Pilot License;   Multi-engine Instrument Rating; Flying Instructor's Rating and Seaplane Rating. She has worked as a commercial pilot, bush pilot and chief flying instructor on both seaplanes and landplanes in the wild Ontario northland. She has flown 20 different types of aircraft.

Jones-Bowman was the chief test-pilot of Ornithopter C-GPTR 1995 to 2001 inclusive, and the first to achieve flight. After achieving the first lift-offs, she resigned in 2001 to start work on my own ornithopter design, which she continues to do.

Chapter 13

Dennis Newton was a test pilot for Cessna, LearFan and the FAA before joining Boeing.

Dennis Newton – LearFan
Race against Time

Dennis Newton was the test pilot for the incredible, but short-lived LearFan. Here he describes the huge rush to get the aircraft airborne before the financial deadline.

I started at LearAvia in Reno on December 2, 1978 and, at that time, was the entire flight test department. We had one large hangar, containing nothing but the late Bill Lear's gull-wing Mercedes. There was no guarantee that the LearFan would ever happen, and it nearly didn't. Going to LearAvia then was a risky career move for anyone. Like most of the others there, I gave up a good job elsewhere to be a part of this fascinating project. I went so far as to forego a year-end bonus in order to report in time for scheduled autopilot demonstrations, which I flew in the prospective vendor's demonstrator airplanes.

The year 1979 was a constant struggle for funding. I was tasked to identify and somehow acquire what we would need to conduct a flight test program. I quickly realized that we would need a crew escape system for the prototype, a stall recovery system (the wind tunnel data revealed a possibility of a deep stall) and, if possible, some sort of simulation to investigate the airplane's flight characteristics prior to actually flying it. It further developed that the engines for which the airplane had been designed would not be available. That was nearly a show stopper, but it appeared that Pratt & Whitney PT6s might work, so conducting engine evaluations was added to my pile.

I found that Stencel Corporation and Stanley Aviation had developed a Yankee rocket crew escape system that could be adapted to our needs; I negotiated a deal and schedule to obtain it. The system would require a hole big enough to pull a pilot out through. Explosive Technology Corporation was contracted to develop a pyrotechnic door cutting system for us. We contracted with Syndex Corporation for the stall recovery system, which was essentially an explosively deployed, and then jettisoned, chute mounted on the tail cone. If we ever had to use it, we would need to jettison the pusher propeller. Explosive Technology also agreed to develop a prop shaft cutter to do this for us. All of this equipment would require development and testing.

I contacted Calspan in Buffalo, New York, about using one of their variable stability research airplanes for simulations. They looked at our wind tunnel data and pronounced it adequate, so we struck an agreement. I shuffled off to Buffalo several times to assist in the data analysis needed to program the system, and spent four weeks at Calspan in November and December of 1979 flying and analyzing LearFan simulations with them. As a result of this work, we increased the tail area about 7 per cent and increased its dihedral four degrees, increased the aileron area about 32 per cent, and modified the pitch trim system with anti-servo tabs to increase the control forces. These changes worked very well, and would have been much more difficult and expensive to do after the airplane had been built.

Everything we did in 1979 was dependent on interim and uncertain funding packages. Then, in February 1980, we obtained a funding package worth about US$50 million from the Northern Ireland Department of Economic Development, together with a US limited partnership of US$30 million. The catch was that the US$50 million in Northern Ireland funding was contingent on flying the prototype by the end of 1980. In many respects, it seemed impossible. As of February 1, 1980, of 237 engineering drawings required for the engine installation, control surface design, and wing design, nine had been completed. In short, large and critical parts of the airplane were not even designed, let alone built. Personally, I was sure that there would be a feast of crow on the table at the end of the year. As it turned out, I would not know until New Year's Day whether I would help serve it, or help eat it.

I went to Calspan again in March 1980, and we flew demonstrations for Bob Harper, co-creator of the well known Cooper-Harper pilot handling qualities rating system, and for Hank Beaird, who had been one of the early

Lear Jet test pilots. Our minuscule flight test organization which, by then, consisted of myself, George Harrison doing test planning and a small test instrumentation group, grew in May, as Hank Beaird came aboard as manager of flight operations.

The escape system came together. A static test was conducted in Phoenix on September 18. All the whizz-bang gadgets worked, and the test dummy descended to the desert surface under a clean, full parachute with no damage. We followed that with a 350 knot sled test. The dummy was extracted cleanly and we again got a full chute. The system worked.

The mated wing and fuselage was rolled out on October 10, but by then it was clear that the only way the we could possibly fly in 1980 was to defer things not necessary for the first flight. The bleed air and ice protection systems went. The electrical system was left incomplete, with only what was needed for the first operational flight. The landing gear retraction system went, and solid bars were installed in place of the retraction cylinders. There was then no need for gear doors, so away they went.

The engine fire boxes weren't ready, so we would use ad hoc fire blankets. The vendor-supplied control surfaces, although unsatisfactory for production, were proof loaded and found to be strong enough. We added external balance horns to the elevators when we could not balance them internally. Well into November, the structure was proof tested to 80 per cent of limit load. The controls were installed, and the yoke twisted loose in my hands during an aileron system proof test. We fixed it. Upon fuel system installation we found that the rivets in the wings resulted in constant leakage. We reluctantly decided to install a ferry tank in the cabin, giving us forty minutes or so of fuel for the first flight. This took up space intended for the flight test data acquisition system, but most of that was not ready anyway, so out it went.

The airplane was painted on Christmas Eve. Finally, on Christmas Day 1980, we did the first engine runs. The PT-6s ran perfectly, as did the drive shafts and transmission. We finally went to our Christmas dinners thinking that we just might fly this year, after all. The airplane was ready for the second engine runs on Sunday, December 28. These were to be the final checks prior to taxi tests. Then, the gremlin struck.

A starter malfunctioned in about the worst possible way. It would spin the PT-6 up, let it light off normally, and then drop out before the engine could accelerate. Had we cooked an engine, our goose would have been in the pot with it. They were not standard PT-6s, and there were no other flight-worthy engines to be had. December 29 was a day of frantic around-the-clock effort, and finally a workaround was found, which bypassed the problem.

Hank and I finally began low-speed taxi tests on December 30. The objective was to verify engine control, taxi handling, initial acceleration, and integrity of the propulsion system (and the whole airplane) to proceed to higher speeds. By that afternoon, we were ready to begin high-speed taxis. We shoved the levers up, and as we accelerated down the runway for the first high-speed trial, both engines quit. We had run the ferry tank partially down during the low-speed work, and the acceleration had pulled the remaining fuel away from the feeder ports. By the time the system was modified to prevent that and the airplane came out of the hangar again, it was 15:00 on December 31. Sunset was 1 hour and 45 minutes away. We had less than two hours to try to do the high-speed taxis and fly for 50 million bucks.

To have any chance at all we knew we would have to ruin a set of brakes and tires. There would be no time to cool them between runs. We put brakes, wheels, tires, tools and fire extinguishers on our chase truck. There then ensued a scene right out of the Keystone Kops, as we, the fire truck, and our chase truck raced the clock down the runway. Rotation tests went easily. We were able to lift the nose wheel below 80 knots, and to control pitch with no tendency for a tail strike. However, full aileron on the first run produced nothing. We tried another run for ailerons. Nothing except warmer brakes. We decided on one more run. I brought the power up and went to 100 knots, trying full aileron in both directions. No aileron response at all, but another high energy stop, and the word from the ground crew that the brakes were smoking. We shut down and got out. A tire deflated, and the hot brake settling down on it started it burning. The ground crew immediately put it out and began changing the hardware. Meanwhile, Hank and I concluded that we could learn no more from taxi tests. The airplane had a wide landing gear stance and small ailerons, and that was that. We would have liked actual test validation of our aileron power to overcome any roll-off, but even with no fuel in the wings it couldn't be had. We would, therefore, trust LearAvia aerodynamics and the Calspan tests. We jumped back in only to find that the ground crew had pulled every circuit breaker.

We were beaten at that point. The cockpit was dim and had no lights. Only about one third of the breakers had ever been tested. We had a hand drawn diagram of which ones to push in, but the others were not banded or otherwise identified on the panels. We could hardly read either the diagram or the breaker panels, and had no idea what would happen if we pushed any of the untested breakers. It was simply too late. It would have been foolish to get airborne with no lights, no electrical system to speak of, only a few minutes of fuel in the ferry tank, and who knew what problems with an airplane that no one had ever flown. Back we went to the hangar, thinking ourselves 50 million dollars poorer. I could practically taste that crow.

The next day, New Year's Day, 1981, the airplane rolled out at 10:00. The ferry tank was filled. Engine starts were routine. We taxied out to runway 14, the longer of the two runways at Stead. Everything had finally come together, and this time it felt right.

The escape system was armed. The maintenance crew looked us over at the run-up area and pronounced us ready. The Stead fire trucks were in position. Clay Lacy and John Penney were waiting overhead to chase us. Communications with our control room were loud and clear. However, the temperature instrumentation didn't appear to be switching properly. All the thermocouples installed in the various locations, including one inside the engine fire shields, indicated about the same temperature regardless of the switch position. We were burning our limited fuel supply messing with it, and we were still suspicious of the starter which had given us problems and didn't really want to shut down, so we decided to go with it as is.

We took a deep breath and looked at each other.

'Well,' I said, 'I guess we get to find out if it's an airplane.'

'I guess we do,' Hank allowed.

We taxied onto the runway and brought the power up. Engines and transmission were normal, Lacy called in position and ready, and we let it run. At

The LearFan was designed to carry eight passengers at jet-like speeds but at a fraction of the cost.

about 120 knots, it flew off with no oscillations or roll-off. However, about the time we became airborne, the thermocouple temperature headed for the roof. The graphite structure was a 350ºF cure, and we wanted to keep it below 200oF. The thermocouple reading went through 300ºF, then 400. I was then nearly certain that we were seeing the one in the engine bay, and that the selector switch was not working. I couldn't imagine the material outside of the engine fire blanket getting that warm that quickly, but if it was we had a serious problem. We had attained about 1,500 feet altitude, so we reduced the climb and pulled the power back. The temperature responded instantly, going back below 300ºF. This convinced us that we were looking at the temperature of the engine itself, but even if we weren't, the temperature was now not dangerous. This was the only real anomaly we ran into. Everything else was absolutely routine.

Hank flew for a few minutes feeling the control responses, then we swapped seats and flying chores and I started looking at speed control and response to flap extension. Controls and trim were good, certainly more than adequate to land. We figured we had pressed our luck (and our ferry tank) about enough for one day, so I lined up on runway 14. The airplane felt just fine at 130 knots indicated, with about 20 knots of pad above our calculated normal approach speed, so that's what I used. I flew the airplane in over the numbers and closed the throttles, then let it touch without floating. We rolled smoothly to a stop after 17 minutes of flight. We taxied back to the hangar area and shut down, and we were surrounded by LearAvia folks, TV crews, dignitaries and well wishers from everywhere. The Northern Ireland representatives jubilantly declared the day to be December 32, 1980, and that the funding would go forward as planned. It was all over but the speeches.

I wish I could say that we all lived happily ever after, but as you undoubtedly know, we didn't. In a sense, the airplane we flew that day was more of

The final day before flight. The team examines the brakes which burnt out during taxi tests.

a full scale flying model than a LearFan. It nonetheless proved to be very useful. During many subsequent flights, it put to bed a lot of doubts about the configuration, it proved that the propulsion system worked, it provided real numbers for performance and handling qualities, and it let us identify a lot of things which needed more work. However, the compromises which went into making LearFan 001 fly on December 32 rendered it unsuitable for certification testing. It could never be conformed to the production design. Two more airplanes, quite different from the first one, ultimately flew but, by then, the program was again in financial trouble. Hank left in 1982. Many others were accepting offers elsewhere by then. I left in January, 1983, subsequently flying for the FAA and then Boeing. The project was shut down in May, 1985. That, however, is another story. LearFan 001 is unique, and its home in the Museum of Flight is appropriate and well deserved.

TESTIMONIAL

Dennis Newton was chief research pilot for the Penn State Department of Meteorology and a test pilot for Cessna, LearFan and the FAA before joining Boeing in 1987. During 14 years at Boeing, he was a training captain, production flight test captain, an FAA-designated engineering representative flight test pilot and assistant chief technical pilot. He retired from Boeing in 2001, and continues to be a consultant DER flight test pilot. Dennis is the author of numerous aviation magazine articles, technical papers and the book *Severe Weather Flying*, now in its third edition. He is a Fellow of the Royal Aeronautical Society, a Centennial Fellow of the Penn State College of Earth and Mineral Sciences, an associate Fellow of the American Institute of Aeronautics and Astronautics and a member of the Society of Experimental Test Pilots.

Chapter 14

After he left A.V. Roe, Blackman joined Smith Industries as an electronics expert.

Tony Blackman OBE – Vulcan Bomber Delta Force

Aerobatic displays from pilot Tony Blackman on the delta-winged Vulcan, one of the most iconic aircraft in the skies pre-empted a tragedy.

The Vulcan was a splendid aircraft and very innovative for its time, the first aircraft to rely completely on electrics to operate the flying controls. The aircraft was the last design of Roy Chadwick and it was his decision to make the aircraft a delta and, therefore, ensure its success. Roly Falk made the first flight in 1952. My first flight in the aircraft was in March 1956 as part of the acceptance team at RAF Boscombe Down and then I joined Avro in August just before the first Vulcan Mk1 was delivered to the Royal Air Force. My job was to carry out all the development work of the Vulcan Mk1 and Mk1A and then, after Jimmy Harrison did the first flight of the Vulcan Mk2, I took over the test flying.

The Vulcan flight deck was very small and the Avro team realized that as the aircraft was going to have fully powered controls there was no need to have a conventional wheel and they fitted a fighter-type stick instead. This immediately solved the pilot ejection problem since, with a stick, there was no need for controls to be pushed forward out of the way prior to ejection.

For me this was a perfect solution as I was left handed and always felt very comfortable in the aircraft even though the forward view through the windscreens was appalling.

Landing the aircraft was always a thrill and a challenge. If the aircraft was a bit fast there was a definite ground effect and it was difficult to get the aircraft to touch down. The initially normal service procedure was to touch down and release the braking parachute, but the RAF pilots soon learnt that it wasn't necessary to stream the parachute. Personally, I always landed the aircraft by coming in at the correct speed but aiming short of the ideal touchdown point and not letting the aircraft land, so the attitude of the aircraft became more and more nose-up. When the elevators were fully up and the wings ran out of lift, the aircraft would subside very gently on to the runway with the nose way up in the air. The drag was enormous, the aircraft slowed right down and there was never any need to stream the chute. If the centre of gravity was aft, which could be controlled using the fuel transfer pumps, I used to be able to turn up the short runway at Woodford with the nose still in the air, wind permitting.

The landing could be made even shorter by stopping the two outer engines before touch down though this required a bit of care. Unknowingly, I nearly anchored the curve one day at Farnborough when landing in the rain. In the Empire Test Pilots School that evening I was teased for landing short of the runway and on inspection the following morning there was a very gentle 10 foot run of wheel marks on the left-hand side of the narrow bottle neck just short of the start of the runway. Pat Hanafin, chairman of the Flying Control Committee, was very good about it, though, in reality, I had absolutely no excuse. These days the pilot would probably be sent home in disgrace.

Tony Blackman (left) and Jimmy Harrison in front of the Mk2 Vulcan. Harrison was chief test pilot before Blackman took over.

At high subsonic speed the aircraft would start to go longitudinally unstable at the cruising speed of 0.85 Mach. By 1.00 indicated Mach number the elevators in the Mk1 or the elevons in the Mk2, all eight of them, would be fully up so there was no way the aircraft could go but down if speed was increased. Avro solved the problem in the cruise by introducing a Mach trimmer so that the aircraft felt stable as speed was increased up to Mach 1 indicated. This enabled the aircraft to be flown manually and automatically at the cruise speed. As speed was increased the Mach trimmer would extend so that the aircraft felt stable but as 0.98 indicated Mach was reached, the Mach trimmer would extend rapidly so the there was a definite nose up trim change to deter the pilot from going any faster. However, it was still possible to increase speed so that by indicated Mach 1.00 the Mach trimmer would be fully extended and the pilot would have his hands full. I say hands advisedly, even though the aircraft only had a stick, since both hands would be need to pull the stick back and prevent the aircraft heading for home.

It always amazed me that there were no accidents due to the aircraft diving out of control but the answer was almost certainly that the drag was so high above Mach 1 that even though the aircraft might dive, the Mach number would not rise significantly. I personally don't believe I ever went faster than about Mach 1.02, but I met a few pilots in the bar who had flown at higher speeds and were even convinced they had gone supersonic.

One of my first tasks at Avro was flying a Mk1 Vulcan, developing the Olympus engines for the Vulcan Mk2. It was important to get things right as the common intake for both engines on one side invariably resulted in losing both engines when an engine surged, which definitely reduced the noise level as well as the altitude. The other interesting idiosyncrasy of the engine was that, when it surged at low altitude, it made the most stupendous noise, which was rather alarming, to say the least, but luckily only damaged our nerves but not the engine. I remember flying the aircraft low level over the development team at Filton one day and surging the engines to demonstrate the problem.

The aircraft had 64,000 lb of thrust at the time, but not the 84,000 lb of later years, and I decided that at the Farnborough Air Show a double roll off the top from a standing start might be the thing to do. The aircraft only weighed 105,000 lb because it barely had any fuel. Applying full power on the brakes and then letting go, the aircraft reached 270 knots at the end of the Farnborough runway and I pulled up for the first roll off the top. The job of my flight test observer, in the right hand seat, was to call out the g, 3g being the target and maximum permitted acceleration. My job was to keep the acceleration at 3g, to try and keep the wings level and to peer through the pillar box windscreens waiting for the ground to reappear, albeit the wrong way up. By the time this happened and the aircraft was upside down, the speed had dropped to 145 knots and applying full aileron was not a lot of good since, at that speed, an enormous amount of adverse sideslip was generated. However, the application of full rudder at the same time helped enormously and the aircraft reluctantly rolled the right way up. I throttled right back, dived at the crowd and did another roll off the top and was back on the ground in 3 minutes 19 seconds; a great way to spend a week.

To my surprise there were a lot of volunteers to fly in the back of the aircraft during the week. It must have been terribly claustrophobic but we were fully booked. Every morning the volunteers were initiated into the escape drills and every afternoon they were given what could only have been described as an extreme fairground experience. My wife, when she came down at the weekend, insisted on having a go and then she travelled back to Woodford in the right-hand seat on the Monday. the first lady to fly. in the right-hand seat.

We never did any more aerobatics after that because there was a tragic accident at Syerston when the first prototype Vulcan, flown by Rolls-Royce and fitted with the Conway engines for the Victor Mk2, broke up doing a fly past. The enquiry assumed that the pilot was flying too fast but it transpired that Rolls-Royce had been doing rolls off the top unbeknown to us, presumably emulating our aerobatics at Woodford. However, it was not generally known that it was possible to damage the nose ribs of the Vulcan doing these manoeuvres and we had a special small man at Woodford who could inspect the nose ribs and carry out repairs if necessary. It has always been my belief that the Vulcan was already damaged when it flew, and pictures of the accident show the right leading edge peeling off.

There was an automatic landing programme for the Vulcan Mk2 and we developed the system on a Vulcan Mk1. Incredibly the automatic throttle system, as initially delivered and developed by the Blind Landing Experimental Unit (BLEU), relied completely on speed error and so was quite useless for a jet-engined aircraft with large power lags when the throttles were opened. As the aircraft pitched up, the throttles needed to be applied immediately, long before the speed started to drop. Once Smiths had added some pitch rate gyros the automatic throttle system worked beautifully but I did wonder about the so-called experts who did the initial design.

BLEU had also decided that it would not be possible to do an automatic landing using just a localizer. Consequently all the bomber command airfields had offset localizers installed, which I detested, particularly as the Vulcan had the localizer antenna in the wing tip. For our tests Bedford had a leader cable laid down in the approach lights and, to be fair, the system worked perfectly, though it was a complete waste of money. However, we had problems longitudinally due to the Vulcan's ground effect on touch down. After wasting some flying hours I realized what should have been immediately obvious, that we needed to vary the approach speed with the headwind component. We increased the approach speed by 1 knot for every 4 knots of headwind component and after that our longitudinal touchdown dispersion became immediately acceptable, just as the programme was cancelled.

Another interesting programme was the Vulcan carrying the Skybolt Air-Launched Ballistic Missile. Each weapon weighed 15,000lbs so all the Vulcan Mk2 wings had to be strengthened which, incidentally, had the side effect of giving the wing a long fatigue life. The ground effect on landing was very pronounced since the air had no way of escaping between the tow missiles, but landing by holding the aircraft off the ground still worked very well. I always remember the first flight with one missile on. We had our normal pre-flight briefing and were assured that there would be no problems at all. A slight asymmetric drag effect, but no worries. I released the brakes and just managed to prevent the aircraft careering off the runway by applying braking, full nose wheel steering and full rudder. I hauled the aircraft hurriedly into the air and all of a sudden my problems disappeared. Incredibly everybody from our chief aerodynamicist downwards to myself had forgotten about the asymmetric inertia effect.

The Vulcan was measurement tested at Edwards Air Force Base in the USA alongside the B-52.

The Vulcan was used in Australia to flight test the Blue Steel Weapon system.

Unusually for a civil pilot, I had two opportunities of taking a Vulcan overseas. The first occasion was on the Skybolt programme, taking an aircraft to Edwards in the USA for measurements. We had to refuel at Goose Bay because though the Vulcan wing was very thick, the fuel was in bag tanks and only carried a relatively small amount of fuel. I enjoyed the trip as it gave me the opportunity to fly their now legendary aircrafts, the B-47 and B-52 and, of course, we reciprocated and let their pilots fly the Vulcan. It also gave me the opportunity to join the very prestigious Society of Experimental Test Pilots. My other trip was to take a production Vulcan Mk2 to Australia for Blue Steel trials. I insisted on having a pair of wheels, our only spare part, and we set off for Aden where we were parked miles from anywhere because of a royal visit. Next stop was Gan and we found we had a puncture due to an Aden nail. The RAF were wonderful and made a wooden ramp, towed the aircraft backwards onto the ramp and so were able to change the wheel. The last leg was from Changi in Singapore, still with the RAF and only 2,000 yards long, to Edinburgh field. We left at dawn, before the ground temperature started to rise, and just managed to get into the air but we did not have a lot of runway left.

At Woodford we had the opportunity to fly and compare all three V Bombers because we had a Valiant for Blue Steel trials and we converted all the later Victor Mk2 into tankers. The Valiant was a very heavy aircraft but had no idiosyncrasies, the Victor had a very nice crew arrangement but, for me, what really mattered was the landing and the Vulcan scored hands down. I was very lucky to have had the opportunity to have been able to test such a great aircraft so thoroughly, right to the corners of the flight envelope.

TESTIMONIAL

Tony Blackman was educated at Oundle School and Trinity College Cambridge, where he obtained an honours degree in Physics. After joining the Royal Air Force he learnt to fly, trained as a test pilot and then joined A.V. Roe and Co Ltd where he became chief test pilot.

Tony was an expert in aviation electronics and when he finished flying he was invited by Smiths Industries to join their Aerospace Board, initially as technical operations director. He helped develop the then new large electronic displays and Flight Management Systems.

After leaving Smith Industries, he was invited to join the board of the UK Civil Aviation Authority as Technical Member.

Tony is a Fellow of the American Society of Experimental Test Pilots, a Fellow of the Royal Institute of Navigation and a Liveryman of the Guild of Air Pilots and Air Navigators.

He now lives in Hamble, Hampshire, UK, and spends his spare time writing books and designing and maintaining databases on the Internet.

Chapter 15

Leland C. Shanle was trained as an EA-6B Prowler pilot and deployed onto the USS Midway *for 'Operation Earnest Will' in the Persian Gulf.*

Leland Shanle Jr. – Target Drones
Oh, to Take a Drone out of El Segundo

It's one thing being a passenger in an aircraft; it is another when the pilot is not in the aircraft, but to be an aerial target too? 'Chip' Shanle suffered all three.

The threat in 'Top Gun' was, 'If you screw this up, you'll be flying rubber dog-squeeze out of Hong Kong'. For my generation, at VT-4 on board NAS Pensacola, it was, 'You'll be flying drones out of El Segundo'. All the students would laugh at the quote; life is funny sometimes.

The J79-GE-8 turbo jet engines rumbled to life, flight control checks complete, I eased the Phantom II out of the chocks. Taxiing to the active runway I passed an A-3D Sky Warrior and a C-130A Hercules being readied for flight. As I continued toward runway 'one two', a flight of four T-33s executed a perfect fan break overhead. Was it 1966, or even 1976? Negative; it was 1996 on board Naval Weapons Test Center, Point Mugu.

I had chanced, by luck into one of the best kept secrets in naval aviation. I was flying F-4 Phantom IIs as a test and adversary (enemy) pilot. As a bonus I was doing it right on the beach in Southern California. How did I fall into this great deal? I had been hanging around the squadron ready room of VAQ-135, NAS Whidbey Island (remotely located north of Seattle in Washington State) and it was raining. Having recently finished my Department Head tour, I was without portfolio and waiting to detach. I got a call from an old friend, Commander Jim Seaman:

'Shantini you want to come to SOCAL (Southern California) and head up my Phantoms?'

'Phantoms? As in the F-4 Phantom II, built in my home town, that I grew up watching and joined the Navy to fly; those Phantoms?'

'Yes.'

'How many you got?'

'Fifteen.'

'Pilots?'

'Five.'

'Wait a minute Spert, how many of them are up?'

'Today?'

'Yea, today; as in, can be scheduled to fly?'

'Hang on let me check the schedule....eight.'

'When do I start?'

Naval Weapons Test Squadron at Point Mugu was a throw back organization and right up my alley. After a couple of hours chatting about the Phantom with Lieutenant Steve 'Icky' Crane and a cockpit check out, I was ready to go. Ten syllabus hours later, completed flying around SOCAL, I got my aircraft check and flight lead check on the same flight. No simulators required or desired.

Having spent most of my time as a fleet naval aviator, I didn't have any experience in flight testing. I would learn through 'OJT' (On the Job Training). Our specialty was weapons separation testing and target presentation for evaluating various weapon systems. For a 'Prowler Driver' who had spent his career very much in the subsonic region, the opportunity to toss around AQM-37 target drones at 50,000 feet and at Mach 1.5 was a dream come true.

At this time I still had not totally comprehended the FSAT designation of our department. FSAT: Full Scale Aerial Targets, whatever I thought, can't possibly compare to 200 night traps (carrier landings at night).

Through the squadron mail one day I received a copy of a letter that was placed in my jacket. It was entitled, 'Category C Flight Test Waiver'. I asked young Lieutenant Crane what it was for and he responded, 'No big deal. You need it for your hop tomorrow'.

With that well reasoned response I acknowledged and we went off to the club for a libation. After a couple of adult beverages, the young Crane gave forth a bit of detail informing me that he would be getting a syllabus 'hop' in the UCC. Risking ridicule, I ventured a question, what's a UCC? The Universal Control Console he informed me, and then further added that I had a drone safety flight in the morning. Not wanting to show any more ignorance I nodded and concentrated on my plate of Lumpia.

There is no free lunch or Lumpia for that matter, and there is certainly no good deal that goes unpunished. I started getting a clue of what was happening about 10 seconds into the next day's brief when Bob Williams, head of targets division, gleefully stated we would get a 'triple X' on the flight. Finally unable to bluff my way through, I asked for an explanation. It seemed I was getting my 'Drone Safety Pilot' syllabus ride, Crane was getting a UCC syllabus event completed and the QF-4N Number 152983 was getting a first flight check as a drone.

The UCC turned out to be simulator-type device located in a NASA-like control room that, when hooked up through a UHF data link, would allow Crane, from his armchair, to fly the QF-4N up to 350 miles from the air-conditioned comfort of his range control room. Mr Williams would instruct him and evaluate his performance. My part in all this was to hook up the system from the cockpit and ride along in the aircraft to insure everything went as planned. Suddenly the realization of what was happening landed. My only solace was the explanation that if it got 'uncomfortable' I merely needed to squeeze the trigger and the mighty Phantom was at my beck and call. Otherwise I felt as much a pilot as Laika the dog, when the Soviets sent up their first rockets.

I wasn't in El Segundo, but it was damn close. I armed the drone panel giving control of the aircraft over to Crane on the other side of the base. The controls flinched, and so did I. Next we ran through the control checks, each flight control cycled normally as the stick moved unaided in the cockpit; Phantom indeed.

The last step was to double check that two small 'Allen' wrenches, attached to the front of

One set of F-4B Phantoms was converted into drone control aircraft; 24 were converted into supersonic target drones.

the throttles, were pulled up bypassing the burner gate, allowing the throttles to move fore and aft freely into, or out of, the burner range. It was a low-tech fix to the problem of physically double-moving the throttles outboard then forward automatically.

The tower had already given us the pattern, so Crane asked me if I was ready to go, I couldn't think of any excuses so the power came up to 80 per cent. The QF-4N had an automatic takeoff mode; it would set an attitude and hold it through the takeoff until the UCC operator turned it off and took control. It did not, however, hold line-up, the UCC operator did. Nose wheel steering was not an option due to reliability and using the brakes would blow the skinny tires on the N-series Phantom, so the only way to control line-up was to modulate the afterburner.

If we started left, Crane would ease back the right throttle decreasing the flow of fuel to the afterburner. The afterburner section of the J79-GE-8 engine contains four manifolds; each can be selected individually by movement of the throttle in the burner zone. Once the line-up correction started to take effect maximum burner had to be re-engaged to lead the re-correction and put the nose back on centerline. That was the theory.

Crane transmitted one last piece of information prior to the takeoff roll.

'It tends to hop a bit before going airborne.'

Hop? Oh I can't wait for this! 'Roger that,' was my creative response.

Crane sat comfortably in the UCC staring intently at the six-inch TV screen he would use to keep me on centerline and pilot me into the air. I sat not quite as comfortably in the Phantom as he selected the ATO (Automatic Takeoff) mode. The light lit up, the stick programmed aft, and throttles ran to full power as the brakes were released. The right engine hard lit a couple of seconds late, creating a slight drift to the right from brake release. I watched as the left throttle slid to mid-range burner. It stayed there for a three count. The nose started tracking to the left as it went back to full burner. The sine wave was now initiated; the Phantom tracked back and forth across center-line as Crane tried to centre the TV camera in front of me on the glare shield.

The Phantom began to erratically hop and skip madly across the centerline of the runway again, and the radio grated as it squealed and squelched loudly in my ears. Already, I was over the runway edge and just barely airborne, when the aircraft began to roll off right getting the wing tip fright-eningly close to the ground. I decided I had had enough fun and pulled the trigger. Leveling the wings I snapped up the gear and climbed away from terra firma, as I searched for the tiny flap switch.

The radio came alive with Crane explaining that the squealing noise in my earpiece had been his repeated attempt at yelling: 'You got it!'

It seemed the data link was lost at takeoff rotation. With the worst of it behind me, I trimmed up the Phantom at 2,000 feet and gave it back to Crane.

The Phantom is not an easy aircraft to fly, nor is it easy to fly smoothly while maneuvering. It is also just my personal observation, that it is nigh on impossible to do it from 100 miles away, utilizing 25-year-old UHF data link technology and a six-inch TV screen.

To say the maneuvers were a tad rough would be generous. The g-force seemed to be applied with an on/off switch. Level-offs were punctuated by an ample use of negative g. Of course the fact that it was only the young Lieutenant's second attempt at this did not improve my mood.

Later when I got my UCC qualification, I realized it truly was the most difficult flying I had ever done. In fact, trying to land a QF-4N from the UCC was the only flying I have ever done that was as hard as or harder than landing on an aircraft carrier at night.

That fun was just about to start. San Nicholas Island was 50 or so miles off the coast in the middle of the Pacific Missile Test Range. Actually, it wasn't much of an island, big enough for a runway and small base; that was about it.

The runway was located on the eastern side oriented north/south, with the southern threshold ending on a 500 foot cliff. There was only 5,000 feet available due to runway construction and repair, so pretty short.

We would start and end NOLO (No On-board Live Operator) missions on the island. The runway was not long enough for the Phantom to land on normally, so we always trapped them by dropping the tail hook and arresting the wire located 1,500 feet down the runway.

The pattern itself was a box pattern like a normal instrument approach except it was a very shallow 1.5 degree glide slope. A normal glide slope was 3.25-3.5 degrees, and thus we got up close and personal with the local cliff edge. You flew the pattern simply by looking up at one of the digital displays and making the little F-4 symbol follow the magenta line.

Once turned on to final approach, the controller aimed for the eastern tip of the island until he could make out the runway with the camera. When the runway could be discerned on the little TV screen you put a white cross hair on it. We called the cross hair the poor man's HUD (Head Up Display). Barney, one of our favorite engineers would give you a GCA (Ground Controlled Approach) by looking at a display located above the UCC. He would simply stand next to the UCC and talk you down the glide slope and keep you on line-up. Unfortunately it was not all that accurate. And I was riding pillion.

Down on the ground, Barney could stand next to the 'flyer' because the UCC was built into an old T-33 cockpit trainer. It was open from the shoulders up; open in a very crowded control room. It was also open to the point where engineers or flight test controllers felt comfortably free to come up and have a nice chat, sometimes at very inconvenient times. And I was up in the cockpit riding pillion.

Meanwhile, a 1.5 degree glide slope, plus a 500 foot cliff, subtracted by a distracting environment, multiplied by extremely difficult flying, equals a potentially interesting approach.

On approach one, turning to 'final'; Bob was instructing, Barney was controlling, observers in the control room were chatting, and I was getting lower and lower on the glide slope, as the Phantom flew closer and closer to the cliff. As I peeked around the camera in front, I gained the unique visual of going below the runway, directly at a cliff face. It was then that I noticed the wreckage of four or five other, less than optimal approaches, on the face of the growing cliff.

Reaching the data point I like to call the 'ASSAVE Point', I keyed the radio. 'Hey...ah, boys, uncle out here! I'm lookin' up at the runway.'

The power came up, the stick came back, and we blew through the glide slope like an elevator from hell. As we crossed the cliff's edge, high even for a normal glide slope, the power came back and the nose went down. I felt like a dog trying to jump into the back of a pick-up truck. As the forward windscreen filled with the runway threshold, and the tail of the Phantom elevated above the nose, I finally squeezed the 'fun killer trigger'. Promptly selecting ASSAVE power, I next explored the high alpha region of the QF-4N Phantom II, in the dirty (landing) configuration.

'Sorry about that Shantini!' came over the radio. 'But, hey it's all good if they ain't shootin' at ya, right?'

Right; this test pilot gig is going be a piece of cake.

It all worked out. 'Smoothly' would be a stretch, but at least nothing was bent. I leveled at 2,000 feet and re-coupled turning the Phantom back over to my sea service pal. The rest of the landings went much better and all three 'X's were achieved.

As I re-took control after the last 'touch and go' I selected full afterburner and let the lightweight Phantom run 50 feet over the runway. Scorching over the end of the runway construction at 500 knots indicated, I yanked on five g and pulled into the vertical. Passing through 15,000 feet I rolled it over pulling the nose down and pointed toward a large sand dune on the coast south of Point Mugu. Flashing across the shoreline and Route-1, I yanked on an 80 degree angle-of-bank four g turn to the north. At 2,000 feet I streaked up the 1,800 foot high ridgeline with a 200 foot separation, indicating 600 knots.

The ridge line ended abruptly with the airfield just below at sea level, crossing at the midfield intersection, I entered the visual pattern and Point Mugu's unique 250 degree break turn to the abeam. Turning to final approach, I glanced down at the migrant farm workers picking strawberries in the fields below. Rolling out after landing with the comforting tug of the Phantom's drag chute pushing me forward in the straps, an uncontrollable smile was hidden on my masked face. That wasn't so bad.

During the debrief we all wore smiles for different reasons. Mine grew exponentially when it was explained to me that the customs and protocol of the Targets Division dictated that Lieutenant 'Icky' Crane would be my Drone Safety Pilot when I started the UCC syllabus. I detected a slight downturn on his smile, as he no doubt knew that his ride would be very similar to mine.

The F-4 would normally deploy its drag chute on all landings.

TESTIMONIAL

Lieutenant Commander Leland C. Shanle Jr. US Navy (Retd), joined Naval ROTC at the University of Missouri and was commissioned an Ensign in the US Navy. He received primary flight training in the T-28B Trojan then completed the 'Strike' syllabus, carrier qualifying in the T-2B Buckeye and TA-4J Sky Hawk.

Designated a naval aviator he was trained as an EA-6B Prowler pilot and deployed with VAQ 136/CAG 5 in the USS *Midway* (CV 41) for Operation Earnest Will in the Persian Gulf. At sea nearly continuously for the late 1980s the *Midway* was the point carrier during the end of the Cold War.

After being assigned as an advanced flight instructor to VT 21 he returned to the fleet in 1993. As a department head for VAQ 137, he flew 40 missions in Operation Deny Flight, from the USS *America* (CV 66) over Bosnia; also transiting the Suez to support US Forces in Somalia. After a quick turn around he transferred to VAQ 135 on board the USS *Lincoln* (CVN 72) and deployed to the Persian Gulf flying 40 missions over Iraq in support of Operation Southern Watch, as an Air Wing SEAD Strike Lead for CAG 1.

Finishing his career at Naval Weapons Test Squadron, Point Mugu (VX 30); he led the QF-4N IPT, where he flew as a test pilot for multiple programs.

Retiring in 1998 Leland returned to Missouri with his wife, Laura, and their four children, where he writes and continues to fly as a pilot for American Airlines.

Chapter 16

Björn Johansson was with the Swedish Flight Test Centre for 18 years, ultimately as Commanding Officer until he left in 2006.

Björn Johansson – Saab Gripen Sent in Spin with Snakes

Back in the early 1990s, Björn Johansson, soon to be the chief test pilot on the Swedish Gripen fighter jet, was seconded to the USA for training. It started a trend to spin.

This story starts in the early spring of 1991 with a bike ride in the Mojave Desert. At the time I was a foreign student of class 91A at the USAF Test Pilot School (TPS), and was spending some of my rare leisure time pedaling my bike and looking at all the flowers that had exploded into bloom out in the desert. Everywhere I looked there were flowers. Most of them were blue and yellow, and, missing home, I was nostalgically thinking they accurately matched the colors found on the Swedish flag. A few were orange, the color that is globally associated with flight testing within the fraternity.

There were a lot of trails out in the desert and I was slowly and nonchalantly riding my bike along one of them looking around, admiring the unfamiliar beauty around me compared to the grey sun burnt base some miles away. Suddenly, a huge snake appeared right across the trail in front, and I was lucky to just stop a few inches short of running over it. After what seemed an eternity of taking in the situation, I managed to get off my bike. What was I to do now? I didn't want to backtrack and I certainly didn't want to make a major detour out into unmarked territory. After some thinking I decided to stamp on the ground, something I had heard would make the snake slither away. I stamped and stamped, but no reaction from the snake. I then started to toss small stones at him, still no response. My third attempt worked better, holding on to the bike rack I pushed on the snake with the front wheel; the snake slowly moved away. Back on my bike, I continued to follow the trail but now much more vigilant with frequent scanning of the trail ahead.

It was now a few years later, 1994 and I was back at Edwards again, thanks to the good relationship between the USAF and the Swedish Air Force. This time I was there to prepare for the spin test program we were about to start with the Saab Gripen fighter project. My colleague Clas Jensen and I were there to get a short refresher course in spin testing and were to spin both the A-37 and the F-16.

I was first out in the A-37 together with 'Trash', an instructor at TPS. We started normally with some stalls and, after emptying our tip tanks, we continued with an aft stick entry from a left turn. After the incipient phase we were stable in a right hand spin and after a few turns it was time to recover. I did as we had been briefed, but the jet didn't recover as we had been told. When I had stopped the yaw rate and pushed the stick forward to break the stall, the jet started to roll quickly instead of flying out of the stall. It was at that moment I knew something was very wrong. The only thing to do was to repeat the recovery procedure and hope that the more dense air at the lower altitude would make it possible to recover the jet. The second attempt gave the same result as before. At this point Trash took the controls and made a few more attempts, still with the same negative result. We very quickly got closer and closer to our pre-briefed bale-out altitude; still no recovery; still rolling. It was then I heard Trash yell out, 'Bale out! Bale out! Bale out!' I grabbed the ejection seat firing handle and pulled.

The next thing I remember was seeing the airplane disappearing below my feet, slowly spinning towards the ground. It was like looking at an old black and white war movie, very unrealistic. It was only after first looking up, seeing a full parachute canopy open above my head, and looking to the side seeing Trash hanging below his chute, that I convinced myself that I actually had ejected from the aircraft.

We had ejected at about 14,000 feet, if I remember right, so there was plenty of time to prepare for the return to earth. In my mind I went through my, before and after, landing check list, and also had some time, as any real test pilot genuinely would have done, which was to check and evaluate the handling qualities of the parachute (why not, it might not happen again) by inputting some 'rudder doublets' to the parachute's steering handles and evaluate the performance qualities. As I suddenly approached the ground, I did actually have to use my new-found knowledge, since there was quite a number of Joshua trees fast approaching in the landing area, but I luckily just managed to steer away from them, before my butt got scratched.

After a perfect landing, I got rid of the parachute harness and then strangely found myself standing like a soccer goalkeeper would, when ready to take on a penalty kick, legs bent, arms out wide. Why? It took a second to figure it out, but when I understood what I was doing I couldn't stop laughing at myself. I was actually listening and scanning for snakes or more correctly, my brain was. Up until this point, my brain had done everything it had been programmed to do since the aircraft starting having problems, and now the brain had taken control since it remembered that there were poisonous snakes in this neighborhood. It did manage to bring a certain amount of humor to a tricky situation.

Both Trash and I survived the accident without injuries to our bodies or our careers. The only one who was unhappy was the commandant of the school who thought it was a little bit embarrassing having me eject from one of his old aircraft. Since all the A-37 were grounded immediately, my colleague Clas didn't get to fly it, instead he got to fly the mighty F-15 Eagle so, he was very pleased. After my mandatory medical check and questioning from the accident investigation board, I had to wait the regulated 72 hours before I could fly again. My planned deep stall demonstration in the F-16 was therefore delayed until the next day; the same day we had airline tickets to take us back home. It was not to happen. However, with a lot of goodwill from many people involved I left Edwards with a great deal more of experience than I had planned for.

It was some time later when I was back home in Sweden that another unplanned incident occurred. It was while I was performing departure resistance testing on the Gripen fighter. Within all the possible parameters that modern flight control systems permit, we were trying to develop a revolutionary aircraft that would not depart or loose control in ways that had been so frequent in earlier fighters. The test card called for a maximum load factor turn at Mach 0.9, in combination with a maximum deflection of the control stick to roll out of the turn for two turns. Everything went well at the starting altitude of 9,000 meters. At 10,000 meters I commented on a slight hesitation in the roll rate, but the engineers gave me the go ahead for the next level altitude after checking their strip charts, trying to predict the aircraft's behavior.

I then climbed to 12,000 meters and set myself up for the next test point. After rolling out of the turn just past wing level I experienced a very quick roll reversal and the aircraft instantly departed from controlled flight. The very first input I gave was completely wrong. Instinctively, I had tried to counter the unwanted roll to the right by a full left stick input.

My excellent training soon automatically took over and, with full stick for the aileron, the spin quickly stopped the yaw.

The next action I took was with neutral aileron, and I pushed the stick fully forward to break the stall. It didn't work.

Suddenly, I was back over the desert, the Gripen just started to spin again. Funnily enough the accident at Edwards came back to me at that moment and gave me confidence that I would be able to handle the situation. I had been 'there', and survived and my mind said I would be able to do so again.

After a few attempts with different techniques, but all with the same negative result, the 'deploy chute' altitude was passed. After managing to stop the yaw rate I reluctantly deployed the parachute.

However, this time I didn't have to leave the jet since we had put a stall chute on the empennage of the aircraft. The chute broke the stall, and I could fly the jet home for a normal landing.

At the debriefing, all the technicians and engineers were very happy. They had got a lot of good data to work with. We learnt a lot from that departure as a team; we improved our tools and pressed on.

Later in the program, I was up in the blue sky again doing what I like most, which was pushing the aircraft envelope. This time we were to test an automatic spin recovery technique which had been installed in the flight control system. We had been working on this for a few years. The digital flight control system was designed, if the aircraft for some reason departed from controlled flight, to first dampen out any roll rate, then stop the yaw rate and finally to break the stall by a full nose down command.

I had deliberately managed to foul the flight control system by performing a pre-designated very steep climb until the speed completely bled off. After that, I established a stable spin with an 80 degree yaw rate. From there I activated the automatic spin recovery system and gently let go of the control stick, contrary to all my training; from that moment I became just a passenger.

It worked perfectly. The yaw stopped and when I felt the shiver in the aircraft that I knew meant the aircraft had returned to controlled flight by itself, I felt very proud. Coming from a test pilot this emotion might be hard to believe, but I genuinely see that moment as the highlight of my career. Even if I didn't do any 'flying pilot crap' at all except sitting back and enjoying the ride, it was a very great moment. All the late hours spent in the simulator, where we had fine-tuned the control laws design and developed and improved flight test techniques, had finally paid off.

For those who are curious as to why Trash and I were unable to recover the

A-37 in 1994, here is the story as I remember it from the accident investigation report.

The Dragonfly was configured with wing-tip tanks. If you wanted to spin the aircraft they had to be empty to make sure there was no weight asymmetry, meaning that the centre-of-gravity should be along the aircraft fuselage symmetry axis. When we entered the spin the tip tanks where empty but, as we spun, more and more fuel was trapped inside one of the tanks due to a malfunctioning fuel valve. With a lot of fuel in only one of the tip tanks the asymmetry became so large that there was no way to recover the aircraft to normal flight again.

What happened over the Baltic Sea several years later? As with most accidents there was a long chain of events that

The name 'Gripen' is Swedish for Griffin, the legendary beast with a lion's body and the head and wings of an eagle.

needed to happen for the accident to occur. As preparation for the high angle of attack testing, we had tried to prepare ourselves as well as we could. Among the questions we had asked ourselves was what would happen if the airspeed became zero. All material group managers had assured us that there would be no problem with any of the aircraft's system. After I had departed and initiated the maneuvers, the airspeed went to zero, and the inertial navigation system declared itself out of order. Doing so there was no way to monitor the airspeed measured by the pitot-system. With an unstable airspeed the feed-back signals to stabilize the aircraft have to be compensated for the actual airspeed. If the airspeed was unknown the flight control system automatically reconfigured itself for a fixed speed, either low or high, depending on the landing gear position. With the flight control system in a reconfiguration mode the nose down response was too low to break a stall, so the anti-stall chute had to be used. One question remains, why did the Inertial Navigation System (INS) declare itself faulty. The answer was simple when we looked at the data. In the INS there was a simple flight management system that we hadn't used but was designed to calculate distance, heading and time to the landing base. When the speed went to zero, the system tried to perform a division by zero and that is an illegal act in the world of mathematics. So the INS system declared itself faulty even though it worked perfectly all the time, except then.

We had, at least, done part of our homework and were very lucky to be able to save the Gripen, since we had prepared ourselves for the unknown and put a parachute on the aircraft. Or as someone once said, 'statistics favor the prepared mind'.

The first Gripen was rolled out on 26 April 1987, marking Saab's fiftieth anniversary.

TESTIMONIAL

Björn 'Tex' Johansson joined the Swedish Air Force in 1978 as a pilot engineer cadet. After getting his Master of Science in electrical engineering from Chalmers University of Technology he began his military basic pilot training.

After being the fighter lead at flight school, Johansson flew the JA 37 Viggen operational at the F4 Wing at Östersund. He was also assigned chief of the aircraft systems division.

After weapons systems school and conversion training to both the attack and reconnaissance version of the Viggen, he was assigned to the Gripen OT&E unit as a pilot and systems engineering officer in 1988. In 1990 he was assigned as a test pilot to the Swedish flight test centre where he stayed for

18 years as a test pilot, Gripen project test pilot, chief test pilot and commanding officer until he left in 2006.

Björn Johansson has flown more than 50 different military aircraft for a total of 2,700 hours. Until recently he was the most experienced Gripen pilot with 1,150 hours in the jet.

He held the rank of colonel in the Swedish Air Force and is currently on loan to Saab for future Gripen programs as chief engineer for the entire weapons system.

Johansson is married to Helen and has two grown up children. He likes to spend his leisure time in the Swedish archipelago paddling his kayak or working on their summerhouse.

Chapter 17

Ray Goudey in a very early version of a pressurised flight suit

Ray Goudey – U2 spyplane
Where Angels Feared to Tread

Nicknamed the 'angel' by its crew, the U-2 spyplane was the first aircraft developed to skip across the outskirts of space and aim a camera onto the Soviet Union.

In January 1955, Kelly Johnson asked me to join the group he was putting together to build a special aircraft. We were only told that no one was to know we were working on this project and no one was to know where we were, even our families. We were also told that when we got to the site, we couldn't tell anyone at the site who we worked for or what area of the country we came from. We had to be careful not to bring magazines, newspapers, or anything else that would give away our area of origin. Kelly's design concepts were so interesting and so exciting that I couldn't refuse. I probably would have done the job even if they hadn't paid.

Back in 1954, it was believed that the Soviet Union was building a war machine that would soon be operational and would include an extensive family of liquid-fuel, nuclear warhead-equipped intercontinental ballistic missiles.

It was under this threat that the pressure grew. The military needed to know what was going on behind the 'Iron Curtain'. As a result, the military began to put forth specifications for a reconnaissance aircraft that could bring back the information needed. It was perceived that it might be possible for an aircraft to fly high enough not to be seen or be brought down by any known weapon or aircraft of the day. The mission would be to fly over military targets within the Soviet Union and return.

If we were caught flying over Soviet airspace, however, we risked being charged with an act of war and subject to retaliation by the Soviet Union.

The threat of World War III was very real, and this threat loomed as the probable outcome if we were caught. Nevertheless, President Eisenhower made the decision to go forward with a reconnaissance aircraft that could do the job.

Kelly and his design team put together a version of an aircraft that could fly well above 70,000 feet with a combat range of 1,400 nautical miles.

The aircraft that was proposed was the CL282. It took the F-104 design and changed the wing. The short 20 feet wing span of the F-104 became an elongated wing of 80 feet on the new aircraft design. Design studies showed that, 'A wing aspect ratio of 10:1, with 500ft^2 of area would attain the desired altitude over the target with the smallest and lightest airplane it should be noted that 1,000 feet of altitude is equivalent to the order of 550lbs of allowable aircraft weight' (from Lockheed Report LR 9732).

Minimizing the weight of the aircraft was critical. The first design eliminated the landing gear to save weight. The airplane would land on its belly like a sail plane. But the final design included a lightweight landing gear, which used a bicycle-type undercarriage with twin main wheels and small twin tail wheels which retracted forward into the fuselage. There were also two pogo-like 'jettisonable' outrigger units fitted beneath the wing at about mid-span, which kept the wing tips off the ground and the wings level while stationary. The reinforced wing-tips were turned down 90 degrees for use as skids during landing.

In order to get to the altitudes specified for the U-2, the pilots needed protection from effects of altitude. This was a new and untested area of our atmosphere into which man would be entering and trying to survive. These would be the first adventures into space.

Advising the Agency on high-altitude survival were two Air Force doctors, Colonel Donald D. Flickinger and Colonel W. Randolph Lovelace II. Flickinger and Lovelace asked the David Clark Company to submit designs for the advanced gear required for the U-2 pilots. The company developed a complex life support system, which was the first partially pressurized 'spacesuit'. The system could maintain pressure over most of the pilot's body to compensate for the lack of pressure in the stratosphere. Flickinger and

Lovelace also helped design the rigorous medical program each pilot went through before he was accepted as a U-2 pilot. These doctors had done a lot of work on the effects of altitude on the human body and the tests they designed would eliminate anyone who wouldn't be able to perform the tasks required.

Believe me, these tests weren't much fun, and involved plenty of torture. Every orifice of the body was probed and examined. Electrical shock stimulus measured reaction time; iced water poured in the ears produced vertigo and the recovery time measured. They gave us a treadmill test while they measured oxygen intake and exhaled gases volume. There were other physical fitness and endurance tests, but the ice water in the ears was the worst test.

Work also went into pressurizing the U-2 cockpit to create an interior environment equivalent to the air pressure at an altitude of 28,000 feet. Without oxygen at 26,000 feet, a man can remain conscious for about three minutes. At 46,000 feet, this time drops to 10 to 20 seconds. At 50,000 feet, the lack of oxygen is compounded with low atmospheric pressure, which causes the waste products of the respiratory system (carbon dioxide and water vapor) to fill the lungs and prevent the intake of air or even pure oxygen. At 63,000 feet, air pressure is so low (about 3 per cent of that at sea level) that liquids boil at 98°F. Since this is the normal temperature of human blood, without countermeasures (pressure) to protect the body, at altitudes above this the blood would boil and the body would explode and vaporize.

In the beginning of the flight test program, we experienced frequent engine flame-outs at altitude. This meant that we would lose power and therefore cabin pressure and the partial pressure suit would inflate. Inflated, the suit would become somewhat uncomfortable and restrict movement, but it did its job. Later in the program, as the flights got longer, it was common for the pilot to lose a pound of body weight for each hour of flight. Many pilots came back eight to ten pounds lighter.

The first aircraft arrived at the test site on July 24, 1955. Personnel flown in from Burbank reassembled the airplane that was referred to as 'Kelly's Angel' or simply the 'Angel'. Two days were required to get the all aluminum aircraft pieces back together and prepared for the initial static engine runs and taxi tests.

Sometime during this initial flight test period, the Air Force assigned the aircraft a number from their log of numbers for utility aircraft. The U-1 and U-3 numbers had already been assigned and therefore the innocuous U-2 designation was given as the official designation. The 'U' is the military designation for 'Utility'.

The taxi tests began two days after the static engine runs on July 29; the preliminary taxi tests. The first taxi test with Tony LeVier in the cockpit went to the 50 knot mark. Kelly said the brakes needed to be broken in. Tony did the second taxi test going to the 70 knot mark. As the aircraft approached the mark, Tony began working the ailerons in order to get a feel for how the airplane would handle. It was then that he realized that the 'Angel' was actually airborne about 35 feet above the lake bed. The lake bed's smooth surface and the lack of runway markings had failed to give any visual indication that the airplane had actually become airborne. The airplane started to buffet, a warning that a stall was imminent. To prevent the stall, Tony slammed the throttle forward. The airplane settled back to earth landing hard, blowing both main gear tires before bouncing back into the air a couple of times, then settling on the ground.

The brakes did little to slow the aircraft during its roll of almost a mile before the flat tires brought the aircraft to a halt, but burst into flames directly under the fuel tank. Johnson noted, 'We were following in radio trucks, and finally got an extinguisher on the brakes. No harm done. The airplane was subjected to terrific tests. Pogo sticks worked real well.'

The first 'official' flight in the U-2 happened on August 4, 1955. The airplane took off and was airborne easily. The long wings were kept off the ground by the pogo sticks installed under the wings about mid-span. The pogo sticks were designed to drop out automatically when the wings lifted during takeoff, but for the first flight they were pinned so that they wouldn't fall out. The landing gear was also not retracted after takeoff. These were safety precautions in case something should go wrong and a quick landing was necessary.

The first flight stayed at a relatively low altitude, leveling off at 8,000 feet and staying below the assigned maximum speed for the flight of 160 knot. The pre-planned flight envelope set the parameters for all the maneuvers, but generally the flight was to check out the control responses, flight characteristics and slow flight capabilities. The only problem was encountered on the landing. Johnson and LeVier had discussed the landing technique that was to be used before the flight. Johnson's view of landing with the main landing gear prevailed. On the first few attempts to land, main gear first, the aircraft wouldn't stay on the ground and instead moved along the runway until it was necessary to takeoff and go around again. Finally, Tony tried his method of tail wheel landing first with a controlled stall and was successful in making a somewhat rough landing. The first flight was over, a total of forty minutes from takeoff to landing.

The first flights were at low altitudes. The flight team tested the aircraft to determine the stall speed of the U-2 in all configurations (flaps up and down, landing gear up and down, etc.). We tried different maneuvers and explored the best way to land the aircraft. We determined that landing on front and rear landing gears simultaneously just before the airplane stalled produced the easiest and best landing solution.

Just before a flight that was to be at altitudes above 50,000 feet, the pilot was required to pre-breathe pure oxygen for two hours. The pre-breathing was done to get the nitrogen bubbles out of the blood stream. Like divers who go too deep into the ocean, pilots who go too high into the atmosphere can suffer from the effects of nitrogen in the blood. The negative effects of nitrogen in the blood include painful joints, tunnel vision or blindness, and cognitive confusion.

The pre-breathing of 100 per cent oxygen was done in a lounge chair with just the helmet on. To pass the time, I would read or try to sleep. After one and a half hours, the technician would help me get into the rest of the partial pressure suit and then the flight suit. He would switch the breathing hose to a portable oxygen bottle and help me to the van, which transported me to the airplane. I would then be helped into the airplane; hooked up to the airplane's oxygen system; and strapped in. This latter part took about half an hour, so I had the required two hours of pre-breathing prior to takeoff. Later in the program we tried to reduce this pre-breathing time to one and a half hours and then to one hour, but symptoms began to appear. I had a bubble in the knee and it was painful for a while. Bob Sieker had a bubble in his eye which produced tunnel vision and he could only see one instrument at a time. We were able to talk him down, but after that, we went back to the two hours pre-breathing requirement for the rest of the program.

The first successful flight to the initial design altitude, 70,500 feet, took

place on October 18, 1955. We had just installed and checked out the new J57-P-37 engine, which was designed to take us to altitude. It was an interesting flight and took a lot of effort and concentration to control the airplane, especially during the last part of the climb.

The first part of a climb in the U-2 is very rapid. It is said the U-2 climbs like a 'homesick

The U-2 came to public attention when Francis Gary Powers was shot down over the USSR in 1960.

angel' – she goes almost straight up. To fly the plane, the pilot needs only to hold a constant indicated airspeed as the aircraft climbs at a very steep angle. The angle of ascent gradually flattens out as the U-2 approaches 40,000 feet.

Then, up to 60,000 feet, it is necessary to start reducing the airspeed a few knots for each 1,000 feet of altitude gained. The climb schedule is prescribed for each flight to get optimum performance and is varied according to fuel load and atmospheric conditions. Above 60,000 feet, a cruise climb is begun. At this point, it is necessary to hold a constant Mach number until maximum altitude is attained. The 'angel' would continue to climb over the next several hours as the fuel burned off. The indicated air speed decreased in very small increments in order to hold the desired Mach number. At altitude, the Mach number is very close to the limiting Mach number of the aircraft (maximum speed). At the same time, the indicated air speed has been decreased to the point where it is getting very close to the aircraft's stall speed (minimum speed). U-2 pilots called this phenomenon 'coffin corner'. At altitudes above 70,000 feet, it took the pilot's full attention to keep the aircraft between the minimum and maximum speeds – there was only a five knots difference.

Improvements in later models expanded the window of acceptable performance from five knots to 10 knots. The window also widens to about a 15 knots spread as the fuel burns down and the airplane gets lighter. At the same time you have to be careful not to over correct and slow down too much or you go into stall buffet. Stall buffet vibration is heavier as the aircraft loses lift; it's corrected by speeding up, but not too much or you hit the Mach limit.

This small window of acceptable performance at maximum altitude (coffin corner) was further complicated by the fact that the air speed indicator reacted sluggishly. Mechanical instruments react differently when they are in the atmosphere at altitude, where air molecules are far apart. The altimeter was especially inaccurate because it had a lot of friction in the mechanism. The inaccurate readings made it even more difficult to hold the airplane at the correct air speed and at a constant altitude.

Subsequently, trying to get better instruments, Kelly placed an order for altimeters with the Kollman Instrument Company and specified that they had to be calibrated to 80,000 feet. Kollman's instruments only went to 45,000 feet, so eyebrows were raised a bit. They were told that the instruments were to be used in a new experimental rocket plane. We got a better altimeter.

In the beginning almost every flight led to a flame-out. If we were at altitude, we would have to descend to 30,000 feet to restart the engine. There were several things that would cause a flame-out: any abrupt throttle movement or sudden pitch were common causes. To help the pilot make small incremental adjustments and avoid flame-outs, we installed a vernier control. This consisted of a large trim wheel installed on the same axis of rotation as the power lever and made it easy for the pilot to make the small adjustments required. Kelly solved the engine cooling problem on the spot. He directed the mechanic to cut off about an inch of fuselage around the tail pipe. This solved the problem by increasing the engine compartment's by-pass air flow.

The first long flight, which took place in October 1955, was also the first flight at maximum weight with a full load of fuel. The goal of this flight was to see how high we could get and how far we could go. The climb schedule had to be followed exactly to get the best performance figures from the aircraft. I used the drift sight pointed straight down to get an accurate reading of the checkpoints as I passed over.

The route of this flight had to have long straight legs to get maximum performance, but we didn't want to get too far away from the site, in case there was a problem. I climbed to 65,000 feet in the test area and then went to maximum altitude and headed to Denver, El Paso, San Diego, Seattle, Salt Lake City, and back to the test site. During the flight there was a lot of data to collect and tediously record. I had to record the time and altitude at check points, and every hour I had to record the fuel used, the altitude reached and oxygen remaining. In addition to the paperwork, I was kept busy checking all the instruments, making sure that I was on course, and staying within the minute five knot acceptable speed window. Time went by very fast.

The duration of the first long flight in the U-2 was six hours plus two hours of pre-breathing. I had many more eight-hour flights as well as some 10-12 hour flights.

After we were confident that the engine would keep running, we flew throughout the USA. We filed flight plans with the FAA with our altitude listed as 45,000 feet. We couldn't maintain constant communication with the test site, but we could contact other ground stations at our designated check points. It was funny at times, because in the course of our normal communications, centers would ask us if we could accept a higher or lower altitude. Of course, we readily accepted, but without changing our altitude. Two areas – Seattle and El Paso – had exceptionally good radar and occasionally asked us, 'What altitude are you really at?' They saw us at a higher altitude and sometimes they were very close. However, we told them, 'Recalibrate your crystal ball!' and continued flying on.

Locally around the site and in the western States, the winds above 65,000 feet were generally light and the air was smooth.

We had weathermen at the site who gave us very accurate briefings before each flight. They gave us the conditions in the troposphere, which we had to climb through to get to our cruising altitude in the stratosphere. The troposphere layer can get turbulent, but the stratosphere is usually smooth. The weathermen could predict the altitudes at which we would leave contrails and where we would hit air turbulence. We had to try to avoid areas of extreme air turbulence and we did not want to be seen, so we avoided altitudes which would produce contrails.

On a clear day at maximum altitudes, we could see mountain ranges that were up to 1,000 miles away. From altitude, the horizon close to earth's

surface looks bright white, but the sky directly overhead looks a very dark
midnight blue. The transition from light to dark starts surprisingly close to
the earth's surface visually and becomes dark very quickly. At night the stars
are so bright that it never seems quite like night. The shadows and the colors
in the light that develops as the sun rises above the curvature of the earth is
spectacular: yellow, orange, red, purple, blue changing all at once. One time,
I was over the Grand Canyon at sunrise and watched the color change as the
shadows came across the canyon; it was a magnificent spectacle.

The original U-2 had a shiny aluminum skin which would reflect a bright
light at maximum altitude, making the aircraft easy to see. Nevertheless, the
U-2s were operational and had flown over their targets for several years
before we began painting them.

It took a while to develop the right paint, one that would absorb light
instead of reflecting it, as well as one that would not add significant weight.
The first black paint job was glossy and looked almost as bright as the bare
airplane at altitude. The second dull matt paint job wasn't much better. The
third paint job was very rough and dull and worked very well, but it weighed
too much and created too much drag. In the end, a compromise was made
with a new blue-black velvet paint. The paint didn't reflect any light and the
color looked like the dark blue sky in which we were flying.

Early in the program I had a hydraulic failure and lost all the fluid. This
meant that the speed brakes wouldn't extend and the landing gear wouldn't
extend normally. I was able to lower the landing gear by pulling the release
handle and letting gravity lower the gear. The descent from altitude took a
long time because I couldn't use the speed brakes to control speed. Instead I
let the plane float down slowly with the engine in idle and made turns to
increase drag.

In the landing pattern, the flaps didn't work so I couldn't use them to slow
down. As I got closer to the ground the aircraft continued to fly down the
runway without slowing down enough to land. It was apparent that idle
thrust was too high. I pulled up and went around again. When I knew I could
make it to the runway on the lake bed, I shut the engine off on final approach
and landed. No harm done. The idle thrust was corrected with a minor
engine adjustment.

Kelly knew we would get better performance at high altitude with a
specially developed fuel. Shell Oil Company developed a fuel which would
burn in low atmospheric pressure. LF-1A was a special low-vapor pressure
kerosene fuel that reduced the possibility of flame-outs at high altitude. The
fuel used ingredients in one of Shell's bug spray products and because
priority was given to provide us with the fuel we needed, there was a nation-
wide shortage of bug spray.

By late 1958 the original U-2s were getting heavier because of added systems, ejection seats, and an extra 58 lb for blue-black paint. Because of all the added weight, the aircraft was no longer getting up to the high altitudes that were originally specified. Therefore, a new engine was proposed and accepted, the J75.

The airplane with the new engine was designated the U-2C. Kelly made the larger, heavier engine fit into the U-2 with some minor modifications. Kelly's log said, 'We reworked five U-2 aircraft into U-2C models'.

On May 11, 1959, I was contracted to fly the performance tests for the U-2C. After the first flight on May 13, 1959, we ran 106 flights on three aircraft for a total of 380 hours of flying time. The new engine really made the airplane climb like a rocket and it reduced the time to climb to altitude tremendously. The U-2C was able to climb to altitude faster than any aircraft of the time. The downside was that the engine pushed the aircraft higher than it should fly and lowered the coffin corner back down to the five knot window we had in the beginning.

In the end, we were able to increase the absolute ceiling of the U-2C by about 5,000 feet. On August 12, 1959, two U-2C aircraft, Articles 351 and 358,

A tribute to the chief test pilot of the U-2 from its designer Kelly Johnson

were deployed overseas for operational over flights. All the remaining CIA U-2s were converted to U-2C models.

In all there were 55 original U-2s built. Twenty aircraft went to the CIA and 30 went to the USAF, and an extra five were built from spare parts. Many of these aircraft were remanufactured into newer models and changed to accommodate the new operational systems as the need arose for different missions all over the world. I flew and tested almost all of the original U-2s built.

On May 1, 1960 Gary Powers was shot down over the Soviet Union in a U-2 spyplane. It caused an international scandal.

TESTIMONIAL

From 1940 until 1943, Ray Goudey was a fight instructor for the Army Air Corp. After a spell with the Flying Circus, Goudey joined Lockheed in 1952 and stayed as a pilot for the organization until 1990. Early on Goudey was a production pilot for T-33A, F-80A, B, and C and F-94A and B. Later on he was the engineering pilot for development of the F-94C and its rocket firing development. He performed the third flight on XF-104, Phase I, II, and III development.

In 1954, he achieved the world speed record of Mach 1.75. From 1955 until 1960, he worked as a test pilot on the U-2 program, setting many altitude records in the process. It included a flight from test site to the Pentagon, taking pictures, and returned without refueling or being observed.

From 1956 until 1982, Goudey test flew the L-329 JetStar and was engineering test pilot on the Electra L-188, RC-121, P-3A & B, F104S, F104G, 1049 G&H and U-2. During this time from 1961, he was a test pilot, rotary wing, working on the CL-475, XH-51A, B, C&N helicopters, L-286 Helicopter and CL-186C Compound Helicopter during which time he again set numerous speed records, becoming chief test pilot (rotary wing) in 1969, concentrating on the AH-56A Compound Rigid Rotor Helicopter. From 1972, Goudey was fundamentally involved with the S-3A Viking submarine hunter.

From 1978, Goudey worked on the ADP classified program of Have Blue (prototype for F117) development, the first fixed-wing aircraft designed from an electrical engineering (rather than an aerodynamic) perspective (stealth).

Chapter 18

As well as test pilot on the Buccaneer, David Eagles was made project pilot for the Tornado aircraft in 1972.

David Eagles – Buccaneer Temperament Take-Off in Temperature

As a test pilot he was deployed to a Royal Naval aircraft carrier in the Far East to simply sort out a 'piloting hitch'. Fifteen seconds after take-off he ejected... .

During the Cold War years, the Royal Navy developed a carrier-based bomber, capable of delivering a nuclear bomb from an internal bomb bay, and designed to fly fast and low, under the defensive radar cover of any sea or land target. This bomber was the Blackburn Buccaneer, and the Mk 1 version flew for the first time in April 1958. It was a complicated aircraft with high pressure air that tapped off the two engines and fed to the wing, flaps and tailplane, to provide Boundary Layer Control (BLC). This 'blow system' allowed the designers to plan a high wing loading aircraft, optimized for high speed low level manoeuvre, while still making it possible to achieve an acceptably low landing speed onto the carrier.

(Explanation: An aeroplane will stay in the air as long as sufficient lift is being generated by the wings. If the aeroplane is continually slowed down, the smooth airflow over the wing will eventually break down and the wing will stall. This breakdown of the airflow, and resulting stall, can be delayed by introducing a high pressure air flow over the wing, tapped from the engine(s) via suitable plumbing, through slots along the wing's leading edge. This arrangement re-energizes the boundary layer and can reduce the aeroplane's stalling speed by 20 or 30 knots).

The Mk 1 version had efficient but low thrust de Havilland Gyron Junior engines (7,100 lbs thrust) which proved to be somewhat unreliable in service. The Mk 2 version, which first flew in 1963, was fitted with Rolls-Royce Spey engines, (11,030 lbs thrust), and was a huge success.

The Mk 1 Buccaneer carried out its carrier suitability trials in 1961 and the first squadron went to sea in 1962. In spite of occasional engine problems, it was well-liked by its crews though it was definitely recognized to be somewhat underpowered. After attending the Empire Test Pilots' School in 1963, I joined the Royal Navy Test Squadron at Boscombe Down, Wiltshire, at the beginning of 1964 for a three-year stint of duty, and walked into the job of project pilot for the introduction of the Mk 2 into Naval service. The two most interesting aspects of the development of the Mk 2 from a test pilot's point-of-view, were the change of the effects of its BLC system, compared with the Mk 1 version, and its very low pitch stability on catapult launch.

With the Mk 1 version, the comparatively low maximum thrust of the engines meant that during a carrier landing, the engines were both set at about 85 per cent to 90 per cent power on the approach. At this power setting, the air pressure, at the point on the engine compressors where air was tapped off to feed the wing and flap BLC system, was high. As the pilot made typical frequent throttle movements during the approach, blow pressure onto the wings remained good, even at the lowest engine revs seen.

With the Mk 2 though, the 'thrust/blow ratio' had been changed. The Spey engine was so powerful that, on the approach, the engine setting was well back in the available power range, and this meant that the blow pressure, tapped off the fourth stage of the compressor, could drop to a dangerously low level during 'throttle jockeying'. If pressures dropped below around 15psi, the slots through which the air was directed over the wing, flaps and tailplane flap, became 'unchoked' and wing and tail lift would be suddenly reduced.

You could easily hear this sudden change in airflow over the wing from the cockpit. For a while there was talk of seeking to change the point of air tapping to a higher pressure point on the engine but this would have been a

The Buccaneer was prematurely withdrawn from service in 1994 after being successfully utilized during the first Gulf War.

very complicated and expensive change. The eventual fix was simply to use full airbrake for the approach to increase drag and so use a higher power setting on the approach.

The down-side of this (and there's always a down-side) was the accompanying airbrake buffet that you then had to live with throughout the approach. To have a permanent buffet in a low-speed flight regime is not a good thing at all since, of course, it tends to mask the buffet which might be the natural warning of an impending and costly stall. However, this was eventually determined to be the best way forward and, indeed in squadron service, this feature never proved a huge problem. Writing up these memories of the thrust/blow ratio problem 40 years later, the item seems trivial when recalling that the difficulty was overcome simply with a procedure change. But at the time a lot of hours and experimentation was devoted to it.

Incidentally, to illustrate the effectiveness of the BLC system, the aircraft's normal approach speed with 'blow' working was 130 knots, but with blow switched off, speed had to be increased to around 164 knots to generate the same lift at the same aircraft weight.

The second interesting problem area was more complicated. A low pitch-stability after catapult launch was not unique to the Mk 2, but changes to the trim indicating system in the 'Production Standard' aircraft, brought it painfully into focus. The initial deck trials of the Buccaneer 2 were flown from the British aircraft carriers, HMS *Eagle* and HMS *Ark Royal*, in the English Channel in 1965. I was very pleased to find some months later, when we were planning hot weather carrier trials, that we were able to use the USS carrier *Lexington*, based at Pensacola, Florida, where, 10 years earlier, I had had my naval flying training. Meanwhile, these deck trials were all flown using the first three Mk 2 aircraft built, the so-called pre-production batch. The UK-based trials and the *Lexington* trials all confirmed the very satisfactory handling of the aircraft both on the approach and landing and during the catapult launch at high weights.

The catapult launch with the Buccaneer was an interesting exercise. Because the aircraft had a high inertia in pitch and low pitch stability, (particularly with faired underwing tanks) the aircraft was designed to be catapulted 'hands-off'. The aircraft was set on the catapult at a nose-up attitude which made it unnecessary for the pilot to make any pitch change for around five seconds after launch.

In fact, the pilot was required to keep his hands off the stick for that time to avoid making any inputs which would get the aircraft pitching in this low-stability area. If the pilot had his hand on the stick during catapult firing, the effect of inertia on his hand could cause an inadvertent back-stick input, so he was briefed to keep his hand on his knee during the launch. The stick was mass-balanced to avoid movement under its own weight. On one of our launches during trials, one of the test pilots involved left his hand on the stick and the aircraft left the catapult with full back stick, and he needed immediate full forward stick to cancel the resulting pitch up.

The key to the success of the launch trials was determination of the tailplane trim setting which would allow the aircraft to continue, hands-off, in trim, after leaving the catapult. This critical trim setting was first arrived at from trials and then confirmed at a range of weights, catapult-end-speeds and outside air temperatures, by day and by night.

The profile of the launch was the aircraft leaving the catapult at 20 units angle of attack, increasing to, and peaking at, around 24 units over the next four or five seconds, and the pilot then going 'hands on' and taking control.

The recommended trim setting was passed to the operating squadrons; and the first squadron equipped with the new aircraft, went to sea in HMS *Victorious* later in 1966.

A few weeks after they had embarked, we began to hear of complaints that the aircraft had a tendency to pitch-up off the catapult, and the first thought was that they might be launching with 'hand-on-stick'. The squadron replied that they were carefully briefing pilots to be sure to have hands off. But what they didn't reveal was that they were invariably pushing forward the stick immediately after launch to counteract regular pitch-up behaviour.

Back at Boscombe, all the trials records were reviewed in an effort to understand the problem. All three pre-production aircraft had been used in deck trials to determine the correct trim setting, so trim setting was not suspected. At this time the company design team came in with some new data (later revoked), that larger angle of attack readings could be expected on launch in conditions of higher ambient temperatures due to an effect on the blow contribution to the wing lift coefficient. All very scientific and technical. This was at the time when 801 Squadron, the first with the Mk 2, were operating in the Far East.

So in the end it was I who was asked to go out to the ship to sort things out and test the aircraft. Armed with this knowledge, I tried to understand the cause. Having been involved in both day and night launch trials and the hands-off technique, I was as much puzzled over the problem as the aircraft designers about the cause of the problem.

My brief was to carry out launches at the minimum launch speed, with the tailplane trim setting confirmed at minus 5.5 degrees (the setting arrived at after our trials) and to keep hands off and allow the aircraft to rotate off the catapult to 25 degrees angle of attack (one degree higher than the normal squadron maximum allowed) before taking corrective action if necessary.

I explained my brief to the Squadron CO and to the Squadron back-seater who had drawn the short straw to come with me.

Back in the UK, the three pre-production aircraft we had used at Boscombe for our deck trials had had a scale painted on the fin against which the tailplane trim setting could be confirmed externally when the aircraft was on the catapult. I found that the Squadron aircraft did not have the luxury of this external scale, so I decided to trust the cockpit trim gauge but to make the first launch at 5 knots above minimum launch speed instead of minimum.

The trial was to be flown at the start of the day's operations and at 06:30 we lined up on the catapult. After the usual checks, I indicated all was well, and the Catapult Officer signalled 'launch'. Immediately after the catapult fired, I concentrated on the angle of attack gauge and was confused to find that it didn't react at all but, stayed at around zero. (normally the gauge moved quickly during the launch to register approximately 20 degrees as the aircraft left the ship).

After about a second it moved up into the expected area above 20 but was moving at such an accelerated rate that it clearly wasn't going to stop at 25. By 24 angle of attack, I had full forward stick on to try to control the pitch-up, but the aircraft continued to rotate nose-up and dropped a wing, at which point I called for ejection and pulled the 'blind'.

Ejection. It was just 15 seconds after take-off.

In fact, it was so swift, the ship had to quickly pull hard starboard to avoid running over us in the water and we were fished out of the sea by the plane-guard helicopter.

I remained on my back for some weeks after that, with the usual Martin Baker (ejection seat manufacturer) disease and, of course, was the number one popular boy. My back-seater initially had no back problems, but I believe he felt the effects later.

My initial signal back to Ministry of Defence, Navy included: 'Squadron pilots reveal that they do not, in any launch configuration, allow the aircraft to rotate naturally to a peak incidence, but rather they take the stick immediately after launch and...reduce the rotation. This...results in a complete lack of information on what "natural" angle of attack peaks the squadron has been experiencing in any configuration and any over trim effects will have been masked. I conclude, temperature effects somehow further reduce stability, since pitch rate was so high.'

It was amazing. An investigation by Boscombe and the design company then revealed that the trim gauging system in the production aircraft had a different calibration to the one fitted in the three pre-production ships we had done our trials on.

Squadron aircraft using our recommendation were in fact all over trimming by around one degree, (setting our recommended -5.5 on the cockpit gauge gave -6.5 degrees on the production standard aircraft), a significant error with the 'blown' tail. But the resulting pitch-up would have been obvious in time to control it if the angle of attack gauge had functioned normally.

The Buccaneer came in two variants, S1 and the more powerful S2, the latter serving with both the RN and RAF from 1965.

I had experienced several interesting launch situations during trials, which had all been satisfactory regarding the angle of attack gauge.

It was concluded that the gauge had been faulty. When the CO of the Naval Test Squadron visited the ship some months later to carry out some launches with the revised trim settings, he found a tool bag hanging from the angle of attack probe on an aircraft in the hangar. (The probe is the delicate sensor which should be handled with great care to avoid damage.)

In addition to a revision of the recommended tailplane trim settings, the design company later redesigned the under-wing tank fairings to improve pitch stability at low speed at the cost of some 2 per cent of high altitude range. And, after my time in the Naval Test Squadron, my next job was as senior pilot of an embarked Buccaneer 2 Squadron, where I was able to experience daily, the joys of the hands-off launch system.

Looking back at that costly incident, there are, of course, lessons to be learned. Certainly the slugged information from the angle of attack system prevented early recognition of a much over-trimmed aircraft, but there was a communication gap too between the squadron's report of, 'a tendency for the aircraft to pitch up off the catapult' against a later explanation that all launches were controlled by pushing forward stick as they left the front.

TESTIMONIAL

David Eagles joined the Royal Navy aged 17 in 1953 and carried out his flying training with the US Navy at Pensacola, Florida and Kingsville, Texas. After serving two years with the Royal Australian Navy flying Sea Furies, he trained as a night fighter pilot flying de Havilland Sea Venom and Sea Vixen aircraft from various British aircraft carriers.

In 1963 he completed the Empire Test Pilots' Course at Farnborough, Hampshire, UK and for the next three years he served as a test pilot at the Naval Test Squadron, Boscombe Down, where he carried out carrier suitability trials on the Buccaneer Mk 2 aircraft. He retired after 15 years with the Navy and, in 1968, joined British Aerospace at Warton, Lancashire, as an experimental test pilot. He was made project pilot for the Tornado aircraft in 1972 and played a major role in the development of that aircraft. He was appointed Chief Test Pilot of BAe (military) in 1977 and director of flight operations in 1983. In 1986 he made the first flight of the EAP, the demonstrator of the Eurofighter Typhoon aircraft. He retired from test flying in 1987 having flown more than 6,000 hours in 61 aircraft types.

David was awarded the Air Force Cross in 1966, the Derry & Richards Memorial Medal for test flying in 1981, and the RAeS R.P. Alston medal for test flying in 1983. He was elected a Fellow of the Royal Aeronautical Society in 1982 and a Fellow of the Society of Experimental Test Pilots in 1988.

Chapter 19

Dave Gollings spent more than thirty years as a test pilot and flew more than 100 aircraft types.

David H. Gollings – Canadair Challenger
The Best of Times, It was the Worst

The sacrifice that test pilots make becomes apparent in the tale of the civilian Canadair Challenger's initial flights.

In April of 1980 the first prototype of the Canadair Challenger crashed in the Mojave desert, killing one pilot while two other crew members escaped with minor injuries. That was us.

To steal a thought from the author Charles Dickens, 'It was the best of times, it was the worst of times': a spring of hope turned into a winter of despair. But, events leading up to this tragedy started several years earlier, so we should start at the beginning.

The Canadair Challenger (once known as the Learstar 600) got off to a rocky start when the original designer, Bill Lear, critical of Canadair's changes to his design, publicly referred to it as 'Fat Albert'. Short and fat as it was, the name stuck and Bill unceremoniously walked out on the project. During the course of the next decade Canadair remained a quasi-government company and nearly brought down the entire Canadian government with cost overruns, until Bombardier came to the rescue with a privatization bid. In spite of this ignominious beginning, Fat Albert morphed into a 90-passenger regional jet and turned out to be a financial success as well as a thing of beauty.

Although Bill was later deemed the father of the Regional Jet (or RJ) he did not get to see its eventual success or even to see it fly; he passed away six months before the first flight of the Challenger.

In 1978 Canadair had been out of the aircraft manufacturing business for many years. So under the auspices of the chief test pilot, Doug Adkins, Canadair set out to establish a world-class flight test centre from the ground up as well as a first class test crew, of which I had the honor to be a part.

Initially, there were only four test pilots, but that soon expanded to an even half dozen test pilots and four flight test engineers when three test aircraft were all flying.

I first met Norman Ronaasen (Norm) in Montreal in the autumn of 1978. Instantly likeable, and in the words of Canadair's official historian Ron Pickler, Norm was, 'A charming, unassuming gentleman'. Like many Canadians I have known, Norm had an enormous sense of humor and, in my experience, he was one of the best engineering test pilots ever. He was a graduate of the Empire Test Pilot School in Farnborough, England and was one of two RCAF pilots selected to fly Canada's pride and joy, the AVRO Arrow.

One of Canada's most distinguished test pilots, Norman Ronaasen, sacrificed himself to allow the crew to bale out .

Unfortunately for Canada (and Norm) Prime Minister Diefenbaker cancelled the Arrow project before his first flight. Norm was later recruited to fly the Challenger early in 1978 and was the first of a small cadre of Challenger test pilots on Canadair's staff. I was hired shortly afterwards, and so it happened that we both wound up in Montreal to fly Canada's first entry into the fast-paced world of corporate aviation.

From its inception, Canadair felt it best to conduct the Challenger flight testing in a more hospitable climate than Montreal, not only for weather considerations but in order to be far removed from government and factory politics.

The choices boiled down to the RCAF test centre at Cold Lake, Alberta and the USAF test center near Mojave, California. Since the bulk of initial aircraft sales were in the USA and, in light of Cold Lake's formidable weather, the choice was obvious. So off we went to the Mojave desert.

Despite the crash, both Transport Canada and the Federal Aviation Administration in the USA certified the aircraft in 1980.

The pace of flight testing was fast and relentless for two years until we were all pretty much exhausted.

05:30 seems like an ungodly time to start work, but that is the world of flight testing. You do it because you love it, and it's unlike any other kind of flying. Somewhat the opposite of the old saying about airline flying: 'Hours of sheer boredom punctuated by moments of excitement...' By April 1980 Canadair test pilots had been doing it for over a year, seven days a week.

Like most days in the Mojave Desert April 3, 1980 dawned bright and clear; a splendid day for flying. I had arrived before sunrise expecting to fly systems tests on Challenger, serial number 1002, the second prototype of the Challenger wide-body business jet.

This plan changed when another pilot telephoned from the nearby ski resort, snowed in, and I offered to fill in as the copilot for him. The flight included a series of stall tests on the first prototype, serial number 1001, most of which had been done many times before.

Stall testing is an integral part of defining the flight envelope of a new aircraft. It consists of slowing the aircraft to the point where the wings no longer produce enough lift to maintain flight. It is not inherently dangerous, but it can be if the airplane's behavior at the stall is not readily controllable. In that event artificial devices may be used to prevent entering this flight regime. Wind tunnel tests predicted this might be the case with the Challenger, however the certification agency (Transport Canada) had decreed that the flight regime must be fully explored before any such artificial devices could be used. This was the order of the day and we should have protested more strenuously.

During many prior stall tests we had performed in Challenger 1001 loud, metallic 'banging' sounds were heard, and we thought the noise was coming from somewhere inside the airplane.

So, it was on April 3, 1980, after completing our 12 planned stall tests at 18,000 feet, that we proceeded to investigate the cause of the noises.

The first attempt involved a slower than normal stall approach in order to try to determine where the noise was coming from. This time, just as the same loud noise occurred, the aircraft angle of attack suddenly increased and the nose pitched-up out of control.

None of the flight controls responded and one engine flamed out as the airplane entered what is known as a 'deep stall' or 'super stall'. Fortunately (or not, as may be the case) the aircraft was equipped with a recovery parachute which I deployed, causing the nose to pitch down sharply and it restored control. At this point it should have been a simple matter to jettison the recovery parachute and return to base. Simple.

This was not to be the case, and things suddenly went from bad to worse.

So, in spite of a carefully engineered redundant jettison mechanism, the parachute failed to jettison. The cause of this failure has been variously attributed to improper hydraulic fluid in the primary actuator and loss of electric power to the back-up explosive bolts. No-one knows for sure. With clairvoyant hindsight, the design was later made more reliable but fortunately never had to be used again.

The cause of airplane accidents has been compared by experts to the game of dominoes, in that the first one to tip begets a chain reaction that goes on until the last domino falls. No one piece in itself is the cause of the accident but all it takes is one domino to start the chain (without the loud banging noise the accident would not have happened). The bottom line is this: When things start to go to Hell they go, not in a hand basket but by the bushel. And it is never a single one thing that causes an accident!

Things suddenly got worse again. During all this excitement, my attention had been focused on the inside of the cockpit trying to sort out the parachute jettison problem. By this time we were descending through 6,000 feet, to which I was completely oblivious (the absolute minimum bale out altitude for such an event was to have been 6,000 feet). Our flight test engineer, Bill Scott was situated in the cabin monitoring altitude and his call of '6,000!' brought us to our senses and Norm immediately called for bale out.

Bill looked wide-eyed at me in utter disbelief, and I nodded for him to get out. His duty then was to get to the rear baggage door, open it and jump out, which he did with some surprising enthusiasm.

Not far behind, I watched him disappear out of the door and observed with some curiosity as he 'fell' upwards. I was vaguely aware that Norm was still around, but, it was at this point my reality began to get really strange.

I dived head first through the hatch, tumbling head-over-heels until, spread-eagled, I wound up face towards the ground. For a brief moment I looked at the trees getting bigger and bigger, when I thought to myself, 'Wait, there are no trees in the desert, those are small cactus, I must be really close to the ground.' I pulled the ripcord like the starter rope on a lawn mower, and life started over again.

The shock of the opening parachute was nothing compared to what was to follow: hanging in my parachute risers, I had a full and complete view of the destruction of Challenger One as it descended rapidly, wings level straight into the desert floor. It was as if a camera was running in slow motion, the way the mind slows things down in a crisis situation. Until it happens to you, through your own eyes, one can never ever truly appreciate something of this magnitude. The brain's time-tracking mechanism slows down and a matter of a few seconds seems like minutes.

To my horror, Challenger One appeared slowly to slide into the desert floor accompanied with a great fireball followed by a billowing black smoke which rose swiftly above the dead aircraft. The force of the explosion tossed great sheets of aluminum and debris high into the air.

Suddenly, just at the moment my parachute fully opened, the ground rose up to meet me with a thump and crunching of bone as my foot suddenly headed in a direction opposite to the rest of me.

As I lay there, trying to collect my thoughts and cope with the pain of a foot that pointed towards my head, I noticed Bill Scott (the flight test engineer) floating slowly down in his parachute. Still in a brain time warp, my mind could not comprehend why he was still in the air when he had clearly jumped out before me. Later analysis showed that Bill had exited around 3,000 feet, while 20 seconds later I had gotten out at less than 1,000 feet.

Adding to the disorientation was the extreme descent rate of the aircraft, estimated by radar tracking at 17,000 feet per minute. The brain cannot correlate these kinds of rates with prior experience, since the airplane attitude had been nearly level.

All told, the entire event took place in a little over one minute. It was later estimated that my parachute opened at about 100 feet. Norm had remained in his seat until the rest of the crew was safely out, which cost him his life. He did manage to get out of the airplane but his parachute did not have time to open. And the airplane we had come to love and hate all at the same time was no more.

In 30 odd years of flight testing I have been in numerous 'uncontrolled flight' situations, but almost always they were accompanied by wild gyrations and excessive g-loads. This particular event was unusual in that the airplane remained with 'wings level', with the nose just slightly above the horizon and descending at a rate that was beyond comprehension. Flight control was regained when the anti-spin parachute was deployed but, with one engine already failed it was impossible to maintain flight.

As luck would have it, I observed a small airplane circling over the crash site, which turned out to be Dick Rutan (later of Voyager fame with brother Burt) flying a local test mission.

Dick alerted the local air force base control tower and coincidentally, the base surgeon just happened to be airborne on a rescue helicopter training mission just at the time. So, within minutes I found myself in the capable hands of not just paramedics, but the USAF Chief Medical Officer.

On this, the last day of his life, my friend Norm Ronaasen had the calm presence of mind to call: 'Bale out,' which most definitely saved my life and that of Bill Scott. Norm then issued a 'MAYDAY' call on the radio and remained at the controls until Bill and I were safely out of the airplane. This turned out to be the ultimate sacrifice, for at that point he was too low to successfully bale out. There is something biblical about such an act, something that words cannot adequately describe. Bill and I have remained close over the years and every April 3 we get together to remember the man who saved our lives.

The Challenger was given a new maximum takeoff weight. A program to reduce the weight was implemented to improve range.

TESTIMONIAL

Dave Gollings graduated from the University of Miami (Florida) with a BS degree in mathematics and a minor in physics. Aviation industry experience included seven years as an R&D electronics engineer, two years as a flight test engineer and more than 30 years as an experimental test pilot.

His flight test experience comprises more than 7,000 flight hours in 110 aircraft types. Gollings unsurprisingly holds an FAA Airline Transport Pilot certificate with glider, seaplane and eight 'Type Ratings', as well as a Transport Canada Commercial Pilot License with two Type Ratings. He has conducted numerous 'type validations' and aircraft certifications including the Canadair Challenger, Douglas MD-87, Fokker Models 50 and 100, Gulfstream IV, V and 550, Embraer Models 135 and 145, Cat III HUD, VLJs and Enhanced (synthetic) Vision systems.

Dave Gollings is a member of the Society of Experimental Test Pilots, The Caterpillar Club, a Charter Member of The Society of Aerospace Communicators, and is presently working on several airplane and avionics certification programs.

Chapter 20

Captain George J. Marrett was a highly decorated Vietnam veteran.

George J. Marrett – Phantom F-4C Don't Kill Yourself

After numerous losses on the Phantom Jet, Vietnam veteran George J. Marrett explains the turning point of a dangerous airplane.

During the late fall of 1967, I was making a grand tour of Europe. Although I was just a captain in the US Air Force, an eight-passenger T-39 Sabreliner jet, usually reserved for generals, was my private mode of transportation. I was flying in glorious style.

The previous three years, I had been a fighter test pilot assigned to the Air Force Flight Test Center (AFFTC) located at Edwards Air Force Base (AFB) in California, flying the F-4C Phantom, F-5A Freedom Fighter, F-104A Starfighter and F-111A Aardvark. I wore an orange flying suit, a bright blue custom flight helmet and high-speed ejection spurs as I accelerated to Mach 2 in my silver beauties over the Mojave Desert.

I had recently completed several extremely dangerous test flights in the F-4C trying to determine why eight aircraft flown by Tactical Air Command (TAC) student pilots crashed while maneuvering at low altitude. Senior TAC commanders were anxious to hear the results of my flight tests. I gave a detailed briefing to them at their headquarters at Langley Air Force Base in Virginia. Fearing that more F-4Cs would be lost, the officers asked me to give presentations to operational F-4C units all over the USA. Interest in my Phantom flight test results also came from the headquarters of the US Air Force in Europe. A request came for me to brief the European headquarters staff in Wiesbaden, Germany and all the F-4C squadrons in England and Germany and the gunnery range at Wheelus Air Base in Libya. So a T-39 was made available to transport me in a very smart fashion with all the trimmings.

The Air Force version of the F-4 Phantom was an outgrowth of the US Navy F4H. The McDonnell Aircraft Company F4H was a twin-engine, 40,000 lb interceptor used for fleet air defense. Armed with air-to-air AIM-7 Sparrow and AIM-9 Sidewinder missiles, the Phantom could orbit 250 miles from the carrier for two hours preventing enemy aircraft from attacking the fleet. The Phantom was the first naval fighter to totally dispense with cannon armament. It was the first fighter that was able to identify, intercept and destroy any target that came into range of its radar without having to rely on ground control.

It was also the first aircraft originally designed solely as a carrier-based fighter to be ordered by the Air Force. The F-4 was built in huge numbers. It was the second most prolific American jet fighter to be built, outnumbered only by the North American F-86 Sabre Jet.

When the Air Force accepted the F-4, they were told to make minimum modifications to the aircraft. Since the Phantom would be landed on a runway instead of a carrier, the Air Force installed larger tires and anti-skid brakes. In addition the Air Force wanted to fly the F-4C in combat in Vietnam both as an air-to-air MiG Cap fighter and as an air-to-ground bomber. Therefore all nine of the under wing weapon stations would be used. For bombing missions the Phantom would be loaded with fuel tanks and armed with bombs, napalm, CBU and rockets. All the fuel and ordnance would be attached to the underside of the wings and fuselage.

In preparation for flying training missions, F-4C aircraft were loaded with small practice smoke bombs, LAU-19 rocket pods (each pod with 19 rockets) and two 370 gallon under-wing fuel tanks. This loading greatly changed the centre-of-gravity (CG) of the plane from the Navy version and ultimately the flying characteristics. The ordnance was fired, or dropped, on simulated targets in gunnery ranges. After takeoff, with a full load of fuel, the aircraft was being flown near the aft CG limit. Within 25 minutes of takeoff, all eight planes crashed on test ranges.

TAC commanders desperately asked AFFTC to run a test program to determine why these F-4 Phantoms crashed. I was given the task to write a test plan, get the plan approved by the center commander, fly the missions and then write a test report.

I prepared my briefing material and showed up at the center commander's office one morning. As I waited outside the general's office I reviewed in my mind questions he might ask. Did we have the correct instrumentation on board? Was the program properly funded? Was the Phantom in good mechanical condition? Did I feel trained enough to perform the maneuvers?

The general's secretary told me he was ready for my presentation. I quickly entered the room and gave my pitch in just a few minutes. At the end I paused for a response. He looked out the window for a few moments. Then he turned to me and talked about the recent accidents and deaths of several test pilots under his command. I listened intently trying to sense the question that would likely follow. Finally he looked at me straight in the eye and said, 'Don't kill yourself'.

During the next month I flew six test missions. For the first flight I had the Phantom loaded at a forward CG. At 10,000 feet and 300 knots I activated the instrumentation system, pulsed the stick fore and aft and recorded the aircraft response. I slowed the speed on the F-4C and evaluated its near stall and full stall characteristics in straight and level flight. This was followed by a series of wind-up turns at speeds from 200 to 550 knots. Wind-up turns were started in stabilized level flight, followed by rolling into a bank, allowing the nose to drop, gradually increasing the g-force without changing the thrust setting and descending to hold a constant airspeed. I maneuvered to heavy buffet that occurred at approximately 18 units on the angle of attack gage. Due to yaw oscillation, wing rock became so bad that precision control of the aircraft was impossible above 20 units. Above 22 to 24 units, any aileron input produced a rapid roll-off in the direction opposite that commanded by the lateral control. McDonnell engineers designed a rudder shaker to be activated at 22 units but it was completely masked by heavy airframe buffet. The only flight control left for maneuverability at a high angle of attack was the rudder.

On following flights I performed the same tests with the F-4C in a mid CG and recorded similar results. The aircraft could be maneuvered, but the pilot had to carefully monitor his control inputs and be alert to counteract stray aircraft motions. Flying near the aft CG was extremely dangerous. Not only was the stall masked by wing rock and heavy buffet, but also the stick forces were so light it was easy to overshoot the desired g. In some wind-up turns, after I had started to apply gs, I actually had to push forward on the stick to keep the g-force from increasing and the F-4C from pitching up. As a result of this terrible characteristic, I came to the conclusion that inexperienced student pilots maneuvered the Phantom through airframe buffet and into a full stall, ending in their loss of control and a crash.

After the test flights were completed I came up with a method to move the CG forward. If the external tank fuel was initially restricted from being transferred into the Phantom's two aft internal fuel cells, the plane was in better balance. Test engineers and I recommended several cockpit displays be modified to alert the pilot when he was nearing this dangerous condition. We also wrote several cautions to be printed in the pilot's flight manual. After my testing experiences, I didn't think much of the F-4C.

Following my tour at Edwards AFB, I flew 188 combat missions in Vietnam in the Douglas A-1 Skyraider. With the call sign 'Sandy', the A-1 was used to rescue downed air force and navy aircrew in North Vietnam and Laos. I also flew as a Forward Air Controller (FAC) in the A-1 and marked ground targets with white phosphorus rockets for F-4 and F-105 jets. It was my experience that pilots flying the F-4 had great difficulty precisely hitting ground targets. It was unusual for them to get a direct hit.

The F-4C made its first flight in May 1963, and production deliveries began six months later.

Also many F-4 aircraft went down during these air strikes. Skyraider pilots always chalked the losses up to enemy ground fire. During the course of the Vietnam War, out of a total loss of 2,254 aircraft, 444 of them were Phantoms. From my flight test experience it is now my belief that more F-4s were lost due to out-of-control maneuvering by the pilot than were downed by the enemy.

I now wonder if the F-4 losses would have been fewer if the Phantom combat pilots had been briefed by someone who said: 'Don't kill yourself,' like the general did to me.

TESTIMONIAL

George J. Marrett entered the US Air Force as a Second Lieutenant from the Reserve Officers Training Corps program. Graduating from pilot training in 1959, flying the Lockheed T-33 Shooting Star at Webb, AFB, Texas, he was then assigned to advanced flying school, flying the North American F-86L SabreJet at Moody AFB, Georgia. After four years in the 84th Fighter Interceptor Squadron at Hamilton AFB, California, flying the McDonnell F-101B Voodoo, he was selected to attend the USAF Aerospace Research Pilot School in 1964. While there he flew the Northrop T-38 Talon, Lockheed F-104

Starfighter and General Dynamics F-106 Delta Dart. Upon graduation, he was transferred to the Fighter Test Branch of Flight Test Operations at Edwards AFB, California and completed three years flight-testing the McDonnell F-4C Phantom, Northrop F-5A Freedom Fighter and General Dynamics F-111A Aardvark.

In 1968-1969 he flew the Douglas A-1 Skyraider as a 'Sandy' rescue pilot in the 602nd Fighter Squadron. He completed 188 combat missions; more than 600 combat hours and was awarded the Distinguished Flying Cross with two Oak Leaf Clusters and the Air Medal with eight Oak Leaf Clusters.

Upon return from the war in south-east Asia, he joined Hughes Aircraft Company as an experimental test pilot. For 20 years he flew test programs in the Grumman F-111B Sea Pig and F-14A Tomcat, developing the AWG-9 Radar and AIM-54 Phoenix missile, the Douglas WB-66D Destroyer, developing the F-15 Eagle APG-63 attack radar, the North American T-39D Sabreliner, developing the F-18 Hornet APG-65 Radar, the McDonnell F-4D/E Phantom, developing the AGM-65 Maverick missile, the F-4D Phantom, developing the F-16 attack radar and a Douglas A-3A Skywarrior on an early version of the B-2 Stealth Bomber radar. He has flown over 40 types of military aircraft, logging 8,000 hours of flying time.

Chapter 21

The X-36 unmanned tailless aircraft on the 'ramp' waiting for takeoff.
(Courtesy NASA)

Larry Walker – X-36 Tailless Aircraft
A Serious 'X' periment

Despite flying numerous combat missions and braving countless test flights, Larry Walker is adamant that the most stressful flying he has endured was an unusual remotely piloted tailless airplane.

One of the biggest challenges I have faced in my test flying career has not been flight testing the many fighters I've flown, but an unmanned aircraft, the X-36. This experimental research aircraft was as new, and as unique as anything I had ever seen or tested before.

I will never forget the day when Dave Manley, the X-36 program manager, introduced me to the program – not only was this jet aircraft going to demonstrate fighter agility at high angles of attack but, uniquely, it had no vertical tails! Worse, it was unstable in two axes, and had to be piloted remotely since it was only 28 per cent scale.

The X-36 was nearly 18 feet in length including the nose boom; weight was approximately 1,250 lb. Wing span was nearly 11 feet; for power it used a modified Williams International F-112 advanced cruise missile engine which supplied approximately 700 lb of thrust.

The control system consisted of canards, split ailerons, leading and trailing edge flaps, and thrust vectoring. Additionally, since it was unstable in both pitch and yaw, this meant that it had to use a highly integrated fly-by-wire control system to create the appearance of normal aircraft stability. Furthermore, as a cost versus risk trade-off, it only had a single-string control system, lacking normal manned aircraft redundancy.

As a footnote, from the standpoint of risk to the program, risk was mitigated by having a second aircraft (redundancy). To reduce the risk to each airframe, an onboard recovery parachute provided a last chance of emergency recovery. However, accepted risk, as it extended to the aircraft and onboard systems, did not extend to processes which included qualification testing of hardware and software, nor did it mean that procedures and training could be shortened. It was also extremely important to have done the necessary work to ensure that the flight test and air vehicle teams were well practiced. The benefit of this increased emphasis on procedures and training was to be highlighted on 'flight 2' when loss of data link created our first major emergency.

Because the effort was to be a low cost demonstration of advanced technology, it drove the decision to make the X-36 a sub-scale demonstrator only 28 per cent of the size of a normal manned fighter aircraft; as a result, it would have to be flown remotely. As a test pilot, I was disappointed to realize that its flight testing would be without the usual joys of actually flying. Also, I feared that my cockpit control suite might consist of a model airplane radio control box but, after selling the advantages of a full-sized cockpit and displays, the program embraced the idea, and it was to contribute strongly to the success of the program. And so, an agreement was made; the pilot station would have all that was needed to create a virtual airplane environment to get the best transfer of flight test experience and fighter maneuverability into this one-of-a-kind aircraft.

With a sub-scale, Remotely Piloted Vehicle (RPV), inclinations might be to reduce the cockpit control and display suite. Actually, the best practice is just the opposite, primarily because the pilot will have fewer natural cues of peripheral vision, sounds and kinesthetic feedback. Therefore, the challenge was to provide replacements for these cues and create an overall situational awareness, comparable to a full-sized aircraft. Ruling out motion bases and buffet simulation cues, we limited our effort to visual and Head-Up-Display (HUD) cues. A full-sized control stick and rudder pedals with their respective feel systems, and a throttle were for primary aircraft control. Secondary

controls included speed brake, flaps, landing gear control and a full compliment of Hands On Throttle-And-Stick HOTAS switches. Proper cockpit
displays included a HUD, Horizontal Situation Indicator HSI, engine instruments and system monitor functions. A video of the outside world overlaid
the HUD to complete the display set. Furthermore, this cockpit was to serve
as both the simulator and airplane cockpit.

As we got into the extensive development simulation, it became obvious
that it was much harder to set thrust and control airspeed than with full-
sized airplanes. Accordingly, we added jet noise and wind noise to our
simulations.

It then occurred to me that we should take this idea a step further and add
it to the aircraft itself by placing a microphone in the X-36's 'cockpit' area so
that sounds could be down-linked directly to the pilot. Not only would this
audio cue help in situational awareness, often an unusual sound will be the
first indication of an unexpected problem.

Unfortunately, audio hadn't been a design requirement, but after a
campaign to add it, the engineers helped me convince management that it
could be added easily. Not only did this audio provide a natural speed cue,
it also alerted us, on more than one occasion, to potential engine problems
such as high power engine screech, and to engine pop stalls in maneuvers
before they might have caused a failure.

Since the pilot's cockpit is in the center of the Ground Control Station
(GCS), distraction by personnel, their movements and sounds within the
GCS had the potential to distract the pilot and hurt situational awareness. We
addressed this problem by creating a tent-like frame over and down both
sides of the pilot's 'cockpit' to keep the pilot focused on the cockpit displays.
Additionally, a 'flight comm' loop was created with the headsets, which
included only the test director, pilot and his external radios, leaving the
engineers free to discuss test results and anomalies without disturbing the
pilot. In my estimation, this emphasis on creating a virtual cockpit was
extremely helpful and at least doubled my concentration on the tasks at
hand.

During the many reviews leading to first flight, many asked whether flying
without motion would be a problem. Since our simulations were without
motion, the actual flying experience should be closer to the simulation, and
therefore would be more representative.

Although it may sound trivial, test card shuffling by the pilot was considerably more challenging than in a manned airplane. The primary problem is
that the HUD and outside world video is the sole suggestion of attitude. With
the X-36's extremely high roll rates and small size, it was more gust suscep-
tible than a larger aircraft, and also had a mild spiral divergence, which made
it roll off in one direction or the other. Therefore, it was necessary to spend
considerably more time watching the HUD than with a manned airplane.

Looking away to shuffle cards on a kneeboard could result in significant deviations of attitude since there was no kinesthetic hint to alert the pilot of these deviations. Accordingly, we made a tray immediately at the lower edge of the HUD monitor to hold the test cards for easy viewing by the pilot and arranged the sheets like a hand of playing cards so that the completed top sheet could be pulled off without looking away from the HUD.

To enhance test effectiveness, we developed a set of canned test inputs such as doublets and sweeps, programmed into the flight control set that could be triggered while the pilot was controlling the overall motion and remaining at the proper flight condition. These were of significant value in determining the effectiveness of each of the multiple surfaces, and something that could not have been done with the cockpit controls due to the extensive control surface integration. Fortunately, to gather this data, I simply had to get to the flight condition, steady the ship, and then trigger the inputs, making as little input as possible while the flight controls went through their canned sequence.

Since the engine used in the X-36 was a cruise missile engine, there was no way to perform an engine air start should the engine have flamed-out. However, since the aircraft did have a battery for back-up hydraulic and electrical power, the airplane could be flown to an engine-out landing, if close enough to the lake beds at Edwards AFB. Unfortunately, this was no trivial task since the landing gear extension speed was only slightly faster than the landing speed, and with the deceleration rate of the aircraft, there was only a six second window to get the landing gear down and locked, but the gear extension itself required five seconds. The bottom line, there was only a one second timing tolerance for extending the landing gear to make a successful engine-out landing.

The other technique investigated, to lower the landing gear early, well before starting the flare, did not work because the descent angle was considerably steeper and there was not enough energy to make the flare. So, therefore, the first technique was adopted and engine-out landings were practiced during every simulation. Since the team was unsure of how much damage might occur to the vehicle if ever the onboard emergency recovery parachute was used, we required all pilots to demonstrate a minimum of 90 per cent success rate in simulated engine-out landings before a pilot would be allowed to pilot the aircraft itself. This was special stuff. The team also had a very detailed list of all possible emergencies which we rehearsed regularly in the simulations. Fortunately, this discipline and attention to detail would pay off in the flight test program.

First flight was on May 17, 1997. After much rehearsal and practice, the test team and aircraft were ready. The scheduled takeoff time was selected to be 06:30 on a Saturday to avoid any conflict with main base traffic. Additionally, winds would be calmer and less of a factor. The UAV (Unmanned Air

Vehicle) operating areas had been extended by special request to the base to provide additional airspace nearer to the data link antenna.

After start-up and BIT checks were completed, I called for takeoff, was cleared, and then added full power. Acceleration was brisk and takeoff was just like the simulation with the aircraft lifting off at the predicted airspeed. I set a climb angle of about 15 degrees to hold the airspeed at the climb target with the gear and flaps left extended, as planned.

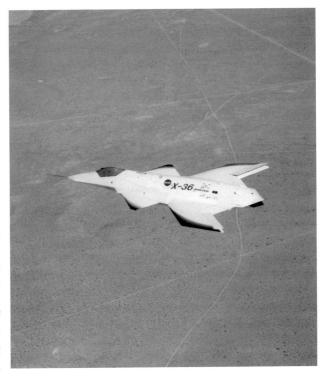

The X-36 successfully completed a thirty-one flight research program. (Courtesy NASA)

I knew immediately from the feel of the jet that the engineers had done a great job, there were no divergences or oscillations; damping and controllability felt good. However, after about a minute or two, a temperature caution ruined our plan. Down-linked data showed that the nozzle bay temperatures were climbing dramatically, therefore an immediate abort was required. Except for this fact, no obvious deficiencies were noted. Unfortunately for the team, there was no time for any of the planned testing as the rest of the flight time was spent quickly positioning for an immediate landing, which ended up floating a long way down the lake bed runway.

Since our velocity vector on the HUD defaulted to an air mass velocity vector, I noticed the first problem with it now; it was not accurate enough for use as an indication of sink rate for landing because the up wash calibrations had not been done yet. The theory was that if an inertial velocity vector (or an air mass velocity vector in no wind conditions) is placed about one degree down, sink rate should be about 1/60th of the true airspeed. And since I had never made a lake bed landing with a sight picture only three feet above the lake bed, I was cautious to avoid the sinkhole illusion and tried to fly the velocity vector approximately one to 1.5 degrees below the horizon line to set sink rate for touchdown. After about half the runway disappeared behind me, it appeared that I had virtually no sink rate and I reset the velocity vector to about 2.5 degrees low. This appeared to do the trick as the X-36 made an uneventful, but gentle first flight touchdown and rollout.

In retrospect, the up wash predictions were about 1.5 degrees too low with the effect that the air mass velocity vector showed about 1.5 degrees lower than the actual flight path. Until the new up wash data could be incorporated, we selected the inertial velocity vector with HOTAS for all remaining landings.

After incorporating two small scoops to aid nozzle bay cooling, flight two gave us our most significant problem. About 10 miles away at 12,000 feet altitude, the video and downlink signals suddenly became very weak with the presence of static and video noise. A break-X then appeared on my HUD, which meant that the X-36 had gone into lost-link autonomous operation. It was almost frightening to suddenly realize that a new $20 million aircraft was suddenly on its own and all I had was this frozen HUD with a big 'X' and a black background! I felt as if I had just ejected into a black night and was no longer in the airplane!

The team instantly went into its recovery procedures to regain the lost link. The ground-based video from NASA range safety showed that the X-36 was still flying in a controlled manner; this was a big help for Terry Weber, our test conductor (but not for me since I was still in the cockpit under a black tent), to track the air vehicle while the GCS engineers attempted to regain links.

As bad luck would have it, the nearest autonomous steering point was behind the aircraft, farther away from the station. A couple of times, the links returned momentarily, allowing me to regain control, but only to lose the links again in a matter of seconds. Each time the link was briefly regained, the aircraft was seen in a turn towards the more distant steering point (it was now flying farther away), but which was closer to the aircraft. Each glimpse of the intermittent link showed it in a yet steeper bank, which was well beyond what we had yet flown, and I was really afraid that it was all over now. Even so, the autonomous autopilot handled it well although it was much more aggressive than we had seen in our simulations.

Fortunately, the X-36 returned to the programmed terminal orbit point where the links and control were finally regained and an uneventful, but stress-filled, landing was made.

At no time in my test flying career had I felt more helpless; the adrenaline level was extremely high and yet I was utterly safe and hadn't even gotten airborne. Only after I went for a short post-flight run around the complex, was I able to settle down. I really hadn't bargained for this.

After much additional ground testing, it was determined that the loss of the link was due to a temperature sensitivity problem in the low noise amplifier. Apparently the LNA was okay at both low and high temperature where it was qualified, but at mid-range temperatures, this LNA lost enough sensitivity to cause link loss. After the problem was finally corrected, we had no further data link problems.

Later in the test program, following many good flights and data gathering, we faced the prospect of being shutdown due to potentially flooded lake beds caused by El Niño; accordingly we wanted to have the option to conduct our operations from the main base runway at Edwards. Surprisingly, when we asked for approval, we were questioned if our landing accuracy was adequate to handle the main base runway which was a mere 15,000 feet long.

I thought to myself, we can have some fun with this. Accordingly, we had the airfield personnel paint a 60 foot long 'H', 600 feet down the right edge of lake bed Runway 23 with a 20 foot wide gap in the cross bar. The object was to land in the center of the H. After completing six precision landings, I was pleased to report an average deviation of only 32 feet, facilitated by the excellent handling of the X-36 and its HUD accuracy. We managed to get approval after that. Landing rollouts using aerodynamic and moderate wheel braking had averaged about 2,000 feet. Too bad we didn't have a tail hook or a carrier landing might have been next

Without a doubt, the challenge of a successful flight test program with a remotely piloted aircraft far exceeded my estimation. Due to the lack of normal pilot cues, cockpit design was especially important as its implementation must help replace the missing flight cues.

The value of a trained test pilot to the operation was, of course, very high. The high degree of agility that was demonstrated by the X-36 required familiarity with fighter maneuvers, as well as familiarity with the necessary cues and displays to do that kind of testing. In retrospect, perhaps the single most aggravating aspect of the program was the idea that the test vehicle was somehow expendable. Although this was really done to make sure that upper management understood the risks, the test team never viewed the aircraft in that light. If a crash had occurred because of accepted risk created by lack of redundancy, this could be accepted. However, if a crash occurred because of a failure to properly prepare and execute, this would never have been acceptable. Fortunately, that 'expendable' thinking did not adversely affect our team's preparation. In the end, process and safety proved to be exceedingly important and were key ingredients in this highly successful flight test program.

The X-36 Tailless Fighter Agility Research aircraft was a 28 per cent scale representation of an advanced fighter.   (Courtesy NASA)

TESTIMONIAL

Larry Walker was a test pilot with McDonnell Douglas Aircraft in St Louis for 25 years and tested many aircraft ranging from the slatted F-4, F-18 full scale development, AV-8B full scale development, Pegasus engine digital engine control development, the F-15 S/MTD and ACTIVE programs, F-15E high angle of attack and spin tests, and the X-36.

Larry is a Fellow of the Society of Experimental Test Pilots; he was formerly a Marine pilot and military test pilot. His decorations include the Distinguished Flying Cross with Gold Star, and 13 Strike/Flight Air Medals for combat action in the Vietnam War.

Chapter 22

Steve Knoblock was part of the initial cadre of C-17 test pilots at Edwards AFB in the USA, first with the military then with Boeing.

Steve Knoblock – C-17 Globemaster Big Head held High

As a novice test pilot Steve Knoblock found himself in the cockpit of one of the largest aircraft on the planet. He experienced some heavy going situations.

The day started in a less than glorious way just like many of the other flight test days in the C-17 program – an 'O dark thirty' wake-up to make the pre-dawn briefing that would allow for the first test run near sunrise. And to make it even more enjoyable, it was a Saturday morning, which made me, one of the two newly graduated test pilots assigned to the program, a prime target for the not-so-good deal of weekend duty. I was fortunate, however, in that I had been assigned as one of the 'loads' test pilots. I figured it wasn't everyday that one got to purposefully fly a huge wide-bodied transport aircraft at -1g for more than a few fleeting tenths of a second.

The C-17 was being advertised as the quintessential direct-delivery air lifter, capable of hauling oversized loads over strategic distances directly to the forward edge of the battle area. That meant unprepared dirt strips for landings, so the aircraft had to be stout enough to handle rugged terrain upon landing.

While I cannot be sure how the day's particular test requirement was generated, someone thought it was important to test and demonstrate the C-17's ability to handle the side forces and lateral g-forces that the airplane may encounter while taxiing on rough terrain. I seem to recall that the end-point for the test was to achieve landing gear and fuselage loads equivalent to near one lateral g while taxiing at the maximum gross weight for austere operations, a whopping 502,000 lbs.

Assigned, as the pilot-in-command that day with me, was veteran McDonnell Douglas test pilot Dick Cooper. 'Coop' was a Vietnam F-4 veteran who had been part of the F-15 test program in the mid-1970s. He graduated from the US Air Force Academy in 1961, a mere two months after I was born. Coop was justifiably cautious about the day's testing, recognizing that the planned test was a bit out of the ordinary and had the potential of becoming messy; an intentional ground loop in a wide body transport.

The structure of the test was not specifically called out in the test plan, so that gave the test pilots and engineers some flexibility in designing the specific maneuver that would generate the desired test condition. From the analysis, it appeared that we would have to essentially execute a 90 degree turn at near 80 knots ground speed. This well may have been possible in some very large, unobstructed open ramp area, but there was not such place at Edwards. Our plan, then, became to use a combination of the main runway and the center taxiway. We devised a 'question mark' shaped maneuver, where we planned to taxi to the target test speed along the right edge of the runway, followed by a 30 to 45 degree left diagonal turn across the runway, finished with a 120 to 135 degree right turn-off onto the center taxiway. While this sounded straightforward, there were some relatively important issues concerning the point at which we make the left diagonal bid and then the right turn reversal which would ensure we would be in a position to make it to the center taxiway. The test required a build up in speed to generate the desired loads, starting first at 40 knots, then proceeding to 60 and eventually 80 knots.

Coop and I discussed the maneuver and added runs at 15 and 30 knots ground speed to warm-up.

During the preflight planning we identified runway markings which we planned to use as action points during the ground test. We initially identified a 'runway remaining marker' that indicated a point about 1,200 feet from the center taxiway as the point at which to initiate the left diagonal cut across the runway. This was the point where I would call out, 'Start turn!' When on the heading and approaching the runway center line, I was to call out, 'Reverse turn!' This would give us about 200 feet to correct the left diagonal cut. Finally, we established the runway distance remaining marker prior to the turn start point were I would call out, 'Stabilize!' This would indicate it was where we needed to be on the target groundspeed for the run.

With a plan in hand, we taxied out for the test. The weather and winds were completely cooperative, and given the early hour on a Saturday morning, we had no other airport traffic to contend with. We were confident that we'd be done well before lunch, so there was a good chance that we could salvage the majority of the weekend, which was important.

The first run at 15 knots was an exercise in yawning. And that's a good thing in a flight test. Coop had no problems controlling the speed, initiating the left turn, and reversing the turn towards the center taxiway. We did note that we lost three to four knots of speed by making the left diagonal turn, so we planned to enter the turn a few knots faster to compensate. We also noted no problems in directing the aircraft at the center taxiway at the end of the maneuver, and that the 45 degrees of heading across the runway may not really be required. Satisfied that we had an executable plan, we taxied back for another run at 30 knots using an initial entry speed of about 35 knots.

The next run was slightly more challenging but was easily executed. After the run, the control room cleared us for a 60 knot run, satisfied that this 'warm-up' met the criterion for the 40 knot build-up run. Good news, we thought, one-third of the way done. Once clear of the runway, we had the tires, brakes, and landing gear inspected as required by the safety plan, noting no anomalies or concerns. On to the next point.

This was where the fun started. Although, little did we know how much!

By now we were in a groove, and Coop and I were satisfied that no further tweaks were required for the test technique. When we hit the stabilization point, Coop was a few knots below the target speed of 60, so he made one last correction to achieve 65 knots at turn initiation. I was monitoring the groundspeed closely, and this last correction was a tad too much. I made a comment to Coop a couple of hundred feet prior to the start turn point, and I think I would say this distracted him at a critical point in his rhythm. He was in the process of correcting the speed when I called out, 'Start turn!' And, surprisingly, he quickly made a pretty aggressive left turn. Before I knew it, we had a full 45 degree bid across the runway at almost 70 knots. I had barely processed this information when the center line was staring me in the face, so I called out, 'Reverse!'

Coop and I were way behind all reason at this point, and all we saw ahead was a face full of desert staring at us through the windscreen. He instinctively applied full right tiller to start the right turn toward the taxiway, but to no avail. The airplane was shaking violently with 60 degrees of right nosewheel input, but we were not turning at all.

For an instant, I felt we were going cross-country straight off the runway. I instinctively took my feet off the floor and went for the brakes, but Coop's years of experience had long beat me to the punch. He was already working the brakes stepping more heavily on the right brake in order to turn the aircraft. Unfortunately, this only served to initiate a skid sideways over to the left towards the edge of the runway. Still shaking violently as the nose-wheel shuddered and skidded across the runway, Coop's experience again took over as he rapidly centered the nose-wheel steering for a split second, then returned it to a right turn at only half deflection. The wheel rapidly regained control, the shaking stopped and the nose began to follow to the right. Coop continued to brake as we dished out the turn, and the airplane came to a stop only a few feet from the left edge of the runway, still about 10 degrees left of runway heading. I noticed it was amazingly quiet as I watched the bluish-white smoke from the skidding tires waft in front of the cockpit.

Both Coop and I were visibly shaken at our near off-road experience, and I noticed he started to push the throttles up to taxi the airplane straight. Only problem was, we didn't move at all, the engines weren't running any more! Somewhere during the maneuver, all four engines had flamed out.

Incredulous, Coop and I looked at each other with that look: 'Hey, what did you just do?' Amazingly, the control room was totally oblivious to our near mishap, and let us know on the radio that, 'data was in progress'. Coop coolly responded that we, 'had had a slight problem,' and went to standby. He had me fire up the APU so we could restart the engines and at least taxi the airplane. Even more incredible than the flame out, was that the engines refused to restart. We were completely perplexed. We had no idea why the engines quit and even less of an idea as to why they wouldn't restart. At this point, we informed the control room of the situation, and told them that testing was complete for the day and a tug was ordered up to tow the now disabled aircraft off the runway.

In the mission debrief, Coop and I had come to the realization that this test point was beyond 'ordinary' and was borderline 'stupid'. This was a highly technical test pilot assessment meaning that we had no business doing that test again. Engineering confirmed that we had generated about 0.6 lateral g during our left skidding stop, but the gear and fuselage loads were nowhere near a level of concern. Coop and I agreed that if that hairy ride had only generated 0.6g, there was no way either one of us were interested in going after 1.0 lateral gs. Based on our brush with the edge of the runway, we all concluded that this test point involved far more risk than necessary for the type of data we were looking for, so we claimed victory and called the test complete.

Further engineering analysis into the engine flameout discovered that we had identified a singe point failure in the engine start panel during the run. The severe vibrations, induced during the taxi test, caused several of the thin metallic traces on the electronic circuit boards in the overhead start panel, to break and short out, commanding a shut down of all four engines, preventing their restart and resulting in a redesign of several computer controller circuit boards.

Nearly a year later I had become fairly proficient at loads testing on the C-17 when I experienced one of my first flight test induced encounters with 'the unknown'. The loads program had provided some excellent flying for me up to this point and given me the opportunities to fly on several aircraft 'firsts' as well as to set some unofficial world records for payload and altitude combinations.

On this particular day, I was paired with test pilot Don Brown. Don was a former Marine aviator, having flown quite a bit of F-18 flight testing while on active duty. After he retired, he joined McDonnell Douglas and flew commercial flight tests on the MD-80 series aircraft. He finally became the director of C-17 Flight Operations for McDonnell Douglas and Boeing in Long Beach (and was my eventual boss when I left active duty). Don and I hadn't flown much together in the loads program, and today he was assigned as my co-pilot on what we called a 'dumbbell' mission. For these tests, we carried various cargo configurations, in the form of cement blocks, weighing anywhere from 10,000 to 160,000 lbs.

The C-17 suffered massive cost overruns in the early 1990s, so that McDonnell Douglas nearly lost the contract.

The test point for today was planned for a 100 per cent Design Limit Load (DLL) condition at 3gs and 350 knots at 22,500 feet (the crossover altitude for the aircraft's limiting speed and Mach curve). As I recall, we were fairly heavy, so the aircraft would barely achieve the target speed in level flight at maximum power. This, therefore, required the test points to be conducted out of a dive maneuver.

After takeoff, we accomplished the obligatory in-flight instrumentation checks. Our tanker was in the hammerhead for runway 22, waiting for our clearance for takeoff. Our plan was to accomplish several build up points at 2.0, 2.25, 2.5, and 2.75 gs. We then planned to rendezvous with the tanker and take on about 20,000 lbs of fuel to make sure we were at the proper weight for the end point.

The build-up points and air refueling were uneventful. As I disconnected from the tanker and cleared to the right, the tone in the cockpit and the control room grew intense as everyone became focused on making the points good, the first time out. I leveled off at about 24,000 feet and 310 knots. The plan was to initiate a dive to about 10 to 12 degrees nose low, allowing the speed to build during the dive with less than maximum power so that as I added the gs during the pull up, I could add full power to keep the airspeed from bleeding off as the load factor increased. It would be a symphony in action, pulling to raise the nose, adding power, and increasing the gs simultaneously so that during the pull-up maneuver I would hit 350 knots, three gs, max power, and 22,500 feet simultaneously.

The first attempt was not quite perfect, as I misjudged the lead point for the pull-up and found myself five knots slow and only approaching 2.8gs as I climbed above the target altitude. I allowed the aircraft to continue its trajectory back up to 25,000 feet to give me a better opportunity to stabilize the dive prior to the pull. This maneuver ended up hiding the problem I was about to encounter. On the second attempt, I started the dive slower with less power, planning to let gravity do most of the work for me to get my speed. With the airspeed indicator rapidly increasing, I was able to start loading up the aircraft sooner to control the acceleration rate, therefore establishing the aircraft at an elevated load factor and 350 knots below the target altitude with the nose still below the horizon. I then used a more aggressive pull on the stick while I added full power to try to further increase the load.

It was at this point a rather odd event occurred, which was not really understood until later when the data traces were reviewed. The stick was almost at the full aft limit, but I was only generating about 2.9g. I continued to pull but could not get anymore gs.

Passing about 15 degrees nose high with the speed slowing below 340 knots, Don called for me to recover from the pull. As I relaxed the stick, the gs backed off, but amazingly the nose continued upwards. I began to push the stick forward, but there seemed to be no response from the aircraft. I continued to push forward until I ultimately hit the forward stop. Speed was rolling below 300 knots and the nose was still going up, now passing 30 degrees nose high. Don was getting worried and started to gently encourage me by yelling, 'Get the nose down, get the fucking nose down!' I looked at him cross-cockpit and told him I had full forward stick, but the aircraft wasn't responding. I suppose he didn't believe me, as I saw him grab the stick as well and push hard forward, but it was already buried against the glare shield. Passing about 50 degrees nose high, I had had enough, so I gently began to roll the aircraft to the right in a desperate attempt to get the nose towards the horizon. The speed had dipped to near 220 knots with the nose almost 60 degrees nose high by the time the aircraft began to gradually respond to my stick inputs. I recovered to level flight and got some speed back while Don continued to use some really colorful Marine language in discussing the last maneuver.

At this point, the control room read back our performance. Bill Norton, our trusty test conductor, with whom I had flown many loads missions, calmly repeated as he had so many times in the past: '348 knots, 2.9gs, 97 per cent DLL, cleared for a repeat.' Don and I couldn't believe that the previous event had gone completely unnoticed by the control room engineers. While I felt like something was not right with the airplane, I think Don was convinced that there had been something wrong with my piloting technique and continued ranting in a colorful manner. But since the control room did not have our cockpit interphone on in the telemetry stream, they had been completely unaware of our cross-cockpit discussion. Don advocated that we should try the maneuver again, and this time he would follow me on the stick. I was game to give it another try. And so we did. Probably not the best decision we made that day.

So for the second time, we set up at 25,000 feet and 300 knots, followed by our dive into the test point. At this point I was more focused on getting a good point than trying to figure out if there was a true anomaly with the aircraft. Consequently, I tried to get a high g-loading in the early part of the pull, followed by a very aggressive pull once I got the power in. This time I know I hit the aft stop with the stick, but I was only able to get 2.92gs. As soon as the speed was below 345 knots, I began an aggressive recovery, moving the stick almost to the full forward stop in less than a half second. Just as before, the load backed off a bit, but the nose kept coming up. Not particularly interested in starting another loop, I rolled into about 70 degrees of bank when the nose was passing through 30 degrees. It ended up being a very nice wing-over, I might add; and this had convinced Don that the problem was not with the junior test pilot, but rather somewhere in the bowels of the flight control system. I had barely begun to roll wings level when Don was on the radio, stating that we had some sort of flight control malfunction and that we were returning to base. At this point, the control room started looking more closely at the data and realized that the elevator was not tracking the pilot stick inputs correctly. By the time we returned to the squadron, the word was already out and there was a flurry of activity. Our debrief was delayed until we could get the appropriate engineers on the telephone. At the debrief, about 50 folk showed up, when normally there would have only been a dozen or so. Apparently our flight had not only generated some good data, but some very curious people as well.

In the debrief, data plots were shown that clearly indicated a problem. During my initial pull-up, the elevator was not tracking with my stick inputs and actually stopped following the stick at about half deflection. A clear sign of 'hinge moment limiting', where the aerodynamic forces created by the airflow over the control surface are so strong that the hydraulic power system in the elevators were not strong enough to overcome them. What was unusual, was that once the elevator became hinge moment limited, it also no longer followed the stick when commanded nose down. In fact, the data traces showed that while I was pushing the stick full forward, the elevators were still commanding the aircraft nose up for about 20 seconds. Suffice to say, this is not a desirable characteristic for an airplane.

Suddenly, all of the test airplanes became available to maintenance (not exactly 'grounded'). It took one control engineer about 10 minutes to find the problem. The C-17 digital flight control system had a glaring flaw that had somehow been overlooked. In laymen's terms, here's what happened: At the speeds we were flying, the hydraulic control system did not possess enough power to overcome the aerodynamic forces on the elevator, so the elevator stopped moving. The integrator in the flight control law recognized that the aircraft was not responding to the pilot control inputs, so it digitally increased the elevator commands in an attempt to force the elevator to move more and make the airplane respond. But the elevator could not move because of the hinge moment limiting situation. So the integrator continued to increase the elevator command with no effect. When this occurs, the integrator is winding up. At some point, when the command is reversed (like

The C-17 has broken 22 records for oversized payloads.

when the stick is pushed forward), the integrator does the same thing-it sees the nose is commanded down and attempts to move the elevator in the correct direction. But since the integrator is all wound-up, it must first unwind itself before it can command the elevator in the opposite direction.

TESTIMONIAL

Steve Knoblock is the lead pilot on the C-5M program based at the Lockheed Martin Aeronautics manufacturing facility in Marietta, Georgia. He received his BS in Aeronautical Engineering in 1983 from the USAF Academy, and entered active duty as a KC-135Q pilot flying the dedicated SR-71 tanker. During the six years of this assignment, he progressed through the ranks of aircraft commander, instructor pilot, and evaluator pilot.

In 1990 he was selected for the Joint AF Institute of Technology / USAF Test Pilot School program. First assigned to Wright Patterson AFB, he earned his MS in Aeronautical Engineering and was qualified in the NT-39 aircraft. His follow-on assignment was to Class 92B at the USAF Test Pilot School. Upon graduation from TPS, he joined the initial cadre of C-17 test pilots at Edwards AFB.

In 1996, he left the USAF to join McDonnell Douglas (Boeing) as a C-17 and KC/MD-10 test pilot. His C-17 work as a project test pilot focused on the avionics and software improvement programs for Blocks 9 thru 13, preparing the aircraft for its initial TCAS, CNS/ATM, and TAWS implementations. He was also a project pilot on the YC-15 cooperative research and development program. In 2000, he joined Lockheed Martin as a test pilot on the C-130J and C-5 AMP and RERP test programs where he has focused his efforts on avionics integration of flight management, terrain awareness, and microwave landing systems.

Chapter 23

The last operational Jaguar was decommissioned in 2007, 35 years after Roger Beazley conducted some of the first tests.

Roger Beazley – Jaguar
A Close Encounter with my Bomb

The low level, strike attack aircraft Jaguar was a mainstay of the RAF's defence capability. However, during tests certain projected assets were soon dropped.

Following graduation from the Empire Test Pilots' School (ETPS) in 1973 I was appointed to the UK's Aeroplane & Armament Experimental Establishment (A&AEE) at Boscombe Down. My main task was in support of the very early work on the Multi-Role Combat Aircraft (MRCA) now better known as the Tornado. I joined the project prior to its first flight when most of the work seemed to centre on endless meetings and conferences, at that time not something to get a recently qualified test pilot too excited.

However, there was much work to be done on other more established programmes including the Buccaneer, Jaguar, Phantom and Hawk with trials support flying in the Canberra and Hunter. These were the aircraft which provided the bulk of my test flying in the mid-1970s, the more exotic aircraft such as the F-111E, F-15 Eagle and eventually the Tornado came later.

The main purpose of the A&AEE was, with the support of the aircraft manufacturer, to provide independent assessments of aircraft, systems and weapon systems to enable a set of 'release' recommendations to be formulated. From these recommendations the UK armed forces could then base their guidance, advice, flying and engineering limitations in support of training and operations. In short, recommendations as to whether the equipment was safe to operate, fit for purpose, and that it met the specification. These recommendations would go on to be the basis of the aircraft's certificate of airworthiness, now called the Military Aircraft Release.

In very general terms the work of the establishment test pilots, and the test pilots at the companies, were usually very much in harmony and often work shared with the aircraft manufacturer in the form of joint trials. It was only when politics, money or timescales became involved that differences become apparent and formal positions were sometimes taken.

Although not a perfect aircraft by any means I particularly enjoyed flying the Jaguar. I suspect the principal reason for my liking the aircraft was that I was essentially an air defence man (Lightnings and Phantoms) and the Jaguar enabled me to experience and I hope contribute, to the development of a low level strike attack aircraft. In those days the Jaguar was deemed to possess a very modern navigation and weapons attack system involving, at that time, a state-of-the-art Head Up Display (HUD), a moving map and an inertial navigation system which was the key to the whole avionics suite; at the time it really did seem very up to date.

Low level navigation trials at 420 knots and 250 feet were exhilarating, weapons system aiming trials required a fair amount of preparation and with the amount of recorded data carried both on board the aircraft, with air-to-ground telemetry and also from the instrumented air ranges at Larkhill on Salisbury Plain and West Freugh in Scotland, there was little if any chance of hiding piloting mistakes. Air-to-air refuelling was something I was very familiar with from flying on other types, although the Jaguar's somewhat moderate performance from the two Adour engines made high-level tanking a trifle limited and a bit sensitive. I particularly enjoyed working on the development of the EMI reconnaissance pod since it meant

The Jaguar had provision for overwing pylons which were used for short-range air-to-air missiles.

a fair amount of high-speed low level flying with the occasional tasking to take pictures which, of course, resulted in the evidence being delivered to your desk in a brown paper envelope merely a short time after landing.

During the mid 1970s British Aerospace was trying to develop a high loft weapons attack software programme for the Jaguar navigation and attack system. Difficulties were being experienced in the automatic software computations which drove the pilot's lateral guidance indicator in the HUD. The loft attack involved approaching the target at low level and at high speed following the system's guidance. At a predetermined range from the target, the HUD format would change and an aiming dot would start moving up the display. The pilot would track the dot (both in pitch and azimuth, that is laterally) and at another predetermined point somewhere near a 60 degree nose high attitude, the bomb would automatically be released, provided of course the various weapon switches were all in the right place.

Operationally, the pilot would then either continue over the top of a loop, or roll and pull down to return in the direction from which he came, getting back to low level as soon as he possibly could. This type of attack had two major advantages, the aircraft did not have to fly over the target and the aircraft was on its way back at low level before the weapon exploded. However, it was not the most accurate of deliveries and was fairly 'sporty' in cloud or at night.

The difficulty the manufacturer was having, was in trying to make the lateral demands of the aiming dot sufficiently smooth to allow the pilot half a chance to achieve a successful attack. Laterally tracking with acceptable accuracy, at the same time, of course, as tracking vertically, and considering a million other things was not working out. The firm's pilots considered the software solution unacceptable but the engineers (known in the British flight test world as 'boffins') were not totally convinced.

I, therefore, found myself at the company's flight test centre at Warton being invited to fly the trials' Jaguar in an attempt to give 'a customer's' view of the problem.

Following a comprehensive brief by the Warton aircrew and boffins, I was airborne in the Warton trials' Jaguar GR1 XX109 heading towards the instrumented West Freugh range. I carried no weapons, the system being electronically fudged to assume a weapon was on board.

The West Freugh instrumented range was situated in Luce Bay in Scotland and controlled from the West Freugh airfield, south of Stranraer. The loft targets were in the form of rafts moored in the bay, numbered 1 through to 6 although number 3 (known as M3) was invariably used; the attack direction was to the south-east. Although the range was controlled from West Freugh airfield, Observation Points known as OPs were situated along the range down the Mull of Galloway. It was from these OPs that the majority of video and film data was obtained including film tracking of the bomb itself.

Attacking M3 on a south-east heading, meant flying swiftly straight down Lock Ryan to the north of Stranraer, overland, high speed, low level and, when the system demanded, pulling up into the loft to throw the bomb high into Luce Bay. High-speed and low level meant 550 knots at 250 feet and in a Jaguar with external stores, meant full reheat and an awful lot of noise. Such attack profiles were kept to the minimum in sympathy with the locals who lived in this gloriously beautiful part of Dumfries & Galloway. Glorious, that was, until a Jaguar turned up to fly loft attacks passing over Soulseat Loch and the people visiting the site of the old Abbey.

With attack checks complete and the HUD camera running, I was nicely set up at 550 knots waiting for the HUD format to change and the aiming dot to start marching up the display and see if it was to be anything like the briefing and the HUD film I had been shown, the lateral demands would start to come in and it would be 'impossible' to track. I was, therefore, pleasantly surprised that I seemed to be able to maintain the dot in the lateral sense, although I was a bit ragged in the vertical plane. Before I realized it, the aircraft was passing through 60 degree nose up and the format changed, indicating that if I had a bomb on board, that was the point at which it would have gone.

What I could not understand was why it seemed so easy to keep the dot laterally controlled. This was, after all, what I had learnt from the Warton test pilots, and had been what all the fuss was about. However, the evidence was there and the essence of a test pilot's job is to report the facts.

I repeated the attack and, in broad terms, obtained the same result. Mindful of the noise I was making over the old Abbey and hoping beyond hope that I had the appropriate evidence in the HUD camera, I set off back to Warton.

On landing, people were keen to hear my opinion but were somewhat taken aback when I suggested that I saw no real problem. The boffins beamed, local pilots were irritated, and I was confused. I was asked what the maximum lateral deflection was to which I replied: 'Well I didn't really see one'.

At this stage I was beginning to smell a rat although I stuck to my guns since I had the evidence of my own eyes and hopefully the whole thing was recorded on the HUD film which had yet to be developed.

I enjoyed a relaxing coffee, got changed out of flying kit, and awaited the call from the cinema room. It came fairly quickly with the reluctant acceptance that I was right, and there was the evidence all captured on 8mm film, or was it 16mm?

My moment of glory only lasted for a few more minutes. The door of the operations room suddenly burst open, and in came a boffin with the news that the lateral software had not been connected, or engaged, or coupled, or whatever you do with software, and therefore it was not surprising that the lateral demand stayed within the aiming circle. In short, whatever I would have done during the loft, the lateral display would have remained centred!

Much embarrassment was suffered by the Warton boffins, I retained the moral high ground and flew again the following day. With everything connected it was clearly unacceptable; I agreed with the Warton test pilots!

Some months after the lateral software debacle I returned to Warton to carry out some similar attacks using practice bombs. The practice bomb is a small (4 kg or 28 lb) device which can be used to develop attack profiles, prove a software aiming system and, in front-line service, forms the basic weapon for range practice. When the practice bombs hits the ground, or hopefully the target, it detonates with a puff of white smoke so its accuracy can be assessed. Against a sea target such as M3, it would either puff on the raft (a hit) or splash alongside (a miss).

Once again after a comprehensive brief by the aircrew and boffins, I was ready to walk out, busying myself in the small operations room with the hundred and one tasks that seem to be required prior to getting airborne and joining the West Freugh range.

One of the pilots sidled up with a boffin in tow and suggested that because the results from West Freugh seemed to take a little time to feed back to Warton (normally, the next day) it would be helpful to spot the bomb myself. It was quite straightforward he claimed, once the bomb had gone, roll away and immediately look back and over to the target M3. After a certain time, the splash or even the white puff would be seen. An early but approximate indication of where the bomb went would, it was claimed, be very helpful.

I gave it all some thought, after all, at 60 degree nose up or more and the speed decreasing markedly there are other things in a trials Jaguar that need to be done. Not least, weapons safety checks, HUD camera management and, in the early development Jaguar, one had to be aware of the rather doubtful attitude indications which could fail or 'topple' if one went anywhere near the vertical. However, I said, showing no great enthusiasm or confidence, I would see what I could do.

The arrival at West Freugh went without a hitch, the range was ready and the OPs had checked in that the visibility and light levels were sufficiently high for the trial to proceed. Light levels were always a consideration with instrumented drops at West Freugh. It was Scotland.

I only had the one practice bomb so it all had to work first time. Down the anchorage of Loch Ryan past Cairnryan ferry port; across the flat countryside to the south-east of Stranraer and, of course, across the Loch and the old Abbey. Speed nice and steady at 550 knots, slowly descending to 250 feet to get the right entry conditions. All went well, the HUD format changed and the vertical and lateral tracking achieved to a satisfactory standard. At or about my 60 degree nose up, the bomb released and the HUD format changed.

Mindful of my informal and last minute task to spot the bomb, I briskly rolled the aircraft right and then immediately left, but I must have pulled or pushed a bit for there, instead of underneath the aircraft, the bomb was just outside the cockpit and not more than a few feet from my head.

Surprised and consequently transfixed, I was not too sure what to do. However, whilst most aircrew at the time considered the Jaguar underpowered (the two Adours pushed out about half the thrust of the two Avons in a Lightning), even at a nose high attitude the aircraft at full reheat could outpace an unpowered bomb.

Slowly, but surely the bomb fell away and I was faced with the post attack checks, HUD camera management, the required RT calls to the range and an almost vertical recovery with not a lot of airspeed. Not surprisingly I failed to spot the bomb which, to be fair was, at that time, not a great priority.

On arrival back at Warton, the ever enthusiastic boffins were keen to know, 'how it all went,' to which I replied with a slight understatement, 'More or less as advertised'. This was followed by the next inevitable question, 'Where did it go,' to which I replied, 'I have no idea'.

My subsequent debrief with the Warton test pilot was a little more animated. As far as I know the high loft attack was never accepted into service.

The RAF accepted delivery of the first of 165 single-seater Jaguars GR.1s with 54(F) Squadron in 1974.

TESTIMONIAL

Roger Beazley CBE AFC BA (Hons) FRAeS served for 32 years in the Royal Air Force initially on Hunters, Lightnings and then the Phantom F4. He graduated from the Empire Test Pilots' School (ETPS) in 1973, following which the majority of his flying and staff appointments were in the flight test, research & development and flying regulatory roles.

On retirement from the Service in 1996 he took the appointment of aerospace adviser at the flight test centre at MoD Boscombe Down; he currently acts as a part time consultant to ETPS.

He was awarded an Air Force Cross (AFC) in 1978 and appointed Commander of the British Empire (CBE) in 1996. He is a Fellow of the Royal Aeronautical Society where he serves on Council and a Fellow of the Society of Experimental Test Pilots in the USA. He is an honorary member of the Flight Test Society of Australia. He has twice been recognized by the City of London Guild of Air Pilots & Navigators (GAPAN).

Chapter 24

Sonja Englert is now a test pilot and engineer and has flown more than 80 types of aircraft.

Sonja Englert – The MD-3 Swiss Trainer Pale Rider

With virtually no experience Sonja Englert found herself test flying a Swiss aerobatic trainer for a demanding boss, when things took a turn for the worse.

During my last year at the University of Braunschweig, with my *Diplomarbeit* for becoming an aeronautical engineer almost finished, I had sent out letters with my short résumé to several aviation related companies. Those that wrote back were polite rejections, except for one. That one came from a company in Switzerland called Dätwyler, inviting me for an interview. They had developed a two-seat, all-metal aerobatic trainer and were still in the process of completing its certification.

The MD-3 Swiss Trainer was designed as a primary trainer aircraft. After performing some of its first test flights, Swiss aerobatic champion Christian Schweizer said he thought it would be suitable as an aerobatic trainer as well. The engine has 160hp and aerodynamically the airplane was quite clean. It had a top speed with a fixed pitch propeller of almost 140 knots. It was capable of a number of positive aerobatic maneuvers including spins.

A friend at the University warned me. He said that Max Dätwyler, the owner of the company, had a reputation of being very difficult to work with and that no one wanted this job.

The MD-3 was his baby and he had designed it, and although he was a pilot, he was no engineer. So it was with some trepidation that I drove to Switzerland in the summer of 1992, to get to know him; the challenge was appealing. During the interview Max Dätwyler asked me a lot of questions, showed me the project and his company, which was mainly in the printing machine business and had about 500 employees. The aviation department had less than 30 people. Currently he had no engineer or test pilot, and needed someone to supervise a structural test they needed to perform for certification. There was no word about flight testing at that time. He wanted to complete the certification, then sell the project to someone who wanted to start production.

He himself was not interested in the production of the MD-3 Swiss Trainer. Max Dätwyler did not seem to be such an unpleasant person, and although he was 76 years old at the time, he was still very active. He seemed reasonably pleased with me, especially when he found out that I also was an avidly keen pilot, because he offered me the job on the spot. After thinking about it for a day, I accepted.

Soon after I started the job, I found out that I would not just be working as a structural engineer. Because I was the only engineer and also a pilot, I got to do a bit of everything, including flight testing. My boss thought he might sell the project more profitably if the gross weight of the airplane was increased and the fuselage height was increased for better head room. He also wanted to offer a second propeller model as an option, and replace the long, heavy exhaust, which was needed for meeting the strict Swiss noise standards, with a shorter, lighter one.

Max had no shortage of ideas and did not consider the effort, time and money needed to certify all those changes. He also had some very strong opinions about his design and was generally opposed to changes anyone else suggested. I had found a problem with design of the wing structure during the testing, and suggested a change to him. He did not look pleased when he said to me, 'I'm sure that there is no problem with the structure. It must be the test fixture which is not applying the load correctly.' I had to collect a lot of data, get a second opinion and modify my original suggestion to make it look more like his original idea before he would reluctantly allow us to make a change.

Before he hired me, he had used several consultant engineers to help out. They would come a few times, get a taste of his temper, and were never seen again. He could get really angry, and yell at people for daring to oppose his views. To me, it all seemed a bit staged. Because I have a fairly thick skin, it didn't bother me as much and I did not take it personally. On the other hand I found him to be a generous person and supportive of those he considered worthy. Max lived on a farm, where he kept animals including sheep and a herd of deer. Every Christmas, he would have several of the deer slaughtered and used for a big Christmas dinner to which all employees were invited.

I had some flight test training, but very little real life testing experience. Nevertheless, I was soon checked out to fly the MD-3. and was lucky to have the occasional help of the famous Christian Schweizer, who had done some of the initial test flying for Dätwyler. He was an absolutely fearless pilot, several times Swiss aerobatic champion, flew air shows, did part time work as a test pilot for various companies and worked as a pilot for the REGA, which is an organization in Switzerland for rescue and medical transport flights. In his spare time he liked to fly war birds like a P-51 Mustang and Max Dätwyler's Dornier C-36, one with a radial piston engine. Schweizer was accepted by the Swiss certification authorities to perform certification flight tests in Switzerland.

I sat down with Schweizer and talked over the test plans and tests I needed to fly when he was not available. Schweizer trained me on the MD-3 performing aerobatics and spins and I flew as a flight test engineer during some of the certification test flights with him. The MD-3 had very good spin characteristics, recovering from a fully developed spin in less than a turn. But because of all of Christian's activities, he was only occasionally available for Dätwyler flight testing and I got to do a fair share of it myself. Switzerland is a small country with less than a handful of aviation companies at that time. The largest one, Pilatus, was going through the certification of the PC-12 at that time, and took up a large share of the resources of the certification office in Bern.

Their project engineer was also working with us, and he entertained us with stories from our neighbors. There was no such thing as an official test pilot in Switzerland, and because of that, even though I had very little experience, I got to do some certification flight tests on the MD-3. I must have somehow convinced the people in Bern that I knew what I was doing.

Our test airplane, serial number 2, got fitted with a raised upper fuselage and canopy, a new propeller and the new short exhaust, which I test-flew. As expected, the maximum cruise speed was reduced by a couple of knots. The changes did not affect any of the normal handling qualities, stability or the position error. I figured

Heading up the test program of the MD-3 was the aerobatic champion Christian Schweizer. He was killed a few years later flying in the Alps.

out a way to measure takeoff performance by positioning observers next to the runway with a camera. The original exhaust had extended the full length of the fuselage from engine to tail. It had a slot at the bottom over the full length, through which exhaust gas was discharged. This resulted in a fairly quiet airplane, but the exhaust was also heavy and expensive to fabricate. Since the target markets were outside of Switzerland, we thought we could trade cost for noise. We had removed the long exhaust and had only two short stacks exiting the cowling.

We soon found out that this modification had other effects besides an increase in decibels. Christian Schweizer took the MD-3 with the short exhaust up to spin it. At that time we did not recognize the contribution the exhaust made to spin recovery. Christian came back from the test flight and disappeared for a debrief with the boss. I did not know what exactly they talked about, but I heard that it was definitely not as well behaved as before.

The spin now supposedly took longer to recover than the allowable 1.5 turns after six intentional turns. Christian left, shaking his head, muttering something about major design changes being necessary. Dätwyler was a very stubborn person and never wanted to believe bad news. He certainly did not want to make changes to his baby, unless they were his own ideas. His tendency was to simply not believe what someone was telling him. He did not agree that the removal of the long exhaust could cause a big difference. I could imagine that he was not in a good mood, and stayed out of his way for the rest of the day.

It was the next day after Schweizer had left that Max approached me and asked me to go up in the MD-3 and spin it. I was not too worried about doing that, after all Schweizer had come back with the airplane in one piece, so it must have recovered eventually. But, I did believe Schweizer if he said it did not meet the certification requirements and needed a major change.

I was more worried about breaking the news to my boss that Schweizer was right, and how we would solve the issue than about spinning the airplane. I took my parachute, did a good preflight inspection and climbed into the MD-3. It started right up as usual and I took off from the 1,500 foot grass strip next to the factory from which we were operating. I flew towards a sparsely populated area to the south-east, which was near enough the Alps to be called mountainous. Once I had enough altitude I initiated a few one-turn spins to the left and right. Reduced airspeed, pulled the stick all the way back, then kicked in full rudder. The airplane would roll and yaw and drop the nose.

The first turn was always fairly slow, and I had no problem recovering. If I pushed the stick full forward and pushed the rudder against the rotation at the same time, the spin would stop. The nose was pointing almost straight down, and a strong pull was required to return to level flight. The g-forces would push me into the seat and drain the blood from my head. Then I would climb back up to the altitude where I had started and try again, to the other side. This was working well, and I increased the number of turns to three in a row. The world was spinning wildly around me, faster with every rotation.

Recovery was now approaching the limit of one and a half additional turns, but it did not feel like it was yet in a fully developed spin. I was maybe getting a little impatient and went straight from three turns to six turns. I climbed a bit higher for this one because during each turn I lost about 300 feet of altitude. Again I reduced airspeed, waited until the airplane stalled, then kicked the rudder to the left. One turn, two turns, the rotation sped up, here came turns numbers three and four, I could hardly tell which way was which, by now the ground was speeding so fast below me and was rapidly getting closer. Now the sixth turn, and the recovery.

Okay, now I pushed the rudder to the right and moved the stick rapidly forward. Nothing happened, the airplane continued to spin. Turn number seven went by, and still there was no reaction as the airplane plummeted to the ground. I mentally reviewed the procedure to jettison the canopy and jump out of the airplane. Turn number eight came and went. At this point I realized that I probably wouldn't even have enough altitude. Did I even have enough altitude for my parachute to open? Then, at last the rotation finally slowed. The nose violently pitched down, throwing me painfully against the seat belts. The rotation stopped and I hung nose down as if suspended by a cable from the tail. The airspeed is came up and I pulled back gently on the stick.

I was still falling at great speed, but the world now looked more normal, green was down, blue was up, and I leveled off feeling very relieved. Clearly, it was no longer a good spinning airplane without the long exhaust. Having now completed the six left turn spins (and more), I thought it prudent not to continue to check out the six-turn spins to the right and flew home.

As soon as I got out of the plane, I saw my boss standing there. He took one look at me, and said: 'What do we need to do to fix it?' I was speechless for a couple seconds, before I told him about my results and spluttered about what had happened. I concluded that we would have to install something that simulated the exhaust on the tail, like a ventral fin. To my surprise he readily agreed. I sat down to design a real ventral fin for the MD-3 and designed it large enough to be effective. I had one made and had it quickly bolted to the tail. I have to admit that it did not enhance the appearance of the airplane, and I had to listen to a lot of ribbing from my co-workers about it. But I never heard a word of complaint from my boss about it. To make a long story short, the ventral fin worked. For certification, Christian Schweizer flew the complete spin matrix with it and the MD-3 recovered beautifully, so the ventral fin was there to stay.

It was only later that I heard why I was spared having to use all my imagination and persuasion to convince the boss to make the design change. When I had got out of the airplane after the spins, the blood that had migrated into my lower extremities from the repeated g-loads during the spin recoveries had not all made the journey back towards my head. I must have looked very pale. My boss had misjudged the reason why my face looked that way, but guessed correctly how the airplane behaved.

To keep cost down, the two ailerons, four flap segments, two elevators, and the rudder were the same part and could be fitted to any of the locations with minimal modification.

TESTIMONIAL

Sonja Englert learned to fly in gliders in Germany at 16 years old. She studied aeronautical engineering at the Technische Universität, Braunschweig, where she was a member of the Akaflieg Braunschweig for the duration of her studies. In the Akaflieg (Academical Flying Group) she helped build the SB13 flying wing glider and design the SB14 glider. She flew all of the Akaflieg's available prototypes including the SB13 and became national female cross-country soaring champion in 1992. She added motor glider and airplane ratings at that time and became a glider instructor. The Akaflieg also provided an opportunity for the first flight test experience.

After completing her studies in 1992 she worked for Dätwyler in Switzerland as structural engineer and test pilot. After the completion of this project, which involved some time in Malaysia, she moved to the USA in 1996 to work for Mod Works, designing and flight testing modifications including engine installations for small single and twin engined airplanes. In 2001 she joined Adam Aircraft in Denver, where she helped design the power plant installations for the twin-engine A500. Since 2003 she has been working for Columbia Aircraft (now Cessna), as engineer and DER test pilot on the development of the Columbia 350 and 400. She has flown more than 80 types of gliders and airplanes with about 4,000 hours of flight time, of which more than 670 flights were test flights. She is an active airplane homebuilder and has published four books on the subject.

Christian Schweizer was killed when the replica Second World War aircraft he was piloting crashed into the Swiss Alps in 1998.

Chapter 25

John Fergione left the F-16 program and accumulated 300 hours on the F-22. The two most 'enjoyable' aircraft he ever flew.

John Fergione – F-16 to the F-22 Raptor Engine Surrounded by a Cockpit

John Fergione conducted some of the most violent maneuver tests to date on the F-16 and later models in order to prove fighter compatibility.

The first introduction to the F-16 came in the spring of 1981. I was a Lieutenant Commander in the US Navy, and had just recently returned from a cruise aboard the USS *Eisenhower* in the Indian Ocean. During this voyage, Kevin Dwyer, a test pilot with General Dynamics, who I had met while I was stationed at the US Naval Air Test Center in Maryland, wrote a letter to me inquiring about my career desires when my commitment with the Navy was complete. I informed Kevin that I had intended to leave active duty and would like to be considered for an interview.

I returned to the USA just before Christmas in 1980. A short time later, I made arrangements with David Thigpen, the manager of flight operations for General Dynamics in Fort Worth, Texas, to come in for an interview. It all went much better than I had expected. In one day, I met and spoke with every pilot on the staff, there were seven of them at the time, was treated like royalty and given a visit to one of the newest F-16 airplanes being built at the facility.

I should note that, as a US Naval officer and pilot, I had very little familiarity with the Fighting Falcon prior to this date. In those days, the F-18 was the US Navy's choice over the F-16, and it wasn't even operational yet. The F-16 was also very new to the USAF inventory.

I remember my initial visit to the F-16 during my interview like it was yesterday. My first thoughts were its small size and gorgeous lines. In pilot terms, this was to me a truly sexy airplane.

It was beautiful, and just looked like an awesome machine, one huge awesome jet engine, surrounded by a tiny sleek airframe. Having recently been current on the A-7E, I was mostly impressed with the massive field of view it afforded from the cockpit, the comfort while sitting in the ejection seat and the simplicity of the cockpit controls. In retrospect, the latter was not good at all, but back then, all we were building were F-16As, and it was a pretty good improvement over the A-7E cockpit. We would make many enhancements in the cockpit over the coming years.

Shortly after my interview, while he drove me back to my hotel, I informed David that I wanted to work for him. Things happened fast after that. My termination date with the USN was May 31, 1981 and we agreed on a start date of July 1, 1981. I never knew just how much in love with an airplane I was going to become.

Shortly after beginning work, and while I was in training, I was scheduled in the back seat of a first company acceptance flight of an F-16B (Serial Number 82-0628) with David Palmer. The date was July 10, 1981. He gave me a chance to fly the airplane for a short time and I quickly adjusted to the side stick controller. The F-16 truly had some nice flying qualities and it was a delight to fly. Shortly after that, I was introduced to the 9g environment.

The maximum g, that I had ever seen so far was 7.3g. In other words, I had subjected my body to 7.3 times the normal force of gravity. I had felt this in both the T-38 and the A-7E but for only a really short time. Not only could the F-16 achieve 9g, it could sustain it. After this first 9g pull, I don't think I had ever felt worse in an airplane, lightheaded, somewhat ill and definitely nauseous. I recovered mostly after a few minutes and the flight was completed without further incident. I wondered, after this flight, and long talks with myself, if I ever wanted to revisit this environment again. My checkout flights began soon afterwards, and were completed in September 1981.

Checking out in the airplane was relatively easy. It had marvelous flying qualities and it was easy to be absolutely precise with it. As many of the engineers who designed the airplane transferred from Vought Aircraft in Grand Prairie, Texas, where the A-7s were built, there were many similarities between the F-16 and the A-7E. Learning the air-to-air capabilities of the airplane took some time, the rest came almost naturally.

I achieved another first for me on my fifth ever front seat flight in the F-16 which was, sadly, my check flight, and actually was a g-induced loss of consciousness. I was flying with David Thigpen, and I was proudly demonstrating the maneuvers required of the company acceptance profile for the new airplanes.

One of these maneuvers was, and is, a hard pull to the 'g-limiter'. This entails an acceleration to Mach 0.9, or above, followed by a full aft stick pull. If the airplane is behaving correctly, it should ramp up in g right into the serious 9g range. It will do this very quickly.

Pilots compensate for this high-g by physically 'straining' (tensing the abdominal muscles in order to tighten blood vessels so as to reduce blood pooling in the lower body). This had never been a problem for me in the past as the airplanes didn't attain these high g levels that quickly, and it was relatively easy for me to compensate for the g level I wanted.

At very high gs, pilots are warned that it may be too high by experiencing tunnel vision and 'grey-out', as the blood is pulled from the head. One's eyesight is the first sense to suffer and, when this happens, pilots generally know and are trained to relax with the pull. On that date, in the F-16, the g ramped up before I could even start to strain hard.

The F-16 is scheduled to remain in service with the USAF until 2025.

I never experienced tunnel vision, or grey-out and, simply stated, went right into black-out and total unconsciousness. Darkness. I...was...not...there.

I regained some consciousness in about 20 seconds, diving at the ground and felt lightheaded and disoriented. Full consciousness returned quickly and I informed Dave that I had just 'blacked out'. Dave, in his calm unemotional style, commented that he was wondering what I was doing. He was also chuckling a little. Needless to say, I gained a renewed healthy respect for the airplane and its true potential on that day.

My first real experimental test mission was with Fred 'Freddy' Haggard, the Operations Officer in the F-16 Combined Test Force on May 12, 1982. General Dynamics had modified a flight control computer with a single digital channel backed up by three normal analogue channels. The purpose of the test was to validate the digital technology in preparation for automatic 'hands off' terrain following and other capabilities that would come a few years later. I was the designated project pilot for General Dynamics for this test program. Fred would fly with me on this test as my flight time was pretty limited. The Air Force Flight Test Center had determined that this test was 'high risk'.

On the day of this test, a number of new engineers had arrived to monitor the flight control data while I flew the agreed procedures. During the taxi, the flight control engineers had noticed that the digital channel was not behaving properly but said nothing. Sure enough, as soon as the wheels lifted off the main runway on the takeoff roll, a caution light illuminated informing Freddy and me that we had a serious flight control problem. We quickly declared an emergency and I landed the airplane uneventfully and shortly thereafter. My first test mission in the F-16 was therefore, barely 10 minutes in duration, and culminated in an in-flight emergency. A baptism by fire and my career had officially begun.

From 1981 until 1985, I flew a number of F-16 test missions at Edwards AFB while permanently assigned to the Fort Worth pilot staff and I also conducted F-16 acceptance flights.

In 1983, I began flying the F-16XL, a new variant with a 'cranked arrow' wing. This was a fun time for me. I was traveling a lot, something I still enjoy doing; I was testing new fighter capabilities and, overall, I was enjoying every aspect of my job.

William B. 'Bland' Smith was the permanent F-16 test pilot assigned with General Dynamics in 1985. Bland wanted to return to Fort Worth with his family and I wanted to stay at Edwards and fly full time there. It was easy talking him into trading jobs. With the approval of Kevin Dwyer, the chief test pilot at the time, I gave Bland my return airline ticket and moved into his desk.

I received my next real trial on June 10, 1988. By this time, I was one of the most experienced test pilots at base and was flying some of the most demanding test flights the Air Force had to offer. High angle of attack is a term that makes all test pilots sit up and listen and I was flying a lot of this at that time.

The afternoon test was a preliminary data flight to gather 'baseline' data before the real test began. It is almost shameful that we had joked just that morning, at a pilot's party, about just how benign this test flight was going to be.

We had introduced the General Electric F-110 engine to the airplane. This engine provided significantly more thrust than the smaller Pratt & Whitney engines of the day, but required more airflow to achieve the benefits. General Dynamics had designed a larger inlet for this engine which changed the shape of the front of the airplane slightly. This was enough to warrant a high angle of attack envelope expansion testing.

The first flight of this configuration was a pretty benign one; even the airplane's center of gravity was placed at the mid-point, the aft limit being the worst case. My job was to conduct a standard set of intentional departures and document the airplane's response in preparation for testing. This would involve more critical loadings and more aft centers of gravity. The first departure was a 60 degree climb to 'zero' airspeed. Once out of airspeed, the airplane nose fell straight through, and the airplane accelerated. It was a self recovery.

The second departure was a 75 degree climb to zero airspeed. Again, the airplane nose dropped dramatically to a self recovering attitude but then it sliced left and the airplane entered a deep stall; a stall at a very high angle of attack, approximately 60 degrees, with large rolling and nose slicing motions. We recovered the airplane from this type of stall by 'rocking' the nose up and down (pitch rocking) in an attempt to get the nose of the airplane very nose down, to effect recovery. In this particular instance, the rocking was ineffective and the airplane remained in the stall while it fell towards the Earth at a high rate of descent in a nearly flat attitude.

I entered the departure at 40,000 feet. The airplane was equipped with a recovery parachute which was to be used at 25,000 feet to recover it if the pilot couldn't. The parachute was packed in a canister which was attached to the back of the airplane and, once deployed, would force the airplane's nose down regardless of what the airplane wanted to do. At 25,000 feet I was still not able to recover the airplane and I was directed by the higher body, to deploy the recovery parachute. For the first time ever in the F-16 test program, and since, the parachute failed to deploy. Hey, just my luck. I was left with an airplane which didn't want to fly, no parachute, no more trump cards and a mandatory ejection altitude rapidly approaching. Life looked pretty good.

With no other options available, I began rocking the nose again. Well, as luck would have it, the pitch rocking became more effective and eventually, I was able to push the nose over sufficiently enough to recover the airplane with barely 2,000 feet remaining before I would have to eject. Why not just say that I had a pretty good hangover the following morning after a night of serious celebration with friends. I was alive.

I have also ejected another time. I'm not proud. August 17, 1985. It was while I was operational in the A-7E flying off of the USS *Forrestal* in the Mediterranean Sea. My only engine decided to lose all of its oil and quit, leaving me in a jet which wasn't going to glide for very long; if at all. The A-7E flew very nicely with a good engine but even with the engine running, it was hard enough to land the airplane on an aircraft carrier. Without the engine, the carrier wouldn't even let me attempt it. So, I grabbed the ejection handle, the face curtain, and left the stricken airplane to crash. I watched it do this from my parachute. I ended up with the face curtain, a souvenir which lives on a wall in my kitchen today, some minor cuts which have healed, a scar on my right index finger which is still visible and a streak of grey hair in the middle of my forehead which is still present, though the grey has moved considerably further around the head since then.

I am convinced that I would have ejected from my F-16 had it not recovered from the stall in which I had placed it. I'm glad I didn't have to. The failure mode I had discovered on that June 1988 day doesn't exist any more. Our engineers designed a fix so that other pilots would not have to experience a harrowing ride such as this ever again.

The F-22 is characterized by a low-observable, highly maneuverable airframe.

Flying is generally described as hours and hours of pure enjoyment followed by a short amount of time experiencing pure terror. I can certainly attest to this description as being accurate. Easily, the joy and challenges I have faced and overcome during my flight testing career in the F-16 far outweigh the few bumps in the long road that I have experienced.

Perhaps some of the most difficult testing I have done was in the Advanced Fighter Technology Integrator (AFTI) F-16, testing an automatic Ground Collision Avoidance System (GCAS). As the title implies, this system was designed to prevent the airplane from flying into the ground with no pilot help. It also worked remarkably well and will, hopefully, serve as a precursor to similar systems in all airplanes in the future. Nonetheless, we had to test the capability and the only way to do this was to hurl yourself at the ground and just let go, letting the airplane recover itself. This was, and is, a totally unnatural act, something I do not look forward to ever doing again. I remember distinctly telling my control room, at the end of one of these more dangerous flights, that the best part of this mission was that I didn't have enough fuel to continue and would be landing soon.

TESTIMONIAL

John Fergione retired in January 2007, and had flown the F-16 for an astonishing 26 years. He had just over 3,400 hours in the F-16 with the majority of it being actively involved gathering flight test data. He left the F-16 Combined Test Force in November 2003 to join the F-22A Test Force as a F-22A experimental test pilot. Following his last flight in the F-22A on January 4, 2007, and having achieved 60,000 feet and more than Mach 1.7, he was able to accumulate almost 300 flight test hours in the F-22A.

Without question, he said, 'These are two of the most enjoyable airplanes I have ever had the opportunity to fly. Exceptional performance, the F-22A is significantly better than any F-16, and that's saying a lot, with a huge engines, and delightful flying qualities. The cockpits are comfortable and the F-22A's avionics system is unquestionably unsurpassed in the world.

'The field of view in the F-16 with its large bubble canopy gives a truly beautiful view of the world. I look forward to flying other new airplanes but will always look at the F-16 and the F-22 as the instruments which afforded me so many wonderful days and experiences.'

Chapter 26

After testing the Gnat, Philip Rajkumar was sent on deputation to the Iraqi Air Force as a Mig-21 fighter combat instructor for two years.

Philip Rajkumar – Gnat On a Roll.

Air Marshal Philip Rajkumar is one of the most experienced MiG-21 pilots in the world. He describes a system failure in the high-performance Gnat trainer.

I joined the Indian Air Force (IAF) in 1962 and flew de Havilland Vampires, French Ouragans, Mystere IV As and Russian MiG-21s for the first nine years, accumulating 1,600 hours in my log book. In 1972 I graduated as a test pilot from the French Test Pilots School (Ecole du Personnel Navigant d'Essais et de Reception or EPNER) at Istres, France and was posted to the IAF flight test centre at Bangalore. The IAF had its flight test centre at Bangalore airfield because India's only aircraft company, Hindustan Aeronautics Limited (HAL), owned the airfield and had its design bureau there. In 1975 I was assigned to be the project pilot for a flight trial in a Gnat fighter to prove some electronic warfare equipment developed in India. The trial was to take place at a base near New Delhi in north India and I had to ferry the aircraft there.

The Gnat was a small single-seat lightweight fighter designed and developed by the Folland Aircraft Company at Hamble in the UK. In the

1960s this aircraft was produced under licence at HAL, Bangalore. The chief designer of the aircraft was Ted Petter who had become famous as the designer of the English Electric Canberra medium bomber in the second half of the 1940s. The Gnat had a wing span of only 22 feet. The high wings had a sweep back of 40 degrees and the basic empty weight was only 4,600 lbs. The maximum all up weight was 8,700 lbs with full internal fuel of 1,590 lbs plus 2,500 lbs of external load. The power plant was a Bristol Siddeley Orpheus 701 turbojet which drew air through side mounted air intakes on the fuselage and produced 4,850 lbs sea level static thrust. The top speed was 620 knots at sea level and Mach 0.95 could be reached at 42,000 feet.

The aircraft had a hydraulically powered flight control system consisting of a powered slab tailplane and ailerons. The rudder was manually controlled. Petter had used some innovative features in his design to keep the weight down. When the tricycle undercarriage was lowered the ailerons drooped down by 22 degrees and acted like flaps (flaperons), though roll control was still available with differential movement of the flaperons. Partial lowering of the undercarriage provided the airbrake function. The 1,800 psi hydraulic system was powered by a single engine driven hydraulic pump and, in case of a hydraulic failure, reversion to manual control was possible.

The slab tail could be split by pulling a lever in the cockpit into a fixed electrically trimable tailplane and a manually operated elevator. The ailerons could be operated manually, though the roll control forces increased quite a bit.

In contrast the manual elevator had very light control forces and flying in manual was tricky because of this total lack of harmony between the roll and pitch axes. The standard emergency actions in case of hydraulic failure was to split the tail, put the hydraulic cock off and exhaust hydraulic pressure, trapped in the pressure lines, to the aileron power jacks by gently moving the ailerons. For some unknown reason these jacks were called servodynes.

Exhausting pressure in the servodynes took about 60 seconds depending on the amount of roll control being used after the hydraulic failure had occurred. Thereafter the undercarriage had to be lowered using an emergency hydraulic accumulator and a landing carried out in manual. The toe brake pedals on top of the rudder pedals had their own independent hydraulic supply sources and were not affected by the failure of the main hydraulic system. There were fairly severe crosswind limitations for landing in manual because of the high roll control forces. The aircraft was fitted with a lightweight ejection seat made especially for the aircraft by Follands.

On 2 August 1975 I had to check general aircraft serviceability of Gnat IE-1071 before the long ferry flight to Delhi. I didn't have very many flying hours on the Gnat, having only recently converted to the type. I, therefore, went across to the office of the deputy chief test pilot of HAL, Wing

Commander Tilak, the previous day and discussed Gnat emergencies with him. In particular we discussed emergency actions at length in case of a hydraulic failure. The monsoon was active over Bangalore with complete cloud cover starting at about 5,000 feet above ground level all the way up to 30,000 feet. The surface winds were about 15 knots gusting to 20 knots, but fortunately right down the westerly runway which was in use.

After start-up at about 10:00 in the morning, I taxied to the active runway, but did not feel happy about the way the stick (control column) was self-centring when left aileron was applied. This was a standard check carried out by all Gnat pilots because there had been more than one unexplained Gnat crash, where the aircraft had rolled into the ground immediately after getting airborne. The pilots had been killed.

There were no crash data recorders fitted in aircraft during those days, and meaningful investigations to arrive at the precise causes of the accidents were not possible.

The Courts of Inquiry had recommended that self-centring of the stick should have been checked at frequent intervals while taxiing to make sure both aileron sevodynes were in power before take-off. It was also found out by the Courts, after discussions with designers both in the UK and Bangalore, that when the ailerons were drooped (the configuration during take-off until the undercarriage was retracted and on final approach after the undercarriage was lowered) and one aileron reverted to manual, it would not be possible for the pilot to control the roll because of excessive control forces.

With these thoughts playing on my mind, I lined up for take-off and did a final self-centring check of the stick before reluctantly releasing the brakes.

The stick stayed stubbornly to the left extreme when I did the check. That was it and I decided to abort the sortie and return to the flight line. I reported the matter to the maintenance crew and my immediate superior, Wing Commander Babi Dey, who was an experienced Gnat pilot, having participated in Gnat development trials in the UK in the late 1950s.

In contrast to Babi's several hundred hours of experience on the Gnat, I had barely a dozen hours on the type. I felt his assessment of the problem and diagnosis would be valuable for rectifying the aircraft. Before the maintenance technicians started to investigate the problem Babi said he would like to start up the aircraft and check out the flying controls. So he went and checked out the controls thoroughly and said he could find nothing wrong with it. I asked him about the self-centring behaviour of the stick and he replied that he had found absolutely no evidence of the problem reported by me.

He then told me to go ahead and fly the routine air test I had planned. The sortie profile entailed a climb to 40,000 feet to check out the cabin pressurization, temperature control and cruise, fuel consumption in the clean configuration, as I had to ferry the aircraft without the 66 gallon drop tanks.

The IAF rarely ever flew the Gnat without drop tanks and these fuel consumption figures were not readily available. I thought it would be a good idea to collect some real flight test data.

It was around noon when I started up the aircraft for the second time that day and this time the aileron servodynes and the self centring mechanism of the stick behaved normally. I shut the hydraulic cock in the cockpit and reverted the ailerons to manual and reengaged power. Self-centring of the stick was normal and I became convinced that both servodynes were now functioning normally under hydraulic power.

I taxied out to the active runway all the while checking the self-centring behaviour of the stick, took-off and commenced a full throttle climb to 40,000 feet.

The clean Gnat could climb to that height in just four minutes from brake release which was pretty impressive for a non-afterburning aircraft, amazingly designed as a small craft in the mid-1950s. I came out of the overcast at about 30,000 feet and relaxed for a moment to look at the clear horizon, the blue sky above and white cloud cover below.

At that moment the control column jerked sharply to the left, and the aircraft had almost 90 degrees of bank in that direction, in an instant.

Even though I was in a climbing attitude the nose dropped quite a bit, quickly, and I lost about 300 to 400 feet of height in a moment. Fortunately, I did not enter the clouds. I rolled back to the wings level position, throttled back and discontinued the climb but I could feel that the ailerons were still in power. I realized that one of the ailerons might revert to manual at any moment. With one aileron in power and the other in manual I would have great difficulty in controlling the aircraft.

With complete cloud cover just below me, any roll control difficulties would make me lose height rapidly and plunge me back into the clouds. If that happened ejection was the only option. I felt that discretion was the better part of valour and decided to pre-empt a possible emergency. I selected the hydraulic cock-off, split the tail and started to exhaust hydraulic pressure to the servodynes by gently rolling the aircraft from side to side.

After a tense minute, I felt both the ailerons revert to manual with a reassuring jerk. With the hydraulic system inoperative the next action was to get the undercarriage down and locked using the emergency accumulator. I pulled the lever and waited for what seemed a long time, and then I had three green lights in the cockpit indicating that the wheels were down and locked. I could not do a very rapid descent through clouds because I was flying in manual with the wheels down and I had to respect the laid down speed limits.

I informed the Bangalore air traffic control that I was returning to base for a priority landing and asked about the surface winds. Fortunately for me the winds were still blowing down the runway in use though it was gusting up to 20 knots. I flew a long flattish approach and carried out my first and only landing in manual control up to that time on the Gnat.

Babi Dey was waiting for me when I switched off at the flight line. He started up the aircraft immediately after I got out. This time when he selected hydraulic power on he was able to see the self-centring behaviour of the stick which showed that the left servodyne was in manual while the right one was operating with hydraulic power. For the very first time in 17 years of Gnat operating experience in India, we had physical evidence available for proper investigation after a serious roll control malfunction had occurred in the air. HAL technicians removed the left and right servodynes and took them for strip examination to the hydraulic shop.

I went with them because I was overcome by curiosity. When the hydraulic filter fitted in the body of the left servodyne was removed we could see the filter element covered with a lot of black stuff, some of which was in the form of strands. The right servodyne filter also had the same stuff but, to a lesser extent. There was obviously a contaminating source in the aircraft's hydraulic system. Microscopic examination of the material found showed that it was probably paper or cardboard pieces. Chemical analysis revealed that the substance was mainly cellulose.

We went back to the aircraft in the hangar and opened out the hydraulic system and started to look for a common source which could contaminate both servodynes. The system had only one common hydraulic filter for both servodynes and was the probable suspect. When the metal housing of the filter element was opened we found that the filter cartridge made of cardboard and paper had burst and sent a lot of debris into the pressure lines connected to the servodynes.

At long last the mystery behind many unexplained rolling flight control problems in the Gnat was solved.

Remedial measures were instituted in the form of reduced shelf-life for filter elements and fairly frequent checks of the filter elements fitted in aircraft on the flight line in operational squadrons. There were no further incidents of this type in the Indian Air Force squadrons. When HAL modified the Gnat into the Ajeet fighter in the mid-1970s, the common hydraulic filter was replaced by two filters and an electric switch was provided in the cockpit which enabled the pilot to revert both ailerons to manual in an instant. There was no need to put the hydraulic cock-off and wait for up to a minute for reversion to occur.

As in all such incidents luck played a major role in letting me bring back the evidence of a flight control system malfunction. If the problem had occurred on take-off, or just after lift-off the aircraft would have rolled into the ground giving me little time to eject. Had it happened during the climb through the overcast I would have been disorientated and would have had to eject.

If it had happened when I broke cloud cover, I would have plunged back into the clouds with the very first sharp roll to the left.

Perhaps the most significant factor was my discussion with Wing Commander Tilak about emergency actions in case of hydraulic and control problems. The incident took place when I had an even chance of saving the aircraft, and I knew exactly how to handle the emergency. Dame Fortune smiled on me that day.

TESTIMONIAL

Philip Rajkumar was born in 1941, graduated with a science degree from the University of Mysore and entered the Indian Air Force Academy in 1961. He received his 'wings' as a fighter pilot in 1962. After serving in fighter squadrons for nine years he was sent to France in 1971 to be trained as an experimental test pilot at the French test pilots school (Ecole du Personnel Navigant d'Essais et de Reception, or EPNER) at Istres.

After returning to India in 1972, he spent 13 years at the Indian Air Force flight test centre (Aircraft and Systems Testing Establishment or ASTE) at Bangalore, becoming the chief test pilot in 1984 and commanding the centre in 1991. He participated in several Indian aircraft development programs with HAL, notably the Kiran Mk I and Mk 2 jet trainers; the Marut and Ajeet fighter and trainer versions, and the HPT-32 piston-engined basic trainer.

In between testing assignments Rajkumar commanded a MiG-21 squadron from 1978 to 1980, was sent on deputation to the Iraqi Air Force as a MiG-21 fighter combat instructor in 1981 for two years, and commanded a Jaguar base in 1988. From 1994, until his retirement from the IAF in 2001, he was the flight test program director of the Indian Light Combat Aircraft (LCA) program. He attained the rank of Air Marshal (three-star General) and flew 5,200 hours (including 2,100 hours on the MiG-21) on 74 types of aircraft.

Chapter 27

John Macready was holder of the world's altitude, distance and endurance flight records.

John A. Macready – LePere LUSAC 11
biplane
Coast to Coast

This story was written by a pilot. She is a pilot and a daughter. She is the daughter of an iconic test flyer from the 1920s. Quoting his log books, diary and notes, Sally, gives a 'first-hand', unique account from an air pioneer, John A. Macready.

During the 1920s, people thought the sky above 35,000 feet was a Stygian darkness, gloomy and hell-like; unknown.

In 1921, as the chief test pilot for the fledgling United States Air Service, I was proud to turn that belief into fiction. It was when I pushed my struggling open cockpit LUSAC (LePere United States Combat) 11 biplane up to 40,800 feet and brought back word, the sky suddenly became more approachable. The air at that height was brilliant, so bright it hurt my eyes, and when I mentioned this fact to Bausch Lomb, they asked me to design special aviator glasses to combat the glare. These would later become known as Ray Ban's Aviator Glasses.

In those days there was no high-tech, specially made, light-weight and toasty warm flight suit to ward off the chilling -80 degree Fahrenheit cold, just several suits of woolen underwear, over which I pulled on a one-piece heavy knit garment of wool, topped by an all-leather flying suit filled with down and feathers.   Several pairs of woolen socks, leather fur-lined moccasins, fur lined gloves and a leather head mask lined with fur, completed the outfit.

The thermometer was affixed to the wing strut outside the plane, and on the first altitude test flights the mercury went completely off the scale. A new thermometer was subsequently designed and installed, that could and did, record temperatures down below -80°. Prior these flights, engineers thought temperatures were the same at all altitudes.

I breathed oxygen straight into my mouth through a tube attached to a welder's flask. The tube occasionally froze up and on one such occasion, as I switched to the emergency flask, I had to pull my goggles off. Since there was no windshield, when I did this the icy blast from the propeller stung my eyes so much that the tears which formed started to freeze. I nearly lost my eyesight on that flight.

Unlike today, there was no way to filter moisture which sometimes froze right in the tubes and, on another flight, my main system did clog up, cutting off my oxygen supply. I hurriedly switched to my emergency bottle. I reached over and 'cracked' the emergency flask by opening the gas valve, and

John Macready set the solo altitude record of 34,509ft in this LePere LUSAC 11 in 1921.

started getting oxygen again. On landing, I mentioned this incident to a newspaper correspondent and the next morning saw, in a Cincinnati newspaper, that, 'At 39,000 feet altitude, Macready felt the need for oxygen, so he reached for his emergency oxygen flask, cracked it over his head, and then felt all right.' In so much as an oxygen flask weighs about 25 lbs and is made of steel, I figured I had a pretty hard head!

Besides the cold and lack of oxygen on these high altitude flights of the 1920s, I flew to altitudes where the pressure on my body varied from 14.7 psi on the ground, to 2 and 3 psi at altitudes above 35,000 feet. This was much worse than the lack of oxygen or the intense cold, and when I tried to explain what happened to the newspaper reporters, their headlines read: 'Macready to Explode for the Benefit of Science.' At the time, the general public thought my body would blow-up and pop like a balloon from the lack of pressure.

The lack of pressure had another fallout. On one particular flight the propeller spun around so fast in the thin air, it flew completely off the airplane. So the engineers, a creative bunch, built a new propeller, one with greater width and higher pitch, but on the first takeoff with this new type prop, on the tail-dragger plane, the tail went up and the nose went down and the prop just dug a big hole in the ground and the plane went nowhere.

During these six years of test flights, it was this first type turbo-super-charger that I was really testing, under orders from my colleague General Billy Mitchell. I held the altitude, endurance and distance flying records, simultaneously for several years, all certified by Orville Wright. All three of us were well-acquainted.

During World War II, when I was in North Africa, I was being checked out on the B-17, as I had been out of the military for awhile. The young Lieutenant asked if I knew anything about the turbo-supercharger? I was quiet for a moment, then said, 'Yes, Lieutenant, I believe I do'.

In the early 1920s when I first climbed into the atmosphere, it was all trial and error and very little 'research and development' money. But the military knew they needed a plane that could climb higher than those the Germans had manufactured in the Great War, and therefore the development of the turbo-supercharger was of the utmost importance.

(Many years later. Macready's daughter recounted that at a meeting at Beale AFB in California, three war veteran B-17 pilots described their bombing missions and how they were able to put 1,000 planes in the air, at one time. The pilots emphasized the fact that they could climb to 33,000 feet and therefore evade the enemy fighters because of the turbo-supercharger, tested and developed some twenty years earlier at McCook Field.)

There is one test honor I would just as soon not have, which was making the first night parachute jump. Parachutes were definitely in the testing stage and not at all reliable. A last resort for the pilot.

It came on a experimental night flight from Dayton to Columbus in 1924. I used flashing beacons along the route to mark the course. The outbound leg was uneventful. It was when I arrived over Dayton on the return flight that the engine quit. My main thought, after fruitless efforts to get the engine started, again, was to head the plane away from populated areas, so I turned toward the Dayton Country Club where there were few homes. Dropping two flares, which failed to ignite, I climbed over the side of the airplane, keeping my hand on the stick to guide the plane, as long as I could, then jumped out.

After waiting the required seconds, I pulled the ring and miraculously the parachute opened and as I floated down in the night sky, I kept yelling: 'Help! Help! Anyone down there?' But, there was no answer. A few moments later a deafening crash reverberated across the sky as the plane plunged to earth on the far horizon, exploding on impact and sending flames high into the air. I yelled again. Still no answer.

I had actually landed on the country club estate of Mr. C. E. Ainsworth. At the time, the Ainsworth's were hosting a convivial dinner party with the usual libations and the guests were about to move out onto the terrace in order to enjoy their brandy.

They had been having a heated discussion about the Bible, and most particularly the *Book of Revelations,* when a mysterious light floated slowly through the night and passed out of sight. They didn't know it, of course, but it was one of my flares which had finally ignited. Moments later they heard the crash of the plane hitting the ground, accompanied by a loud explosion. This was followed by a strange sepulchral voice calling for help, which floated down to them from 'the heavens'. It was just too much. They froze in their seats. One of the men said later that, although he was a student of the Bible, he did not really believe in the ultimate chapter until that very moment, 'When the Angel Gabriel was calling for help from the heavens above as the earth was going up in flames'.

They finally pulled themselves together and I was rescued, dangling from a tree by my parachute on the edge of a ravine.

Meanwhile, Oakley G. Kelly, a fellow pilot at McCook field and I, were making plans for the first non-stop flight across the USA. Although several pilots had attempted this, no-one had succeeded, until May 1923.

We chose the Fokker T-2 for its reliable Liberty engine and the fact that it could be reconfigured to carry enough extra fuel to make the 2,700 mile flight. The thick-winged monoplane would normally carry 180 gallons of petrol, enough for about six hours of flight. But because the flight would be at least 30 hours, we installed an extra 410 gallon tank, along with a 40 gallon oil tank and a ten gallon reserve water tank, a booster radiator, and an oil radiator.

A second set of controls was welded inside the cabin near a door close to the third window which was where the rear pilot sat, at the ready, to relieve the forward pilot. We planned to take six hour shifts. The pilot sat out in the elements eight inches from the exhaust stack. The absolute ceiling of the airplane with 11,000 lb total load was…the ground.

When we took off, we had only 150 lbs to spare with a 10,850 lb load. There were maps to collect and most important of all, besides enough fuel, was the weather, so we haunted the US Weather Bureau.

Since the prevailing winds are from west to east across the United States, we planned our flight from San Diego, California, to Long Island, New York. We made some reconnaissance flights over the more mountainous country we would have to traverse out west.

As it happened, on the first try in October 1922, we only got as far as the Tehachapi Mountains on the east side of California…the low clouds and fog made it impossible for the heavily loaded plane to climb out of the weather and over the mountains, so we returned to San Diego and proceeded to make a record endurance flight.

Not to be deterred, at daybreak on November 3, 1922, with a favorable weather forecast, we took off for a second attempt. This time we were prepared with a well-stocked supply of chicken sandwiches, hot soup and coffee for the long flight. As the country around Tucson, Arizona, was approached, it became a continuous struggle, with the climb practically

United States Army Air Service Fokker T-2 flown by Lieutenant John A. Macready and Lieutenant Oakley G. Kelly.

hitting the absolute ceiling of the airplane in order to cross over the big passes, mountains and elevations. The atmosphere was very rough and bumpy with numerous air currents, which would raise the airplane 100 feet or more at times, then let it down quickly. Many times it seemed that the T-2 would not be able to get over these high plateau areas. For long periods, we flew within 40 or 50 feet of the surface of the ground. It was a period of considerable stress.

A short distance beyond Terra Haute, Indiana, Kelly passed back a handwritten note, explaining that a forced landing seemed probable because of the rapidly decreasing water supply due to cracked cylinder jackets on the engine. 'Mac, another cylinder has burst. Lucky if we get to Dayton,' he wrote. There was no other way for us to communicate except passing notes through a tube.

We changed front seats at this point. I immediately observed, when taking the front control seat, that conditions were extremely bad. The water was shooting from both sides of the engine in small streams. The loss of water was so great that it was almost immediately assessed that a forced landing would be necessary.

About 50 miles from Indianapolis the temperature began to rise rapidly and I turned back on course to a field which had previously been observed, with the intention of landing. Kelly, in the rear, had been pouring all the drinking water, coffee, consommé and all other liquids in the radiator, and with these additions, the airplane was flown to the Indianapolis Speedway where we landed. The newspaper headline the next day read: 'Transcontinental Flyers Make Flight On Soup'. We had failed again.

The third, and successful, attempt was in the opposite direction, from Long Island, New York to San Diego, California. This was again a weather decision. Once a year there is a weather phenomena that comes down from Canada called a Hudson Bay High, during which period the winds reverse and blow from the east to the west. It was decided to reverse the order of the flight so as to minimize the early encounter of high mountainous terrain when our load was the heaviest.

The first attempt at takeoff using this route, however, was another failure. After rolling at top speed for almost a mile over the ground, the huge, heavy transport displayed no sign of rising into the air and had we continued we would have crashed into the wires and trees ahead. The T-2 was taxied to another position and with the nose of the plane pointed toward the hangars two miles ahead on the adjacent field a few feet below, we again waved goodbye to the group of anxious spectators, and the plane lumbered heavily across the ground, gathering speed and momentum as we went.

The big monoplane bounced and bounced, but did not rise. It was still on the ground when we came to the 20 foot drop-off from Roosevelt to

Hazelhurst Field. When we came to the drop-off, I wondered whether we would go over the ledge and settle down to the ground. Over we went and settled down, but not quite to the earth. The T-2 was flying, but without any apparent climb, and the big hangars were straight ahead. The people at the takeoff said we flopped over them and went down out of sight on the other side. From there they started to run to pick-up the pieces.

The heavily loaded plane could hardly maintain itself in level flight. For 20 minutes over Long Island our climb was hardly appreciable. In fact for the first few miles we only barely cleared the poles and wires.

Our only instruments were a magnetic compass, an altimeter and an airspeed indicator; navigation was by section lines, railroad tracks, highways, cities and lakes or rivers, the smoke from bonfires for the wind direction, but at night it was a different story.

We arrived at Dayton about dusk and I took over. Across the Mid-West the weather closed in and heavy clouds cut off the moonlight. Shortly after leaving Terre Haute, Indiana, I noticed a dim flicker of light on the propeller in front. The faint flicker seemed to come regularly, and grow stronger. Then a little later when we were 70 or 80 miles from Belleville, Illinois, a mysterious shaft or beam of whiteness, apparently coming from some far distant point, broke through the black clouds and mist ahead and swung from side to side across the sky in front of the T-2.

Shortly after, we could see where the light was coming from, and headed in that direction. Sure enough, it was our fellow aviators at Scott Field who had rigged up a searchlight on top of the hangar to guide our way through the storm swept night. That was a very welcome sight, because we then knew we were on course. We passed over Belleville where we knew our friends below were hoping for the success of the attempt. It was an oasis in the desert. They threw the light on the T-2 as we shot out of the blackness south of St Louis, toward the foothills of the northern Ozark Mountains. Then the night closed in around us again; the drizzle was continuous. We had to fly within only 400 to 500 feet of the ground in darkness, mist and low clouds. This period was a very trying one during the transcontinental flight...in fact, the most trying of all for me.

The T-2's engine droned on steadily through the long night, but a little after midnight we suddenly came out from under the dark, dismal clouds into the bright moonlight. As we flew over Tucumcari, New Mexico, we could see the little square cubes of earth below and, as the sky got lighter we realized they were the adobe huts of the Indians.

While we approached St Johns, Arizona, the ground seemed to come up faster than the plane could climb; we were very close to the ground and the T-2 was at its utmost elevation. Our maps had shown the country in this vicinity to be about 8,000 feet, but our altimeter registered 10,000 feet which was correct because it was an area that had not been surveyed. We had to change our course and fly to the south, but even this proved hazardous as we had to cross what, at first, we thought were lava beds but actually proved to be a dense forest and the T-2 had to fly for 75 or 80 miles just above the tops of the trees to get to the valley on the other side.

Crossing the Imperial Valley, the T-2 was at 8,000 feet and we could see San Diego in the distance. As the wish was to reach Rockwell Field and land in less than 27 hours from takeoff, we contemplated no flourishes over the city and besides, we were just about empty with only the last fumes of petrol.

Diving down from 8,000 feet with power on, we reached San Diego, cocked the T-2 up on the wing to swing down the Main Street, and passed about 100 feet above the tops of the buildings. We learned afterward that thousands of people were standing on rooftops and in the streets, waving sheets, blankets, throwing their hats up in the air, amid car horns blowing, ships in the harbor sounding their horns, fire engines screaming. Everyone was excited but Kelly and I. We had been working in grease and dirt, without rest, for such a long time previous to the flight that we had not had an opportunity to think about it from the standpoint of an accomplished fact.

We had just successfully completed the first non-stop flight across the USA. The flight took 27 hours 50 minutes and we averaged 92 mph.

To deal with the extreme sub-zero temperatures Macready wore several suits of woolen underwear topped by an all-leather flying suit filled with down.

TESTIMONIAL

John A. Macready was the second of three sons born to Benjamin Macready and Mattie DeLaHunt Beck Macready. He was born in San Diego, California. The family later moved to Searchlight (near Las Vegas) Nevada, where his father at one time owned the largest producing gold mine in the state. John graduated from Stanford University and worked in the gold mines during summer. He and partner Jim Cashman owned and operated the first freight line between Arizona and Nevada for the shipment of ore.

In 1919 Macready joined the fledgling US Air Service and, in 1920, he was promoted to chief test pilot and as such, did all the in-flight testing of the turbo-supercharger, reaching a world altitude record of 40,800 feet in the open cockpit LePere Biplane. During this period he held the world altitude, endurance and distance record; made the first non-stop flight across the USA; became the first crop duster; flew the first aerial photographic survey of America, and managed to develop the Ray Ban Aviator sunglasses.

He was the only three-time winner of the Mackay Trophy; awarded the Croix de Guerre with Palm (France); enshrined in the Aviation Hall of Fame, Dayton, Ohio, and the International Aerospace Hall of Fame, San Diego, California. His daughter (and supplier of the original article), Sally M. Wallace, is also a pilot, holding private, instrument, multi-engine and borate bomber ratings. She is an active lecturer in the USA about her father, has written a book, and in 2003, re-created her father's non-stop flight, in a Piper Aztec in 17 hours, New York to California.

Chapter 28

Justin Paines as he hands over to Flight Lieutenant Terry Parker.

Justin Paines – XW175 – The VAAC Harrier
Stalwart of STOVL

Development of the revolutionary STOVL flight control concepts was not particularly straightforward, explains RAF test pilot Justin Paines.

It's funny, but a lot of people who have heard of the VAAC (pronounced with a hard 'a' like 'vark'), haven't the first idea what it stands for. Indeed, the acronym is a little contrived. But it's nevertheless a name people recognize. With all the aircraft has achieved, it's perhaps not surprising.

The Vectored-thrust Aircraft Advanced flight Control (VAAC) had its origins in the earliest days of electronic flight control research at the Royal Aircraft Establishment, Bedford, UK. In those days, they called it Active Control Technology, before phrases like fly-by-wire became more commonplace. Prior to becoming the VAAC, Harrier airframe XW175 was actually the second-ever two-seat Harrier constructed, one of two 'Development Batch' prototypes build at Hawker-Siddeley's Dunsfold factory in 1969. The sister aircraft to XW 175 crashed on Salisbury Plain training area shortly after it first flew, which makes the VAAC undoubtedly the oldest flying Harrier in 2008, as she approaches retirement this year.

I had the good fortune to be closely involved in the VAAC, and all the research she performed from 1996 onwards, based at Boscombe Down in Wiltshire, UK, about 100 miles south-west of London. I'd like to think that the bulk of the aircraft's contribution to aeronautical research has come on since that time, but that would not be easy to argue. During her time at RAE Bedford, VAAC had pioneered early research into Head-Up Displays, the famous ski-jump launch, nozzle nudge control, Microwave Airborne Digital Guidance Equipment and many other things which were incorporated into the Sea Harrier. Of course, the Sea Harrier's finest hour came in the Falklands conflict of 1982, which established the Harrier in British aviation mythology, second only perhaps to the Spitfire.

But it was in 1996 that the VAAC Harrier emerged from an extended modification programme which had given it full authority 'active' (fly-by-wire) control in all axes, with integrated thrust, and

The VAAC pioneered early research into the famous ski-jump launch.

thrust-vector control. The key to the VAAC as a research tool, however, as in other, so-called 'variable stability' aircraft, is that the experimental, digital flight control is effected only from one cockpit (the aft cockpit) leaving the aircraft captain with conventional Harrier mechanical flight controls. By ensuring the safety of the aircraft in this way, the experimental flight controls did not have to be tested to normal safety-critical standards, but could instead be developed and prototyped rapidly, allowing extremely fast research progress.

Where this aircraft is really different from other 'variable stability' research aircraft, is in the dangerous nature of the flight regime of interest for this line of research, namely, the semi-jet-borne region between about 30 and 150 knots.

In the semi-jet-borne region very large trim changes occur with power and speed, the aircraft is neutrally stable longitudinally and unstable directionally, but with a strong dihedral component at moderate angles of attack and above. Very little excess lift performance is available from either engine or wing and, without going into too much detail, disaster lurks for any Harrier pilot that does not fly plumb down the middle of this dangerous regime. Stray towards the boundaries of sideslip, bank or angle of attack, and you may not recover. Harrier pilots are not, therefore, accustomed to experimenting with the semi-jet-borne flight envelope.

Safety of the VAAC, when it was being flown from the rear cockpit with simplex, untested flight control software, was assured not only by the skill of the safety pilot, but also by a monitoring computer called the Independent Monitor which, among other things, monitored for exceedance of various flight envelope limitations. These limits were designed to allow safe recovery from the worst possible flight control upset at the worst possible time, while leaving a sufficiently wide envelope so as not to prevent sensible experimentation in flying qualities.

As a new graduate of the USAF Test Pilot School (on exchange from the UK), testing and clearing the IM was my first real job. Of course, it was a two-pilot job and my deputy, Paul Stone, was also the Sea Harrier (or 'Shar') project pilot and often away on 'Shar' business. I was, therefore, in the habit of pressing often-unhappy colleagues from the Fast Jet Test Squadron at

Boscombe Down into the rear cockpit to assist me with these clearance flights.

One of the most reluctant participants was my good friend Johnny Lawson. Johnny, was an acerbic fellow at the best of times, and on this occasion we were looking at lateral control run-aways at around 80 Knots Indicated Air Speed (KIAS). Given the

The first automatic ship landing by a STOVL aircraft was achieved during a test on HMS Invincible.

dangers of the semi-jet-borne regime, this did not please him at all. Flying in the rear, experimental cockpit, Johnny would make progressively larger flight control inputs, and then wait for me to take control and effect a safe recovery. By doing this in a controlled and progressive manner, we would be able to ascertain whether the current flight envelope limits, at which the IM would intercede, were safe enough, or needed redesign.

Because of the lack of available lift at 80 knots, any large bank angle was likely to give rise to a rapid acceleration towards the ground and a very fast build-up in sideslip, which could cause the aircraft to depart from controlled flight. Careful coordination of controls would be required to recover from any large bank angle upsets. I remember Johnny referring to it as, 'falling off the bubble'.

And so it was, that at about 1,500 feet (engine thrust would allow no higher) and 80 knots, Johnny was in the rear cockpit, making what he saw as senseless lateral control inputs (moving the centre-stick to the left or right), relying on my wherewithal to take control, pick up the wing and recover to level flight. One quarter aileron in...aircraft rolls...Independent Monitor limit gently reached...I recover without problem. One half stick input from the back, a slightly faster roll rate but no great overshoot in bank angle. Three quarters stick and 'WHOA!' – an unexpectedly large bank angle overshoot ensued.

Well, the recovery was without issue with properly coordinated rudder and aileron inputs but for Johnny, the 40 degrees of bank reached was quite enough and he categorically refused to continue the sortie.

Suffice it to say that after some refinement and further testing, I was able to bully Johnny back into the cockpit and soon the aircraft was cleared for use as a flight control research aircraft.

The VAAC was always manned by a 'can-do' team. In fact it was a 'can-do-it-yourself team'. We never had any help, it seemed, we were the Cinderella programme, with ugly sisters like Tornado and Jaguar getting all the glory. No giant test team with one man for each job here. It was a small test team with several jobs for each man. But really, I think we liked it that way. It meant no one else, including our lords and masters, really knew what we were doing!

As a result we made rapid progress in developing a revolutionary form of flight control for Short Take-Off Vertical Landing (STOVL) aircraft. But the nature of pilots is to defend and believe in what we know. Pilots are very conservative – drastic change is not normally on the agenda. So when radically different concepts were introduced into the cloistered and hallowed halls of STOVL pilotage it was not going to be easy. In fact, very emotive arguments began to develop between those who favoured Harrier-style flight control and those who saw the advantages of the VAAC's innovative approach.

It was very good for us as a test team, because it taught us the discipline of absolutely objective handling qualities research, where results would be robust enough to withstand any probing. It also led us to the need to perform a back-to-back evaluation of the various STOVL flight control concepts in the most demanding and testing of environments, the graduation exercise if you like, namely, on board ship with a pitching, rolling deck.

In November 2000, we were privileged to conduct an embarked trial, evaluating the flying qualities of the advanced control concepts on board HMS *Invincible*. For the evaluations we needed special markings on the deck to assist the test pilots in their assessments. How were we to achieve this? You don't just wander out, paint brush in hand, and start defacing one of Her Majesty's capital ships. So, with trepidation, we approached the Captain.

'Oh yes, no problem,' he said, as we made our way out of Portsmouth Harbour, 'My man will show you the paint store.' So, with the Captain's permission, as the VAAC was airborne on its flight out to the ship from Boscombe Down, there we were: pilots, flight test engineers, even the US programme office representatives, paint-brushes in hand, throwing paint across the deck of one of Her Majesty's aircraft carriers.

Landing during the test on HMS Invincible.

Nevertheless, a landmark evaluation was successfully carried out onboard HMS *Invincible*. It ultimately led to the adoption for the F-35B Lightning II of the radical STOVL flight control strategy which we had been developing.

Another of VAAC's endearing qualities was the aircraft and team's tremendous capacity for, 'down-to-the-wire last-minuters'. It seems inevitable that only days before some big test programme, everything would be falling apart, inexplicably not working or, mostly, just not ready yet.

This occurred most dramatically in early 2005. For over a year, VAAC team engineers had been developing an 'autoland' system, a guidance device that would allow the aircraft to land itself on a moving aircraft carrier without any help from the pilot. Just weeks before we were due to embark onboard HMS *Invincible*, and with no sign of any of the autoland equipment working, the Harrier's engine suffered a minor issue and needed to be changed.

The hangar team worked tirelessly, and the engine was changed in record time. But that only put us in a position to start development of the autoland technology with just a few weeks to go before we were due to embark on HMS *Invincible*.

We were given a two week period on board, and they were the only two weeks available. The trouble with experimental, ground-breaking guidance and navigation equipment is that it never works first time, or second time, or third time, fourth, fifth, sixth…

In fact, we never got it working on one single occasion before we were due to pack up the VAAC and fly out to HMS *Invincible*. Not once. So, should we nevertheless embark, continue working on the autoland system and risk wasting two weeks of HMS *Invincible*'s valuable time? Or, should we cancel the embarkation and admit defeat?

Well, the Ministry of Defence wanted us to go, so we went. The boffins worked away on their software, finding and fixing one problem after another. We were able to do some other, related, flight control testing early in the first week on the ship, giving the scientists a little more time. And then we were ready to have another go with the autoland system.

But, embarrassingly, it still didn't work, with the aircraft swaying like a drunken sailor in the hover alongside HMS *Invincible*, when it should have been gently setting itself down on the deck. But the scientists were up-beat, 'We've found the problem in the software,' they said. What they meant, of course, was that they had found one problem in the software, but not the only one. The next day we went shooting past the ship, under the careful direction of the autoland system, without even stopping. Not good.

But despite all the furrowed brows, the long working days began to pay off. Problems were found and fixed and, on 15 May 2005, Chris Gotke and I piloted the VAAC (or should I say, the VAAC piloted herself with us in it) for an automatically guided recovery to a precision touchdown on the deck, within a few inches of the target location, all at the press of a button.

'No problem!' We all shouted in glee. But it had not seemed that way a week earlier. Nevertheless, the old girl had pulled it off at the eleventh hour once again.

Refinements made to the control concept using VAAC since 2002 continue to influence the Joint Strike Fighter control law design. But the significance of the work done belies the lack of high-level support for the VAAC project, the do-it-yourself test team, and the last minute triumphs, in a most characteristically British way. The VAAC aircraft will be in a museum soon, for a well-earned rest. The test team likewise should be in a museum soon, but are hoping to postpone that eventuality a few more years.

Justin Paines with passenger John Farley, the pioneer of Harrier test flying in the 1960s. (see Chapter 2)

TESTIMONIAL

Justin Paines joined the RAF in 1988, serving on the front line with No. 1 (Fighter) Squadron, flying Harrier GR3, 5 and 7. His front-line experience included working with 1 Squadron as the first RAF night electro-optical combat ready squadron, the first operational evaluation of the Harrier GR7 family on HMS *Illustrious*, and peacekeeping duties in northern Iraq. In 1995 he attended USAF Test Pilot School on exchange, graduating as top in the class; before serving for three years as a test pilot at Boscombe Down, where he was project pilot for the experimental VAAC Harrier programme. He was selected as the UK military test pilot to fly the X-35 Joint Strike Fighter Concept Development aircraft, from 1999 to 2001, before returning as a Fixed Wing Tutor at the Empire Test Pilots School. He left the RAF in 2004, joining QinetiQ as a test pilot, where he flies the VAAC Harrier in support of JSF technology development.

Chapter 29

John Knebel was among the first military pilots to check out in the first production jet fighter, the P-80.

John Knebel – Convair F-102
Seek and Destroy…Oneself?

John Knebel, Convair chief engineering test pilot, who did early VTOL testing, recalls the unexpected ending of an early rocket firing test in an F-102 Delta Wing Interceptor.

I was anticipating a day with a bit of excitement as I enjoyed winding down the mountain from Cloudcroft to Holloman Air Force Base in my new homemade sports car in September 1955. The car was a Glasspar G-2, which I had just completed in San Diego before driving it to New Mexico to participate in the armament testing of the Experimental Convair F-102 Dagger.

My wife and I had found a comfortable cabin up in the mountain resort town of Cloudcroft, high above the scorching desert around Alamagorda, the town nearest Convair's test installation at Holloman AFB and the White Sands Rocket Test Range over which we were conducting our rocket firing tests. The 30 mile commute was fun in a car well-suited for this kind of mountain driving.

I was on assignment to Holloman for the F-102 armament testing during a lull in test programs at the San Diego Aircraft Factory where the F-102 was built.

The XFY-1-VTOL, (Pogo Program) was on hold while we built an oil rig tower suspension system for Chuck Meyers and myself to learn to fly the Pogo in a rig, without wrecking it. The powers that be had decided to postpone my training there, in our haste and concern to get the XFY-1, (Salmon) going, which never did a VTOL flight.

The other flight test programs on which I was doing test work in San Diego were busy without me: the R3Y Tradewind Flying Boat was in a redesign phase; the F-102 at Edwards Air Force Base was fully staffed, and the 6 to 10 engine B-36 Bomber reconfiguration at San Diego, on which I had flown forty hours, plus un-refueled max endurance flights at Fort Worth, had been completed. I was now on loan to the Convair armament test detachment at Holloman AFB to help complete F-102 rocket testing.

The airplane I was to work with, was on the first phase of its armament firing test. This was Convair's answer to the US Air Force's competition in 1950 for a complete interceptor, fire control system, in a single seat super-sonic fighter plane. This was during the fears prevalent in the Cold War days, after Russia had developed the atomic bomb, when citizens were building bomb shelters and bombing attack survival drills were being encouraged. This plane was intended to intercept large bombers flying the North Pole and Arctic route from Russia over the North American continent carrying nuclear bombs. It had to be fast enough, and carry firepower deadly enough, to find and destroy these bombers in any kind of weather before they could reach our major cities and destroy them. Some Air Force officers in the Pentagon originally wanted it to be a Mach 2 airplane. A few of them even envisioned it as a pilot-less aircraft – half a century ago!

Convair won the competition on September 11, 1951, with a proposal for the F-102 that was basically a 1.22:1 scaled up version of the XF-92A Delta Wing Research Aircraft, built and tested by Convair in 1948.

The Delta platform had been researched in Germany by Dr Alexander Lippisch in gliders during the war, but the XF-92A was the first powered delta wing aircraft to fly.

The F-102A had a troubled development history. It was initially expected to be a Mach 2 machine using the Wright J-67 engine. The J-67 was to be a British Armstrong Siddeley Sapphire engine built in the USA under license. But, the Pratt & Whitney J-57 was substituted as the power plant when the J-67 was not produced due to time schedules. Since the Pratt & Whitney engine produced only about two-thirds as much thrust as had been predicted for the J-67 engine, the F-102 airframe design was almost 2,000 pounds heavier than it needed to be for the new J-57 Mach 1.2 machine.

When the XF-102, was first flown on October 23, 1953, it was soon understood that it was incapable of reaching supersonic speed in level flight, an absolute requirement of the contract. The program was saved when Convair was quickly able to build a lighter, longer version using the Whitcomb area rule with a thinner wing.

Richard T. Whitcomb was an aeronautical scientist working for the National Advisory Committee for Aeronautics (NACA), the forerunner of NASA. He had been doing research on supersonic flight, and after ten years of studying transonic drag rise, postulated his theory in 1953. He said that an airplane designed to go supersonic should have a total cross-sectional area that increased from a long pointed nose, and then maintained the cross-sectional area continuously all the way to the aircraft's tail. Any attachments, such as the wing, had to be compensated by an accompanying reduction of cross-section.

Convair, in desperation, built a lightened 'wasp-waisted' fuselage F-102A. This gave the original fat fuselage a 'coke bottle' effect, the curvature of which was popularized in the aviation community as the 'Marilyn Monroe' look. So naturally the newspapers were playing up our new curvaceous airplane with that name.

During the development time for the F-102, several of the early performance deficient planes were turned over to Hughes Aircraft, who had the contract to provide the MG-10 weapons control system on the F-102. This system was to enable the F-102 to locate and destroy an enemy bomber at supersonic speed in all weather conditions, day or night. It took over control of the aircraft and automatically opened the armament bay doors, signaled the Falcon (GAR) missiles to sling down on their launching rails into the air stream clear of the airplane's structure, and fired the rocket motors, sending them on their guided way.

The guided missiles that Hughes were building used two types of guidance. The AIM-4F was an infrared heat-seeking missile which was attracted to its target by the radiated heat energy of the target's engine exhaust.

The other guidance system used radar sensing, which honed in on its target using signals generated by picking up reflected radar waves between the target aircraft and the F-102 radar system.

In addition to these six guided missiles, which were the primary target killers, the F-102A was also armed with 24 attached 2.75 inch folding-fin unguided rockets, which were carried in the weapons bay doors. The F-102 was the first Air Force fighter designed without guns aboard. We were now finishing the firing tests of this 24 rocket package, preparatory to entering the guided missile firing phase. This improved fuselage fineness ratio, with its pointed nose and wasp waist, was the beautiful new fighter plane on which we were now testing the armament. And the aircraft was finally meeting its speed requirement of Mach 1.2.

The previous day had been a discouraging one. My F-102 had been armed with a full load of 24 of the 2.75 folding-fin, 'Mighty Mite' rockets for our first attempt at a salvo firing of all 24. Higher priority military tests had preempted our time on the range, which required us to have the base armament people remove the rockets from my aircraft. We had been assured by Range Control that we would be rescheduled and I was looking forward to flying the test that day.

Upon arrival at my office, I learned that we were still waiting for a range time, which needed to be far enough in advance for us to get the base armament personnel to load the rockets with sufficient time for us to complete our flight test instrumentation checkouts and hopefully arrange for an Air Force photo chase plane to document the test firing patterns. Time dragged on until late afternoon and we had almost given up the operation for that day when we received the go ahead. The armament crew surprised us by promptly loading the rockets and our test instrumentation checked out. We couldn't get a photo chase plane for our assigned range time so we elected to go without; a decision I was later to regret.

After the usual radio contacts with the Holloman tower and the range safety officer, I was cleared for engine start, taxi and takeoff. The flight progressed routinely and although previous tests of selective firings of rocket packages had gone well, I was excited to be doing the first salvo of all 24 rockets in automatic sequence. It was the whole works!

Our aircraft was the first to be purchased by the USAF as a one-man, radar interceptor fighter, following the decision not to carry guns and to be armed only with missiles. The 24 unguided missiles were also carried internally in an unusual in-line arrangement in tubes within the missile bay doors that opened for firing and to release the large missiles carried in the internal missile bay. The most destructive of these was to be a nuclear-headed one.

Memories of previous firings flitted through my mind as I entered the range corridor awaiting the Range Control Officer's clearance for my firing run. I was on the right test speed, at the right altitude, had been cleared for my run, and was relieved that the most troublesome part of any flight, getting everything working at the same time and been given the 'clear to go', was behind me.

Now, all I had to do was turn on cameras and instrumentation; arm the rocket launching system, and push the firing button on the control stick.

All hell broke loose when I did! The airplane jumped and the cockpit pressurisation fluctuated as I witnessed the various warning lights that immediately sprang to life and began to flash across the flight deck.

The expected spectacular smoke trail of the rockets I had fired did not appear ahead of me.

Had the engine failed? No, it had rolled back only to idle, I hoped, as I retarded the power level to that position. I now recognized that one of my two hydraulic flight control systems had lost pressure but the other seemed to be holding. I called out a 'May Day' while trying to gather my wits about me so that I could analyze the situation. Why hadn't I held out for the chase plane?

I very gingerly (minimizing control inputs until sure of my remaining hydraulic system's condition) headed my crippled bird toward 'High Key for Holloman' (the point from which a jet pilot executes a flameout landing if an airport is within reach). I told the tower of my intentions, notified my flight test people and tried to analyze my choices. I knew that one of my two hydraulic systems was gone, the F-102 had a redundant irreversible control system; but if both were out the aircraft was uncontrollable. I also realized that my remaining system may have been damaged and could be slowly leaking out all of its fluid, in which case I must eject. In addition, that was the system that lowered the landing gear.

If any of the lines leading to the three landing gears had been taken out I would lose control upon actuating the gear. This meant that I needed to consider extending it early in the pattern while shooting my flame-out approach to landing to give me more time to eject and insure enough altitude for my parachute to deploy.

The few times that I have been faced with leaving a crippled, but still flyable aircraft (luckily I never had to) I found it to be a very difficult decision to make. In such cases, as in this one, the cockpit was intact and a much more comfortable environment to be in than what's outside.

Also, in the mid-1950s our ejection seats were still propelled by explosive cartridges which, unlike later rocket systems, hit you in the butt so hard that sometimes pilots suffered major spinal injury. I made a decision to kick out the gear fairly high and accept the greater sink rate, because of its added drag, to give me that altitude and time to eject, if that action took out the remaining hydraulic system. Luck was with me, the gears came down, the system held, and I made an uneventful landing from that point on.

The reliable old iron Pratt and Whitney J-57 engine gave enough thrust at idle that I was able to taxi back to the Convair ramp, fire trucks and ambulance in formation with me. I figured that my machine probably didn't look too good, but I wasn't quite prepared for the looks of horror and utter dismay on the faces of my ground crew. After I had shut down the engine and joined them looking at the underside of my plane I was as shocked as they were. The missile bay doors that, when closed, constituted the entire bottom of the fuselage were mostly gone, only shredded remnants of the hinge attachments points remained. The explosion of my rocket motors had blasted me out of the sky. The engine had continued to run only at idle because the fuel lines had remained intact but the fuel control regulator had been damaged.

Investigators, looking into what went wrong, revealed that the rockets, after being unloaded from the plane the previous day, had unaccountably been left lying on the transport for the remainder of the day and night until being loaded on my aircraft late the following day. Instead of being taken to the proper storage area the missiles had been outside, baking in the desert sun, all that time. This may have caused cracking of the rocket motors creating an explosive burn.

There was some disagreement as to whether this triggered a malfunction in the firing circuitry, or vice-versa. The unconventional loading of the rockets in line was also looked upon with suspicion, because any disruption in the sequencing of the fire signal to the individual rocket motors could have been catastrophic. In this case a very comprehensive investigation of the damaged armament bay area seemed to pinpoint the cause of the failed test and prompted some changes in the firing system.

Eventually the Air Force concentrated on the six large, guided missiles and, finally, on carrying two, even larger, nuclear-tipped missiles in the F-102. The latter were capable of destroying any aircraft without a direct hit. No surprise there.

The F-102, and its faster successor, the CV-F106 Dart, proved to be superior interceptors although they were never forced to fire upon enemy strategic bombers. The amazing F-102 became operational in April 1956, and was phased out by the end of 1976.

The manned, heavy bombers were largely replaced as the delivery system for nuclear bombs, by intercontinental ballistic missiles.

The F-102 was designed as an interceptor, and the first aircraft to be considered a 'weapons system'.

TESTIMONIAL

John Knebel grew up on a farm in Illinois near Scott Air Force Base, the same airfield his father had flown out of in the US Army Signal Corps during the Great War (1914-1918). He received his pilots license when he was 19 years old and taught naval cadets at Millikin University in Decatur, Illinois, until he joined the Ferry Command as a civilian pilot. After accepting a commission in the US Army Air Corps, he served in the North African Campaign, until Field Marshal Erwin Rommel was defeated.

John flew most of the production fighters and bombers of World War II and was among the first military pilots to check out in the first production jet fighter, the P-80, at Muroc. At the time he received his degree from San Diego State University.

A retired Lieutenant Colonel USAF command pilot, John flew professionally all his life until he controversially retired out of the captain's seat in Trans American DC-8s, after flying for them for fifteen years.

Previous to that he had been operational director and instructor captain transitioning Lebanese International Airlines from props to jet Convair 990s from 1965 to 1967. He left Beirut when the Israelis, following the Six Day War, made a helicopter raid on the airport and burned two of the three ex-American Airline CV-990s that he had taken there.

He retired from the USAF as chief engineering test pilot in 1965 to go to Beirut. In 1964 he flew the first flight on the P-38 look-alike STOL aircraft, the Charger, which was the last aircraft ever built at the Convair San Diego plant. Together with Don Germerad, Knebel set the transcontinental speed record for water-based aircraft in an R3Y Tradewind on February 24, 1955, of six hours from San Diego Bay, California to Patuxent River Naval Air Station, Maryland. That record still stands and is unlikely to be broken

Chapter 30

Henshaw experienced a total of seven skew gear failures in Spitfires.

Alex Henshaw MBE – Mk V Spitfire
A Deafening Silence

The revered and legendary Second World War Spitfire test pilot Alex Henshaw MBE, recounts a mysterious failure that almost cost him his life.

On one beautiful day in England during the spring of 1942, without a cloud in the sky, I was completing flight trials on a Mk V Spitfire with a Merlin 46 engine. I decided to swiftly climb towards Warwick, drop down to 10,000 feet for a full throttle speed run and then finish off with the dive on a reciprocal course to bring me back to Castle Bromwich. The exercise would take only 10 or 15 minutes, after which I expected to inform AID that the Spitfire had cleared all flight trials. Visibility was perfect, the aircraft was smooth and stable throughout the range and, as I moved my right hand from the elevator trim tab to bring back the throttle, I suddenly felt the change in thrust. I could not accept what immediately entered my mind. At about 470 mph IAS there is, of course, a great deal of wind noise, and it is not always easy to distinguish between this and the engine roar. I glanced at the instruments as I eased the nose into a climb. Oil pressure was 90 lb/in and temperature 75ºC;

glycol coolant was 87°C, rev counter read 3,000 rpm, and boost was just a shade under 12 lbs. A photograph taken of the instruments at that moment would have proved the engine was running perfectly. With the machine now in a steep climb, the wind noise dropped in seconds; there was no response from the throttle and it was becoming awfully quiet. All temperatures were now dropping rapidly and I surveyed the whole scene in a kind of silent hypnotic stupor. I do not know how other pilots react, but in the case of a piston or con-rod failure there was always considerable noise, smoke or steam and generally you were left in no doubt that you had to do something.

My immediate response in this case was to over-stall the aircraft and arrest the wind-milling airscrew to stop churning up the engine, and also to prolong the glide. In the awful lonely silence of a skew-gear failure I had plenty of time to think, and it did not improve my morale.

The bright sunny day meant that all the EFTS Tiger Moths were in the sky, crowding round their respective airfields. At that moment they were of more danger to me than was the task of landing with a dead engine. I was lucky; but as I stepped from the machine after it had rolled to a standstill, any elation I might have had in

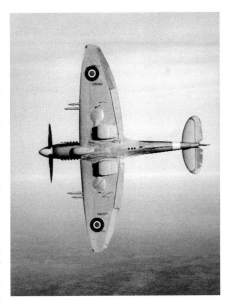

The Spitfire Mk V was the most common type, with 6,487 built.

getting down safely was taken over by burning anger and resentment that we still continued to get these failures in an engine with a reputation as the finest in the world.

The next flight on which I experienced a skew-gear failure might easily have been my last. I had flown to Cosford to commence flight trials on one of the dispersal unit's Spitfires at the end of a dull and dreary day. The machine I had taken over there was another Mk V with Merlin 46 engine, and this short trip to Cosford and back would also complete the trials on this particular machine, which could then be handed over to AID at Castle Bromwich for delivery clearance. As I landed at Cosford in the normal manner, the starboard wing of the aircraft stalled prematurely on the final 'float-off'. It was nothing and I doubt whether many would have noticed the slight shaking as the machine touched down. The camera door on the starboard wing near the fairing was fastened by an Oddy fastener and if, for any reason, this was not locked properly the door would be drawn up as the wing approached stalling incidence and disturb the flow over the remainder of the wing and possibly the tailplane.

I made a mental note to have this door fastened before I returned to Castle Bromwich but something cropped up as I stepped from the machine and I forgot about it. This might have been the costliest lapse I ever had in my life.

Later in the day, with my work completed, I took off for Castle Bromwich on a direct course. As the cloud was ten-tenths and at about 80 feet I did not follow normal practice and shoot up into it for such a short flight but, being tired, I decided to return quite leisurely in clear conditions. As I gazed over the dense conglomeration of pylons, slagheaps, belching chimneys and railways, interspersed with pockets of tiny rows of houses, my lethargy was interrupted: without cough or spit, the engine stopped. There I sat in an awful ominous silence, with even the swish of the slipstream diminishing as the machine slowed and went into a normal glide. I looked down for a landing space in desperation, but in the Black Country there are not many to choose from. I was now over a huge area of terraced houses; there was a thin snake-like canal threading through more railways and electricity pylons, but no clear road or gap to be seen. For a split second a wave of terrifying, uncontrollable panic surged through me. On reflection I do not think this was because of the knowledge of the possible consequences, so much as of the fatal decision – and to make at once. I could bale out, but would I make it and would the aircraft plunge into a factory or public building crammed with people?

Once I decided upon my course of action I became coldly calm, but I felt in my heart this was my last fight. I must at all costs avoid the foundries, factories and electricity pylons, and more importantly, the compact row of houses and buildings crowded with people.

I finally chose a small gap between two rows of houses on which were garden shed, vegetable plots and the odd yards of lawn, with a small paddock in which there were a few solid trees. At the end of the rows of houses was a narrow canal and I reasoned that if the cabbages and garden sheds did not bring me to a standstill, the canal banks certainly would. In the last few seconds as I sat in the machine for the final turn I prayed hard. My final movements were to pull the Sutton harness with all my strength so that the straps cut into my shoulders, and then to adjust the seat to its lowest position so that I could barely see out of the cockpit. Just at the most critical stage when concentration was at its highest, I was about to congratulate myself on having hit off the exact spot on the vegetable patch when the starboard wing suddenly stalled, fell away, and I remembered with extreme bitterness that I had forgotten about the camera door.

Everything was now in the hands of the Almighty; as the machine snaked off to the right, the starboard wing caught a large oak tree and snapped off like a carrot; the nose then swung into the house whose cabbage plot I had tried to take over, and the engine tore a gaping hole, exposing the kitchen furniture to wholesale view.

As the airscrew dropped onto the floor, the port wing plunged into the soft ground and it also snapped off. The unrestricted fuselage then tore through everything in front of it and the earth, vegetables and debris cascaded over the cockpit in a terrifying crescendo. I prayed silently that it would all be over soon without too much pain.

The engine-less blunt nose of the cockpit bulkhead must have struck something hard, for it suddenly lurched over and

Spitfire V EP615 lying in pieces at Willenhall on 18 July 1942.

round, tearing the fuselage in half just behind where I sat; but as it poised to bury me upside down, it suddenly paused, hung for a split second or so, and then fell back. There was dead silence.

I was dazed; I saw blood trickling down my left hand; the arm felt numb

The Merlin engine had been wrenched away and the starboard wing snapped by a tree.

and I guessed it had broken. My legs and thighs hurt like hell and I dared not look at them to see how mangled they were. Blood was also trickling into my mouth. I was grateful to be alive.

I must have remained quiet and still for a couple of minutes, closing my eyes as I thought about my injuries. As my senses slowly cleared I was appalled to notice petrol swashing all over me, and for the first time to realize that the fumes were becoming overpowering. In a flash I thought, 'Oh God, I am going to be roasted alive'. In sheer panic I instinctively undid my parachute and Sutton harness, pulled on the cockpit hood release lever and in split seconds I was out of the cockpit and onto the beautiful firm earth.

I was bruised and cut but, considering what had happened, I was miraculously unscathed. The next morning the managing director came on the phone, with deep concern in his voice as he said, 'I have just been through to Rolls-Royce, Derby and Ernest Hives would like to come over for a working lunch and discuss the skew-gear business with you'.

I was in no mood for a public relations exercise, but fortunately Lord Hives was not only a highly qualified technical engineer with vast experience, but had worked on the shop floor and spoke the language of the man on the job.

I was surprised when he showed such a depth of knowledge on flight testing, and the concern that he and all his staff felt over the skew-gear failures and the high risks involved when dealing with such a vast output in difficult conditions. Hives knew where the problem lay; he did not at this stage know how to cure it. He finished by saying, 'We are going to live on the job until we locate the problem, and one of our finest engineers, R.W. Harvey-Bailey, is now doing just that!' True to his word, some considerable time later in the year, my secretary ran out to me on the tarmac and said 'Mr Harvey-Bailey of Rolls wishes to speak with you urgently'. As I lifted the receiver a voice said 'By here; you will be pleased to hear that we have located the cause of the problem and you should now have no further skew-gear failures'. He then went on to give an explanation that was almost unbelievable. In simple terms the remedy consisted of raising the reduction gear pinion so that its locating bore was 0.0015 inches above the rear bore.

Having a number of engines to examine helped in the detail analysis, and it began to appear that there was a relationship between the backlash in the skew-gears, but this did not tie-up completely. A failed engine with only a new skew-gear fitted was tested with what for the time was a lot of instrumentation. It was found that on some engines the crankshaft was shuttling rearwards with considerable force, to the extent that it distorted the centre bearing panel in the crankcase by 0.01 to 00.012 inches. In the Merlin the crankshaft was located by flanges on the centre bearing and it was the load on the flange that was distorting the centre bearing panel which, in turn, meant that, with the friction in the splines, there was end load in the wheel case that was pushing the main drive bevel out of mesh with the mating gear on the upper vertical drive. Thereby, due to the wide clearance on the driving bevels, the skew-gear was exposed to the heavy loads generated by the torsionals present and, in consequence, failed. It was clear that if engines could be built so that the main drive bevels had half the backlash of the skew-gears and this could be maintained under running conditions, the skew-gear failures would be overcome.

I have been extremely fortunate to have the generous cooperation of Alec Harvey-Bailey who, as a young man, worked with his father on the skew-gear problems. He told me: 'My company had recognized the hazards of this problem and had put in continuing effort, but had been hampered by the development of special instrumentation. Statistically it is remarkable that, after the very scattered nature of the failures, our Crewe factory should have had a sudden spate of them. That they were confined to Castle Bromwich in numbers never before experienced did enable us to examine each failure with a wider perspective than was previously possible. The fact that this occurred in the darkest days of war no doubt gave a stimulus not previously experienced.'

It is estimated that Henshaw flew at least 10 per cent of all Spitfires built.

(Photos courtesy RAF Museum London)

TESTIMONIAL

Alexander Adolphus Dumfries Henshaw was born in Peterborough on 7 November 1912, entered the 1933 King's Cup air race in a Comper Swift and was awarded the Siddeley Trophy. He won the 1938 King's Cup in the fastest time and speed ever for a British aircraft, flying a specially modified Percival

Mew Gull. He broke the solo records for flights from London to the Cape and back in February 1939 and, in recognition of this, the Royal Aero Club awarded him the Britannia Trophy.

During the Second World War, Henshaw worked as a test pilot with Vickers Armstrong at Weybridge and Southampton. Initially he flew the Wellington but then got involved with the development and production of the Spitfire, Walrus and Sea Otter. In June 1940 he became chief test pilot at Castle Bromwich factory, which produced Spitfires, Wellingtons and Lancasters. For his contribution to the war effort, Henshaw was made a Member of the British Empire.

In 1946 he moved to South Africa and worked as a technical director for Miles Aircraft South Africa Ltd. During his two-year contract he made several sales tours and deliveries of Miles aircraft across Africa.

After returning he concentrated on his family, business interests and writing a trilogy of books on his aviation experiences. In 2005 he gave his collection of papers, objects and art works to the RAF Museum. Alex Henshaw died on 24 February 2007.

To mark the 70th anniversary of the first flight of the Spitfire, in March 2006, the 93-year-old Henshaw flew over Southampton in a two-seater Spitfire, taking the controls once airborne. His pilot commented that Henshaw could have landed the aircraft but for the prohibitive insurance conditions.

Chapter 31

Onboard the F-86. After leaving the Naval Service, Harper served as an aeronautical research pilot with NACA.

John A. Harper – B-45 Bomber
The Wingless B-45

From John A. Harper's flight log for August 14, 1952...a true and humble test pilot.

While I was serving as the aeronautical research pilot at NACA Langley (precusor of NASA), we were flying a four-engine B-45A, which was the first ever jet bomber, on the first flight of a research program to measure the distribution of load between wing and tail under various flight conditions. The bomb bay was fitted with a pallet full of NACA instrumentation. Herbert H. Hoover, chief of flight operations at NACA Langley, was the pilot. I occupied the rear seat, operating the instruments. The bombardier station was not occupied, it was just the two of us. This was an instrument calibration flight.

The first part of the test was to push over to a negative half g, then pull up to 2g positive. Herb's first attempt didn't reach negative g, so he tried again. This time he reached it and pulled up to attempt the specified '2 positive'. But the airplane went right-on straight through it and shortly thereafter, came the sound of breaking aluminum and the airplane shuddered violently.

I saw that the right wing was gone from the engine nacelle outward and the wing root was on fire. The scene to the left was the same. It was apparent that we had overstressed the airplane, which was making for terra firma in a steep dive. I felt wind in the cockpit but the canopy stayed on. Herb called on the intercom, 'Pull the handle, John!' I had already raised the seat armrests while preparing to eject, so the trigger was exposed when I reached for the canopy eject handle. The canopy went and the swirling wind forced me into a bent-over posture. I pulled the seat eject trigger and both elbows scraped the cockpit rails and the front of the seat struck my face. The windblast was overwhelmingly violent, as our air speed was approximately 500 mph (the USAF had not yet converted to knots). I found out later that my ejection was made at the highest airspeed to date.

Our escape system had neither an automatic seat release nor automatic parachute rip cord. Once clear of the aircraft, I released the seat belt and shoulder straps and I remember seeing the seat fall away. Within moments I pulled the ripcord and felt the shock of my 24-foot parachute pulling my shoulders. But, almost immediately I landed in a tree. After extricating myself from the branches, I hitched a ride on a nearby road and asked the driver, a young woman, to take me to the crash site clearly marked by a column of fire and smoke perhaps a mile away. The girl was horrified by my bloody appearance, but readily complied. Our B-45 had made a big hole in the ground between two houses in Burrowsville, Virginia. The homeowners were lucky, as the houses were only about 150 feet apart.

The accident investigation concluded that a bit of metal had lodged in the electrical junction box during the negative g event in such a way as to drive the longitudinal trim in the nose-up direction, carrying the aircraft to five or more gs until the wings came off. A simulation of the incident we conducted on a B-45 borrowed from the neighboring USAF squadron showed that the wheel forces would have exceeded 400 lbs, too much for my friend Hoover to overcome.

B-45 Tornado was the United States Air Force's first operational jet bomber, and the first jet aircraft to be refueled in the air.

As for Herb Hoover, the investigation concluded that when he raised his seat armrests to eject the canopy, it did not fully separate from the airplane. He unstrapped and manually knocked the canopy off with his left hand. As his right hand was still on the trigger, the seat fired with Herb about a foot above it. It struck him, throwing him out of the airplane. He also contacted the tail, probably knocking him unconscious and he struck the ground in a free-fall.

A little more research revealed that the B-45 squadron across the field from us at Langley had experienced five unexplained crashes that closely resembled ours. All crew members were killed in those crashes, so I was the only live witness to see how the crashes might have occurred.

After I escaped from the hospital that same evening, we had a celebration at our house and a wake at the Hoover home across the street.

The USAF bought a total of 142 B-45s including 33 for reconnaissance.

TESTIMONIAL

Born on December 25, 1920 in Benton Harbor, Michigan, John A. Harper entered the US Naval Service in April 1941. After being designated a naval aviator he was immediately ordered back to Miami as a fighter gunnery instructor in Grumman F3Fs and Brewster F2A Buffalos, then to Landing Signal Officer training and assignment in just four months as the senior LSO on the carrier USS *Belleau Wood*. In this role he officiated at more than 8,000 carrier landings and, while flying the F6F Hellcat with VF-21, shot down two Japanese intruder aircraft.

At the end of World War II Harper was separated from naval service in 1945 and joined the Organized Naval Air Reserve program to command two fighter squadrons, two carrier air groups, and one attack squadron.

After leaving the regular Naval Service in 1945, Harper served as aeronautical research pilot with NACA, where he flew the transonic wind tunnels mounted on P-51 wings. He continued his work with a leading role in the development of an early version of the Navy's A-7 Corsair automatic flight control system, flying the Vought F8U-1P Crusader. He ended his career as director of missile and space program development at McDonnell Douglas, before retiring with wife Peggy, in 1985, to manage their California avocado ranch and other real estate holdings. They had four children who have given them ten grandchildren and three great grandsons, so far.

Harper accumulated 3,700 flight hours in 61 different aircraft models and made 70 carrier landings.

Index

Page numbers in *italics* refer to illustrations